Global Innovation, Finance, and International Commerce

This book analyses the historical context and progression of "significant innovations" beginning with the industrial revolution, starting around 1750 to the present. It explores the interrelationship, causes, and evolutionary process of contemporary "disruptive" inventions and the role played by global finance and international commerce to support these.

First, the authors examine the environment and circumstances surrounding the inventors and explore their backgrounds to determine, why at a specific time, they identified a need that became the seed for invention and, what was their method of successfully commercializing their innovation. Secondly, they focus on the financing of the inventor, the innovation, and the commercialization of the invention(s). They analyze the changes in finance during the shift from a labor-based production process to a more capital-intensive production process, and what new financial products or financial markets were created to facilitate this transition. Third, they explore the impact of global commerce on the inventor country's innovation environment and international competition impacting the innovation's production, distribution, and sales, as well as, investigating any financial impact from the demand side and whether that impact was domestic or global in character. Furthermore, they consider if and how global finance and international commerce including the migration of people, together play a role in helping the disruptive invention satisfy a need in society, whether from a production or consumption perspective. Finally, they search for common elements that repeatedly inspired inventors and their disruptive innovations over time.

This book will appeal to global government officials, business leadership, early career professionals, and students across a number of disciplines including finance, economics, business, engineering, and technology.

F. John Mathis is an emeritus professor of global economics, banking, and finance and the former director of the Global Financial Services Center at Thunderbird School of Global Management, Arizona State University, USA.

Raja M. Almarzoqi is Chief Economic Advisor at the Ministry of Economy and Planning and a faculty member at the Institute of Diplomatic Studies, previous Adjunct Professor at Thunderbird School of Global Management, Arizona State University, USA; and King Saud University, Saudi Arabia, and Former Advisor at International Monetary Fund, USA.

Routledge Studies in the Economics of Innovation

The *Routledge Studies in the Economics of Innovation* series is our home for comprehensive yet accessible texts on the current thinking in the field. These cutting-edge, upper-level scholarly studies and edited collections bring together robust theories from a wide range of individual disciplines and provide in-depth studies of existing and emerging approaches to innovation, and the implications of such for the global economy.

The Political Economy of Digital Ecosystems
Scenario Planning for Alternative Futures
Meelis Kitsing

China's Innovation Economy
Artificial Intelligence and the New Silk Road
Jon-Arild Johannessen

The Dynamics of the Innovation Divide between China and Europe
National and Regional Dimensions
Edited by Arkadiusz Michal Kowalski

A Systemic Approach to Continuous Change in the Innovation Economy
Jon-Arild Johannessen

Industrial Revolution 4.0
Economic Foundations and Practical Implications
Edited by Stanisław Mazur

Global Innovation, Finance, and International Commerce
F. John Mathis and Raja M. Almarzoqi

For more information about this series, please visit: www.routledge.com/Routledge-Studies-in-the-Economics-of-Innovation/book-series/ECONINN

Global Innovation, Finance, and International Commerce

F. John Mathis
and Raja M. Almarzoqi

Routledge
Taylor & Francis Group
LONDON AND NEW YORK

First published 2023
by Routledge
4 Park Square, Milton Park, Abingdon, Oxon OX14 4RN

and by Routledge
605 Third Avenue, New York, NY 10158

Routledge is an imprint of the Taylor & Francis Group, an informa business

British Library Cataloguing-in-Publication Data
A catalogue record for this book is available from the British Library

Library of Congress Cataloging-in-Publication Data
Names: Mathis, F. John, author. | Almarzoqi, Raja, author.
Title: Global innovation, finance, and international commerce / F. John Mathis and Raja M. Almarzoqi.
Description: Abingdon, Oxon ; New York, NY : Routledge, 2023. | Series: Routledge studies in the economics of innovation | Includes bibliographical references and index.
Identifiers: LCCN 2022030080 (print) | LCCN 2022030081 (ebook) | ISBN 9780367456696 (hbk) | ISBN 9781032398839 (pbk) | ISBN 9781003024675 (ebk)
Subjects: LCSH: Technological innovations—Economic aspects. | Inventions—Economic aspects. | Finance. | International economic relations.
Classification: LCC HC79.T4 M363 2023 (print) | LCC HC79.T4 (ebook) | DDC 338/.064—dc23/eng/20220906
LC record available at https://lccn.loc.gov/2022030080
LC ebook record available at https://lccn.loc.gov/2022030081

ISBN: 978-0-367-45669-6 (hbk)
ISBN: 978-1-032-39883-9 (pbk)
ISBN: 978-1-003-02467-5 (ebk)

DOI: 10.4324/9781003024675

Typeset in Bembo
by Apex CoVantage, LLC

Contents

Figures, Tables, and Case Studies

Chapter 4

Chapter 5

Chapter 6

Chapter 7

Chapter 8

Chapter 9

Part I

Innovation of First Industrial Revolution Sets Foundation – Industrial Capitalism

1 Survival in a Shrinking World

Innovation is a crucial ingredient in increasing productivity, sustaining economic growth, creating new jobs, and improving living standards. Internationally, innovation can build a substantial competitive advantage and enhance a country's terms of trade creating new jobs and further promoting domestic growth. Countries that engage in international trade benefit and receive what both trading countries need to contain inflation, boost GDP per capita, and learn from each other. Innovation and entrepreneurship have similar meanings as entrepreneurial activity applied to an invention represents starting a new business or industry. According to the Merriam-Webster Dictionary, an invention is a discovery or product of the imagination validated by scientific research. Innovation refers to a new product or service that may result in the launch of a new industry generating strong industrial or consumer demand.[1] A January 2021 *World Economic Forum* report on "Strategic Intelligence" describes innovation as turning innovative ideas into value in the form of new products, services, or ways of doing things and includes the practical steps necessary for adoption. Innovation has fueled most of the world's productivity and economic growth. Financial reward, while important, is often not the primary driver for innovation as there is also an innovator's desire for personal accomplishment, social benefit, and recognition.

Joseph A. Schumpeter (1883–1950, a Czech economist) is the foundational theorist of innovation and economic development, and he identifies entrepreneurship as the vital link between them. He described innovation as being "creative destruction in that innovation must happen to replace inefficient and outdated, uncompetitive companies." The replaced companies faced declining demand and were often subsidized or protected by import restrictions resulting in a tax on consumers. They represent wasted resources by society. A necessary process in the economic growth cycle is to increase productivity and guide a country's limited capital investment into industries that will sustain and build a country's international competitiveness. And provide an attractive real return to entrepreneurs and investors. This process of economic renewal creates jobs, productivity growth, and economic development with higher standards of living. There is a risk that successful major innovations might become monopolies, and therefore new entrepreneurial endeavors must

DOI: 10.4324/9781003024675-2

be supported by continuous capital investment in new innovations. A country's economic development is defined by constant investment in new innovations that become internationally competitive leaders.

History of Innovation Since 1750

This book takes a historical approach to analyze and uncover the primary drivers of innovations and global competitiveness. Humans have had ideas that have been shared verbally since the beginning of humanity. Many of these ideas were never assessed or used and disappeared. Innovation involves developing and proving that an idea or invention works and consistently does what the inventor promised. If the invention provides real value, consumers will want to purchase it, and the cost is often less than what they were paying for a previous product or service. Or the innovation provides an entirely new product or service that consumers find desirable and are willing to purchase and use because it gives them value. Innovation goes beyond intuition or predictions. It is learning what works and why, requires a detailed record of what was done and how, and why the experiment turned out the way it did to be a proven success. Innovations must perform as promised and advertised, or the seller violates the law.

First and Second Industrial Revolutions

The First Industrial Revolution began in Britain, followed by the USA. Both countries experienced a unique period of entrepreneurial creativity that continues today and has spread to other countries through immigration, international commerce, and foreign investments. Most early innovations were based on people's experiences, trial and error, or what they learned from further personal experimentation to fix or improve production or make work less burdensome. The more often a person does something or uses something, the more they learn about its strengths and weaknesses. People often have biases based on their perception of the invention's relationship to past experiences. It is believed that as much as 80% of the time, this 'experience' reasoning may be misleading. Innovation often is an entirely new experience and technology.

Significant Creative Disruptive Innovations

Innovations around the First and Second Industrial Revolutions (1750–1850 and 1850–1914) in Britain and the USA were primarily based on working experience and how people thought things happened or functioned. Finding a solution to a problem often took many years of trial and error before the expected outcome was accomplished and repeatable. After the buyer used the new product or service, modifications and improvements often came from users' requests. As seen in early textile and other industries, there were many changes along the way based on what fabricating devices, materials, and energy sources were available. Many early innovations were based on modifying an existing process to produce the desired product or service more efficiently, reducing its use of labor time and cutting operating costs. Accomplishing something more efficiently with fewer people increased worker productivity and was critical to expanding farm output to satisfy growing demand. This improvement often meant developing a new technology or energy source. For example, **Cyrus McCormick's (1809–1884, an American inventor and businessperson)** reaper innovation replaced human labor with a mechanical device. It increased productivity and lowered marginal and average costs. One laborer could now do what previously needed two workers, thus freeing up a worker to produce additional output. The innovation's value is based on what was saved in costs to produce the same amount as before measured in time, quantity, or quality, and whether these savings could be continuously and consistently accomplished. Market demand was based on the number of farmers who could afford the product and trusted that the machine would always perform as promised. Thus, guarantees and warrantees were initiated to give the buyer peace of mind if a problem arose. The innovation's cost could be equal to a worker's pay for several months or years, but there would be no cost thereafter, as the new device continued to function correctly. Rising food demand from emerging urban centers was the primary driver of agricultural, textile, and energy innovations to expand output.

A significant disruptive innovation was the steam engine, which replaced horse-powered travel with coal-burning steam-powered locomotive railroads. The steam engine was more flexible, mobile, and powerful than waterwheels or windmills as a new energy source for manufacturing and mining. It was a more robust and efficient power generator for expanding railroad transportation. The steam-powered locomotive reduced the time and expense it takes to travel while increasing its transport load. The steam engine's higher efficiency and increased power lowered manufacturing and transportation costs to supply more products and services to growing urban centers. This creative innovation was based on higher knowledge, research, and discovery of solving a problem and accomplishing something more efficiently. It is how innovative technology by reducing costs for energy expands the demand for more products and launches an economic growth cycle based on using more advanced scientific knowledge to boost employment output and create new markets.

One of the problems with an entirely new technological innovation from the buyer's perspective is whether the new product or service will work for the buyer or whether they are willing to learn how to use the new product correctly. The buyers' background, sophistication, and culture may make new technological products a culture shock or perceived as too complicated, dangerous, or risky to operate before potential buyers are comfortable buying them. Some buyers may also be concerned about whether the new product or service will offer sufficient value to offset the purchase cost. These buyers' concerns about the innovative technologies may take years to overcome before they are convinced to buy after many other users share good experiences. Increased education became required, and training sessions, demonstration programs, and third-party recommendations helped reduce buyer concerns. Magazines, manuals, and books became essential parts of this education.

Other examples of significant disruptive innovations are presented, from the invention of the telegraph, followed by telephones to accelerate two-way communication speed. And the invention of electricity as a new power source for lighting and powering motors for manufacturing. Electricity brought much more flexibility to workers in terms of working hours with lighting and working on a production line with power tools. Innovative technology disrupted communication by mail through a postal service transported by people on horseback or horse-drawn wagon. The telephone was a cultural change for people to share and respond much more rapidly than writing a letter and waiting weeks for a reply. The phone was also a significant development for financial and commodity trading markets and marketing and sales. Information could be transmitted immediately with explanations enabling better-informed decisions. Similarly, electricity was a critical disruptive invention replacing the steam engine as a more efficient and less polluting power source. Both innovations required higher education and time to understand how they worked and digest the innovation's usefulness before their entrepreneurs were rewarded for their knowledge and creativity.

In an address to the Mathematical Association of England on the importance of education in 1917, **Alfred North Whitehead** argued, "the basis of the invention is science, and science is almost wholly the outgrowth of pleasurable intellectual curiosity." The scientific method is an empirical method of acquiring and confirming knowledge that has characterized the development of inventions since at least the 17th century. It involves careful observation, rigorous skepticism about what is observed, and formulating hypotheses which are then repeatedly assessed to determine their factual truth.

Innovation's Impact on Productivity

Countries' average annual growth rate of real (removes inflation) Gross Domestic Product (GDP) per person has varied significantly over the past 150 years. In part because nations have diverse resource endowments. Some countries like Britain and the USA are rich in resources. In contrast, some countries have one or two significant resources, like Saudi Arabia and other Middle Eastern countries with large oil reserves. However, Japan has few or no known natural resources. Yet, Japan has a remarkably high average annual real GDP growth rate per person of 2.6% compared to the US 1.9% average for the past 150 years because of its emphasis on international trade. Japan imports raw materials and transforms them into higher value-added products for export. The differences between a country's GDP growth rates per capita result from productivity and innovation differences.

Productivity measures the output per worker per hour and determines laborers' standard of living and wage rate based on their production complexity, uniqueness, product value, and labor value-added. A country's worker productivity level is influenced by physical capital (plant, machinery, and tools), human capital (workers' knowledge, skills/education, determination), natural resources (land, water, forests, minerals, raw materials), and an increase in the level of technical ability and entrepreneurial skills (education, knowledge, creativity, management, leadership). These all make up the 'factors of production' as they influence the growth in Real GDP and the production of goods and services. Production transforms raw materials with the help of labor, capital, technology, and many intangible factors into finished products. GDP measures the sum of the final value created by the factors of production in a nation during a period. These inputs, including labor, add additional value to the final product. Thus, output per labor unit is driven by the physical capital per worker, knowledge level per worker, a country's natural resources, and the significance and application of technology affecting output. Each input unit will differ in importance based on its value added to the final product.

Physical capital (plant, machinery, tools, etc.) is a produced factor of production affected by the technology developed by people with appropriate skills and knowledge. This ability was acquired from education, experience, training, coworkers, and individual's own deep thinking and creativity. These factors comprise and define proficiency in innovation and entrepreneurship. Natural resources are raw materials, of which some are renewable (forests and trees), and some are nonrenewable (coal and oil). The level of technology and expertise determines the most efficient way to produce goods and services. Technology improves physical capital, machinery, and tools to free labor to make additional goods and services. The application of technology to increase output is dependent on the amount of savings invested to finance and install technological innovations. The level and application of technical knowledge are dependent on human knowledge and understanding. Knowledge, experience, deep thinking, persistent analysis, and creativity produce inventions, and entrepreneurship and financing create innovations.

The Entrepreneur and Innovations

Entrepreneurship refers to imagining and creating a new enterprise and accepting its uncertainty, risks of failure, and the possibility of profit. An entrepreneur must understand how to start and run a business, arrange financing, manage people, apply modern technology, and identify market opportunities. The actions of innovators or entrepreneurs reflect creative thinking about an improvement in productivity or the launch of a new product or service. It involves arranging inputs such as land, labor, and capital, applying the modern technologies that result in improved efficiency or a new product or service, a lower cost of output, and identifying new revenue sources for the enterprise. There are various forms of ownership protection of innovations, including proprietary ownership by a company or legal patent protection. Both formats provide additional incentives for undertaking and promoting innovations.

Innovation and Productivity Drives Economic Growth

Historically for advanced developed and developing countries, labor productivity is the most critical contributor to output produced by a labor unit in a specific time. The more skills or education workers have, the more they can add value per unit of time. As the economy develops, labor output increases as workers learn to use more sophisticated factories, equipment, tools, and machinery, called capital, to produce more output per period. The costs of investments in capital, which help make labor more productive per hour of work, are recovered in the estimated return or profit paid to entrepreneurs or companies for their products or services. Thus, total productivity improvements come from three sources. First, the worker that most directly produces the product or service. Second, the investors that finance the process create new capital facilities that help workers achieve more output per hour. Third, technological advances from inventions, discoveries, and innovations make more efficient capital equipment. Labor working with different skills and education contribute to all three components responsible for productivity improvements.

One of the significant benefits of innovation is its contribution to economic growth via productivity increases. Productivity is the number of goods and services produced from each unit of a person's input in a period and is the driver of the rise in humans' living standards. As productivity rises, more goods and services are produced, and the economy grows. Even in using more robots with artificial intelligence and smart machinery and tools, people who make, operate, maintain, and repair the robotic machinery and compose AI software controlling the intelligent machinery receive increased compensation for their creativity. Innovation and productivity growth yield vast benefits and lower costs for consumers, and as productivity rises, the total number of service jobs and salaries increases. As labor's income rises, more goods and services are purchased, making businesses more profitable and enabling them to invest in innovations, expand, and hire more employees.

The Pace and Cycle of Innovations

Innovation usually starts on a small scale, for example, when innovative technology is first applied in a company where it has been developed. However, for the full benefits of innovation to be realized, it must spread throughout the economy and benefit other companies in various sectors. The diffusion of innovation to different countries happens at different speeds due to its complexity and acceptance as influenced by culture, traditions, beliefs, customs, behaviors, values, morals, religion, knowledge and education level, and economic and income groups. A second factor influencing the diffusion of innovation is that inventions often go through a series of development stages encompassing multiple transitions, technical improvements, and cost reductions before they become acceptable to the general population, as illustrated in Chapters 2–5. This process, if done correctly, may enhance a company's and its products' international competitiveness and reputation. The relationship between output growth and the rise in labor and capital inputs accounts for around 15% of the GDP increase in developed countries. The remaining 85% is due to a broad combination of advancing and improving technology and the other factors mentioned earlier. Acceptance in developed countries tends to be faster than in developing countries, resulting from the latter's lack of an educated labor force, capital resources, and well-developed middle-income population and marketing channels.

Large corporations in developed countries have become the primary source of inventions and innovations, and their amount of R&D expenditures have been rising with the advance in technology. These increased expenditures have not always yielded major innovations or top-rated marketable products. Sometimes the CEO's or Chief Investment Officer's tenure is shorter than the expected invention or innovation period. In this case, the leadership may see no benefit in maintaining R&D expenditure in that area. Expectations about a new product or service may be distorted, especially if there are high implementation costs. The product or service may be a great idea but not where the marketplace is now. Therefore, demand does not materialize no matter how many adjustments are added until market sentiment improves. Many issues can disrupt a marketplace atmosphere for a new product. Increasing environmental concerns and climate change questions are now being asked about the latest innovations. Health issues, medical changes, and medications impact the market response to new drugs and other health innovations. The most prominent fear by investors comes from high uncertainty. This uncertainty often results from fear of war, financial crises, and economic and political cycles. For example, during the second half of 2021, the spread of the COVID-19 pandemic increased, climate change was a growing concern, economic recovery was in an early, vulnerable stage, and global supply chain bottlenecks were contributing to rising prices and inflation fears. In part, this uncertain situation was due to the persistence of the COVID-19 pandemic and its variants disrupting companies' output which curtailed the supply of goods and services. This disruption hindered the return to full employment output, and the ending of the COVID-19 pandemic continues to be a significant uncertainty for many sectors of the global economy. As a result, production, distribution, employment, and consumers' lives and education have been severely disrupted.

Most governments are unsure about the most appropriate policies for this worldwide, prolonged shock, and nations' social fabric has become more frustrated and hostile. Supply chains are backlogged, ports are overwhelmed, critical product shortages persist, and rising prices are causing widespread inflation uncertainties interrupting investments and employment. Governments' stimulative fiscal and monetary packages are being re-examined with continuing tensions about how they can be adjusted to normal non-inflationary, full-employment levels. Under these uncertainties, planning new investments are challenging for every economic sector, and the short-term outlook for innovation is uncertain. The potential negative impact of the pandemic on population growth rates may have a longer-term negative effect on the labor force growth and consumer demand. One bright spot is the re-shoring of many multinational companies' offshore production facilities, including the production of computer chips, which is expected to boost employment and output. However, re-shored companies will face higher labor costs resulting in higher product prices and inflationary pressures unless robots are substituted for labor which appears likely in advanced industrial countries.

Inventions, technological progress, and innovations are not continuous but tend to come in waves or cycles as one moves from one major technological change to the next. Each significant technological change requires understanding how and what it does, digestion of its benefits and uses until scientists can see its constraints, and then removing these problems with new modifications or new inventions. The ongoing advancement in technological innovations to expand physical and human capital per worker requires financing and investing in human and physical capital to grow productivity. This investing requires that people or companies save more and channel these funds via financial markets into future innovations. The primary source of investment increasingly comes from corporations' Research & Development (R&D) spending rather than stock re-purchases to boost senior managers' benefits. R&D spending began increasing in 2021.

How Governments Help Empower Innovators

Governments can provide incentives to promote increased innovation investment by reducing or eliminating taxes on investment returns, such as lowering the short-term and long-term capital gains tax. Governments can also improve human capital development by providing low-cost or free educational programs in specific areas of study such as Science, Technology, Engineering, Mathematics (STEM), and Medical and Biological Sciences. Governments can also pursue policies to attract increased foreign investment in domestic innovation companies that support physical capital and human capital improvements. Supplying better health care programs to promote healthier and more nutritious meals for school children helps improve student performance and learning outcomes at all levels of education. Government support of property rights, political stability, elimination of corruption, and improvements in establishing an effective and fair judicial and legal system also help foster innovations and economic growth. Promoting free trade and technology transfer via imports promotes higher incomes and education levels. The government can also establish programs to fund research and development activities in areas where it believes it has or desires a comparative advantage. Finally, an open immigration policy can also invite international college graduates from STEM and Medical and Biological Science advanced degree programs and encourage them to relocate to the country to work. Governments can provide a haven for trained, well-educated scientists interested in pursuing their research in a safer, more accessible, and supportive environment.

Increasingly, growing innovations require a more sizable number of well-educated researchers in various fields. Also, the more varied their backgrounds and experiences, the more empowered and freedom they feel, and their inventions will be more significant. The next step is identifying the business opportunity and use for the invention. This process can also be reversed engineered with the entrepreneur recognizing an opportunity and engaging scientists to discover alternative ways to realize the opportunity. The greater the number of scientists, including women and international immigrants, the greater the chances for different creative ideas to establish and maintain a momentum of innovations. The number of scientists today is male-dominated, and a more balanced perspective requires that more women be encouraged to enroll in STEM, Medical, and Biological Sciences educational programs and be equally recognized and accepted as scientists and similarly compensated. There is also a need to add more women entrepreneurs to gain a better perspective of both halves of the consuming population.

Significant Disruptive Innovators Case Studies

How do we define and identify significant disruptive innovations? These innovations are determined to be implemented and widely used, and they change and contribute to civilization's advancement. The characteristics of the inventors, inventions, and innovations are summarized, including their environment, background, education, and how they financed their discoveries. We also explore the role played by global commerce in supporting significant innovation, enhancing the value in human living standards domestically, and impacting the global economy's economic development through international trade. Several common factors emerge.

An invention is often defined as a unique or novel device or process that arises from a pressure point. The invention process is often an engineering and product development operation, which emerges from a mental visualization, followed by the fabrication of a prototype. Historically, this process was done in machine shops very slowly and at great expense, depending on the material and the number of follow-up adjustments and modifications. **Chuck Hall (1939–, an American engineer and inventor)** invented the **SLA 3D** (dimension) printer or **stereolithography (SLA)** in 1984. 3D printing represents a significant improvement in the machine shop fabrication process as a final product image can be viewed in 3D on a laptop screen. It may also be projected in a hologram, rotated, and modified as required. Many modifications can be electronically made on a computer using **Computer-Assisted Design (CAD)** software visualizations before a 3D printer produces a working prototype in hours via **Computer-Aided Manufacturing (CAM)**. The 3D additive printing process has also become a new industrial machine production method. It is an essential part of the production process, and in emergencies, it can produce replacement parts on-site, including body parts for health purposes. It is also used to replace obsolete parts for expensive specialized machinery and is increasingly used in space stations and the front lines of military activities. Software for products can be emailed and produced in hours, cutting the shipping costs of sending a finished product. In recent years, the focus of innovations has shifted toward developing and launching new services.

Disruptive innovation is an invention that is successfully implemented by an entrepreneur(s) and changes how a product or service is produced or performed and significantly impacts people's behavior or culture. It is a new way of doing something and creates value for humanity's standard of living. Innovations often displace market leaders' established products or services and may affect their distribution and supporting infrastructure. Think of how online marketing and shopping is closing the big-box shopping outlets such as Sears and Penny's. The term 'significant disruptive innovation' was defined and analyzed by **Clayton M. Christensen (1952–2020, an American academic and business consultant)** in 1997 in *The Innovators Dilemma*, Harvard Business Review Press.[2] More recent sources also include 'significant positive societal or cultural impact' as an aspect of disruptive innovation such as online shopping and Amazon delivery for almost anything you desire. Amazon does not produce products but provides pictures, prices, and comparisons and sells what other companies build and quickly delivers the product to you.

Critical and Deep Thinking

Disruptive innovations increasingly involve critical thinking, including evaluating previously accepted standards and applying a positive attitude, facts, deep thought, reasoning, and logic skills. Critical thinking is increasingly required with the advance of science and the scientific method. Technological innovation increasingly requires higher levels of formal education, including college and beyond in specialized subject areas and years of on-the-job training skills. **Diane Halpern (1950–, an American psychologist and former president of the American Psychological Association)** in 2003, *Thought & Knowledge*, Lawrence Erlbaum Assoc.,[3] identifies five steps in developing a critical thinking attitude. These are willingness to plan, the flexibility to consider new options and clarify complex issues, persistence to start, engage, complete a thoughtful task, willingness to self-correct and change your mind when evidence changes, and being mindful or drawing mindful conclusions. Commercialization involves consensus thinking, which requires high-level communication skills and compromises so that thoughts become actions.

Before the First Industrial Revolution, innovators were Guild members, especially in Britain and the more advanced Western European countries, and others were artisans or craftspersons. They had natural talents and had learned and improved their trade from parents or family members, who had trained them in a profession that became their career and often a family business. However, the guilds tightly controlled what members did, primarily repeating what they had been doing. The guild's purpose was to keep its membership employed against non-guild creative work. The market for guild craftsperson was limited to the very wealthy, a small economic segment.

Other potential innovators were employees: workers, farmers, miners, or service people that labored at various trades. Their firsthand 'on-the-job' experiences working hard for long hours to survive and make a living drove them to look for easier ways to increase their output for a better life. Most had little formal education, and if they had gone to school, it was at the level of grammar school to learn the basics of reading, writing, and their mother's homeschooled arithmetic. Few children attended high school or college except wealthy families living in or near major cities, and they already knew how to read.

While books did exist, they were available in Britain and the major cities of Europe. Until the 19th century, there were no public libraries and few private libraries but only open to institutions or wealthy families. Commercial subscription libraries gradually spread throughout Britain, western Europe, and the USA. Britain's modern public library system started with the Public Libraries Act of 1850, giving local boroughs the power to establish free public libraries. It was the first legislative step toward creating an enduring national institution to provide universal free access to information, knowledge, and literature.

The first tax-supported public library in the USA was opened in 1833 in Peterborough, New Hampshire. The 1700s ushered in the beginning of increased literacy and intellectual curiosity. Society's hunger for knowledge enabled magazines to become a popular cultural staple. The first American magazines were published in 1741, and by the end of the 18th century, there were more than 100 magazines. However, early periodicals were expensive, and only the wealthy could afford them, and consequently, were geared toward the most learned, cultured, and sophisticated individuals of the day. Thus, new developments and knowledge did not spread rapidly, but primarily by word of mouth shared locally between business associates, neighbors, and friends. Communications from Europe were from travelers, ship crew members, or immigrants, and Americans had little information about Britain's First Industrial Revolution details. Britain had banned the First Industrial Revolution's innovations from being exported to colonies in America.

The USA Joins British Industrial Revolution

As the First Industrial Revolution progressed in Europe, the USA also started its own Industrial Revolution. It began in the agricultural, textile, and clothing sectors to meet early immigrant settlers' survival needs. Thus, wheat production spread in the Northeast, and cotton was grown and processed in the South for export to Britain to produce clothing. Some of the later immigrants to the USA came with more current knowledge about agricultural production-enhancing techniques. Eventually, some immigrants arrived from the UK and Europe knowledgeable about industrial developments. Each nation of the immigrants had its unique relative comparative advantage in industry knowledge to share in its exports and immigrants to America.

Immigration of Knowledge

In 1790, the US Congress passed The Naturalization Act that allowed any free white person of good character living in the USA for two years or longer to apply for citizenship. People without citizenship were denied constitutional rights, including property ownership, voting, and legal right to testify in court. Non-citizens were not allowed the opportunity to be innovators. A US census showed that the English immigrants were the largest group of 4 million people. There were just under 800,000 people from Africa and the Caribbean, primarily in the Southern part of the USA. The British brought many enslaved people to work on Southern cotton plantations to produce cotton for export to Britain since cotton could not be grown in the UK. Imported cotton supplied Britain's largest textile industry to export cotton textiles to the USA and other countries.

After the War of 1812 with the British, immigration from Western Europe increased. Over the next 40 years, people from Ireland represented about one-third of all immigrants. Five million German immigrants arrived to buy farms in the Midwest or settle in St. Louis, Cincinnati, and Milwaukee. After the US Civil War 1861–1865, the Federal Government established and enforced immigration laws. In the late 1800s, the USA began its Second Industrial Revolution, with growth in urban centers. These metropolitan cities became home to immigrants from Southern, Eastern, and Central Europe, including about 4 million Italians and 2 million Jewish people. Immigrants settled in major eastern and midwestern cities and worked in the new factories of industrialization. In the mid-1850s, Chinese immigrants moved to the USA's western states to help build the transcontinental railroads and worked in California gold mines and farms. In 1882 Congress passed the Chinese Exclusion Act, which stopped further Chinese immigration. The Immigration Act of 1891 excludes the immigration of people convicted of certain crimes, sick and diseased people, and polygamists.

Ellis Island opened, and between 1892 and 1954, 12 million immigrants entered the USA, with 1.3 million arriving in 1907 alone. Simultaneously, concern about Japanese immigrant workers in California replacing local workers and depressing wages resulted in an agreement with Japan to limit immigration to specific businesses and Japanese professional categories. In New York City in 1910, an estimated 75% of the population were recent immigrants or first-generation Americans. At the beginning of World War I, the Immigration Act of 1917 set literacy requirements for immigrants and stopped immigration from Asia. During World War II, labor shortages resulted in the USA and Mexico establishing a program that temporarily allowed Mexican workers into the USA for seasonal farm work, and this program continues today.

The US Immigration Act of 1924 established a limit on the number of immigrants allowed to enter the USA through nationality quotas based on the 1890 census. Three countries account for 70% of the visas awarded: Britain, Ireland, and Germany. The Act excluded people from Asia. After WWII, the

USA passed the refugee and resettlement law for the inflow of Europeans seeking permanent residence, and in 1952 the USA ended its exclusion of Asian immigrants.

Innovation Promotes Economic Development

Innovation and creative endeavors are indispensable elements that drive growth and sustain the relative competitive advantage for an economy by increasing its productivity and lowering production costs. It also supplies new products and services to be exported, improving the US international trade balance, and increasing its competitiveness relative to other countries. Innovation becomes even more critical if it helps reduce pollution and moves the world toward sustainable growth with broadly distributed benefits to everyone in society. Remarkable innovations have improved living standards during the last century and promoted sustainable development. They have reflected improvements in health, communications, transportation, economic wellbeing, and overall quality of life worldwide.

US Role in Global Innovation

The USA is a leader in world innovation, as shown in Figure 1.1 compared with other countries depicted in Figure 1.2. US companies have relied on intellectual property (IP) as one of the most important techniques to promote

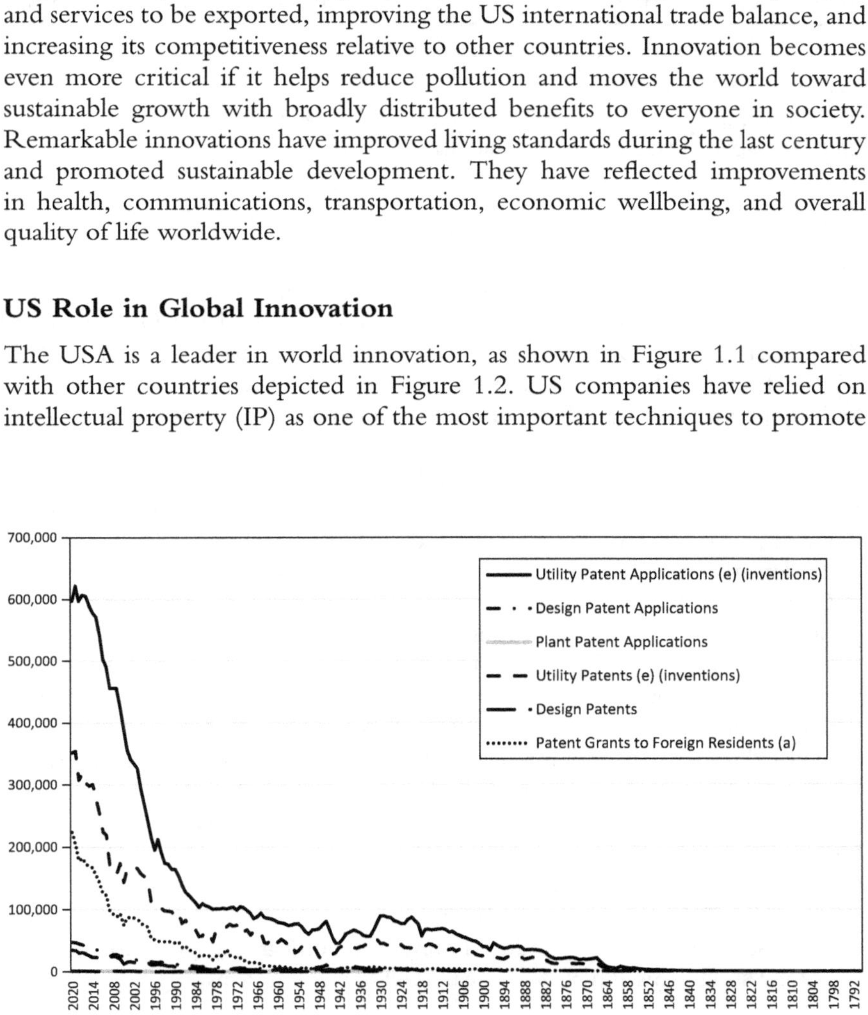

Figure 1.1 US Patents: Applications and Grants

Source: US Patent and Trademark Office

Origin[1]	*2011*	*2012*	*2013*	*2014*	*2015*	*2016*	*2017*	*2018*	*2019*	*2020*
EPO[2] states	32,580	32,625	33,608	33,042	36,562	48,727	50,680	57,906	60,570	58,656
US	13,391	14,703	14,880	14,384	14,955	21,939	24,960	31,136	34,614	34,162
Japan	11,650	12,866	12,135	11,120	10,574	15,395	17,660	21,343	22,423	20,230
China	513	791	941	1,186	1,406	2,513	3,180	4,831	6,229	6,863
Korea, Rep.	1,424	1,785	1,989	1,891	1,993	3,210	4,435	6,262	7,247	7,049
Others	2,560	2,895	3,159	2,990	2,939	4,156	4,720	6,147	6,701	6,755
Total	62,108	65,655	66,712	64,613	68,419	95,940	105,535	127,625	137,784	133,715

Figure 1.2 European Patents Granted and Published

Source: European Patent Office

[1]Geographic origin is based on the residence of the first patent issued.

[2]EPO states include 27 states of the European Union

technological advances and the intensity of IP's use in the global economy. Patents, trademarks, and copyrights are the primary means for setting up ownership rights to the creations, inventions, and brands used to generate tangible economic benefits to their inventor and owner. The latest US Patent and Trademark Office (USPTO), *Intellectual Property and the US Economy: 2016 Update*, finds that Intellectual Property (IP) intensive industries are an essential and integral part of the US economy and help promote its economic growth. These IP industries account for more jobs and a growing share of US GDP. USPTO identifies 81 IP-intensive industries, representing a quarter of all industry categories. Companies in IP-intensive industries employed 28 million workers in 2016, rising 3% since 2010, contributing to 40% of GDP.

Trademark-intensive industries supplied 24 million jobs in 2014. Copyright industries contributed 6 million jobs and patent-intensive industries 4 million positions. With an additional 18 million supply chain jobs created by IT-intensive sectors, they account for 30% of all employment or 46 million jobs. Employer earnings are also 46% higher in IP industries than in non-IP industries. IP-industries exports of goods and services totaled $1 trillion in 2014. Corporate innovations, as opposed to new startup innovations, continue to grow. In a study by A. Arora, S. Belenzon, and L.A. Rios, "The Organization of R&D in American Corporations: The Determinants and Consequences of Decentralization," *NBER Working Paper* No. 17013, 2011, just under 1,000 or 16% of manufacturing firms introduced a new product, and 42% reported patenting their most significant innovation. More intensive R&D investment firms, or 63% of large manufacturing firms, patented their most important new product innovation, compared to 47% for medium R&D investing firms and 36% for small R&D investing firms.

Higher Education Is Increasingly Critical to Innovation

Higher levels of education are becoming increasingly important to all industries, particularly IP industries. The higher the technology level, the more elevated the necessary level of knowledge in the STEM, Medical, and Biological Science fields. The USPTO 2016 update shows that the percentage of workers with a college degree or higher in IP-intensive industries was 40%. In patent-intensive IP industries, the percent of employees with a college degree or higher was 42%, in trademark-intensive 37%, and copyright-intensive workers were the most educated, with 21% having Masters and Ph.D. degrees, and a sizable percentage of BA college degrees at 46%, for a total of 66% of all workers.

Low STEM enrollment emphasizes a growing problem for future US innovation requirements. For post-college education, US students going into STEM, Medical, and Biological Sciences is only about 20% of total enrollment in ranked colleges and universities. Consequently, in 2020 USPTO launched the National Council for Expanding American Innovation (NCEAI) which is committed to increasing the opportunities for all Americans to participate in innovation. The OECD ranking of quality and level of graduate and higher education in the 24–35 age bracket (high invention and innovation bracket) shows South Korea recorded 70%, Canada 61%, Japan 60%, Russia 58%, Lithuania 56%, and the UK is ranked eighth at 52%. In contrast, the USA ranked 13th at 48%. According to the OECD, higher education is more important than ever as technological advancement increasingly disrupts lower-skilled jobs. Furthermore, preparing students in grades K-12 for future learning in STEM, various UN and WB reports indicate that US students are not among the top-performing countries like China, India, Singapore, South Korea, Taiwan, Israel, and several Eastern European Countries.

Characteristics of IP-Intensive Industries

Value-added US IP industries versus non-IP industries show a 30% increase in value to $6.6 trillion, which resulted in a rise in its GDP contribution to 38% in 2014, up 3.4 percentage points over 2010. The bulk of this increase came from Trademark intensive industries, and the revenue associated with using intellectual property rights totaled $115 billion in 2012 from 28 industries deriving income from licensing. The following three sectors accounted for 78% of all direct revenues from IP licensing: Motion picture and video industries (NAICS code 5121), Cable and other subscription programming (5152), and Lessors of nonfinancial intangible assets (5331), according to the USPTO report.

The impact of IP industries on US international trade has also been significant. In 2014, IP-intensive industries' merchandise exports equaled 52% of US merchandise exports, or $438 billion. US IP-intensive industries imports were about 59% of total merchandise imports or $825 billion. Exports of service-providing IP industries totaled $81 billion in 2012, or 12% of US private sector service exports. The top three IP-intensive manufacturing exports were necessary chemicals, semiconductors and electrical components, and pharmaceuticals and medicines, which accounted for about 21% of total manufacturing exports. The largest share of IP-service-providing industries was software publishers, portfolio management, computer systems design and related services, motion picture, video production, government, scientific, and technical consulting services, accounting for 72% or over $58 billion according to the USPTO Intellectual Property 2016 update (the latest data available).

Shift From Individual to Corporate Innovations

An accelerating pace of technology advances today comes from corporate research laboratories, corporations' R&D departments, universities' research centers, and to a lesser extent, startups. Over 60% of innovations come from corporations with more than 500 employees. In the past, innovations tended to be very specialized by the source of power or industry manufacturing. Today's technological advances have a much broader impact on how things are accomplished in all sectors, particularly the expanding service sector. Innovations continue to change how we live, and their effects are increasingly comprehensive. The ramifications are most visible in developed countries and their crucial raw material suppliers and lower labor costs in developing countries, but eventually, they impact all nations through global trade. Innovations' pervasiveness raises concerns about how their use will serve and not abuse us.

Innovation and Competitiveness

A country's competitiveness depends on innovation driven by investment in R&D and its business application. Together, they drive economic growth and build strong, competitive nations. But not all innovations are good for an economy when they harm the environment. Many private and public investors now require environmental studies on the impact of every investment, from supporting startups to major infrastructure projects. The potential environmental damage is measured and treated as a liability remediation cost against the project, detracting from the investor's estimated return. Fear of this potential damage can cause financing to be withdrawn or the cost of financing a project to be raised to a much higher level preventing it from being viable.

During the 1800s, wealthy families, rich merchants, and entrepreneurs funded significant disruptive innovations. Occasionally, a government grant was offered to develop a new weapon or communications technology to support a monarch or government's war effort. A study by Ufuk Akcigit, John Grigsby, and Ton Nicholas, "When America Was Most Innovative and Why," Harvard Business Review, March 6, 2017, analyzed inventors' characteristics. It found that they were highly educated, likely to have had a father who invented, came from high-income families that invested in education, and were likely to have lived in New Jersey, Massachusetts, and Connecticut. These states produced many patents during the First and Second Industrial Revolutions. They also saw a meaningful improvement in the inventor's education level from the early 1800s to when the First Industrial Revolution was entirely underway. Advanced degrees in the inventor's expertise require more advanced and specialized graduate study in science and technology.

The relationship between innovation and real GDP growth per capita is also understandable because of the labor force's expansion as production shifted from cottage output to large factory production. And as manufacturing machinery became more complex, labor required more skills and earned a hirer wage. Better paid workers enabled improved nourishment and health and increased education. There was also increased worker specialization in the advanced production process, requiring more on-the-job skill-based training along the line of the certifications provided by the various guilds (apprentice to master craftsman). The formation of labor unions also supported this process to ensure labor received its fair share of the benefits.

The incentive to innovate was greater recognition and a more certain income level. A higher living standard enabled the inventor's children to attend higher education at better colleges and universities with more advanced degrees. In addition, some students arranged to spend time in universities overseas to learn a different perspective or gain more advanced knowledge on the subject areas of their career.

Early Innovations Trigger a Sustainability Shock

The history of humans before the industrial revolutions was a struggle for survival. Death at birth was high, proper nourishment and nutrition were limited, and life was short. Survival was further shortened by droughts, wars, accidents, catastrophes, plagues, and diseases. Industrial Revolutions came in cycles, and the major disruptive innovations were often made with many less critical contributions in previous inventions and discoveries as steppingstones. Today, survival is increasingly dependent on technological advances that sustain people on Earth and improve their living standards. However, in some cases, significant early technological advances have complicated humanity's survival by polluting the environment and contributing to global health problems. Developments on the horizon of increasing robots and artificial intelligence to replace various worker professions have elevated labor stress and uncertainty and contributed to growing cancer cases and deaths. These same technological advances widen the gap between the upper 1% of the wealthy population and the rest of the middle and lower-income levels whose spending created the upper 1%.

Innovations are necessary to satisfy rising consumer demands for survival and improvement in the quality of life. Achieving this objective is a challenge, and in times of crises, we learn quickly how increasingly widespread and dangerously narrow the line is between barely surviving and the unfortunate alternative. Humanity, driven by mentally narrow-minded politicians, is witnessing a growing air of hate, fear, and conflict with nations turning inward to support themselves with a nationalistic, self-interest focus.

Sustainability is the ability to exist continuously without damaging the Earth's environment and jeopardizing people's health so that the environment can support future generations. Sustainable development is defined as growth that provides present needs without compromising future generations' ability to meet them. This outcome requires stopping climate change now. The switch to using coal as the source of heat or energy to power machinery is an example of innovation from wood for power as Europe exhausted its forests. In 1938 **Guy S. Callendar (1898–1964, a Canadian-born British steam engineer and innovator)** published research data showing that the USA and Canada had warmed significantly due to CO_2 emissions generated by the First Industrial Revolution. He continued tracking temperatures into the 1960s, recording that the Earth's greenhouse effect was underway. In the late 1950s, a continuous series of CO_2 readings again confirmed his global warming finding. After decades of expanding an infrastructure based on coal to power industrialization, it is challenging and costly to move to a new and cleaner fuel now available to power more sustainable growth. For example, the continued use of coal is a significant problem today in China and India. Both nations face societal rigidity to change because it is culturally and financially challenging for current users to switch. Even the USA is still a significant source of pollution because of its reduced but continued reliance on coal.

In late 2021, with more than half the world vaccinated, corporate R&D investments in new innovations are starting to rise again, with developed countries recovering GDP growth and schools reopening. The innovative corporate use of Zoom conference meetings is now an accepted way to work from home for many companies. The education industry is similarly video conferencing many classes. COVID-19's harmful impact on business and society is causing a rise in M&A. Meanwhile, Central Banks keep liquidity ample and interest rates low but warn of increases in 2022. During the fourth quarter of 2021, prices rose because of the backlog of supply chain disruptions, including petroleum shortages. Although consumer prices increased by 7% over year-earlier levels in December 2021, the Biden Administration projected a return to 2–3% by mid-2022.

Innovations to Control COVID-19

Examples of how innovations during the First and Second Industrial Revolutions disrupted sustainability are the Coronavirus variants beginning with SARS[i] followed by COVID-19 and its increasingly harmful variants. Scientists believe these viruses are related to climate change due to the pollution of the Earth's environment, causing rising temperatures. Record-breaking global pharmaceutical innovations are beginning to reduce COVID damage. For example, the new COVID-19 vaccines (Pfizer-BioNTech and Moderna) formulated mRNA-based modifying genes to recognize and fight the pandemic. The speed to develop COVID-19 vaccines is reenergizing a series of innovative technologies in the medical field. At the same time, there is a renewed interest in what scientists can discover as we re-enter the Fourth Industrial Revolution. And, while people arrange appointments for their booster vaccine shot, suddenly a spaceship has put a land explorer-rover on Mars, and two entrepreneurs are sending people on space flights to prepare for future colonization on planets.

In 1800, there were an estimated 900 million people globally, with China and India representing 520 million or 58%. Today the total world population is 7.9 billion, and China and India represent less than 36%. It took over 2 million years for the world's population to reach 1 billion and only 200 years to grow to 8 billion. The net increase in global population is over 80 million people per year. Since 1800 an additional 6.9 billion people are inhabiting the Earth and require the basics of food, water, clothing, housing, jobs, education, medical care, etc. Before COVID-19, global population net growth rates (births less deaths) slowed from over 2% per year in 1970 to 1% today. Over 4.4 billion people, or 56% of the total population, now live in urban centers, increasing from 800 million or 30% in 1950.

The Earth's land area is about 29% of the Earth's surface area of 14,894 million hectares. Only 37% of this surface is arable, or about 5,511 million hectares (13,617 million acres). Of this amount, 23% usually is used for producing crops, while 77% is used to feed livestock. This arable land is a finite constraint. Supplying sufficient food for the world's growing population was accomplished by applying modern technology innovations to improving productivity per acre. International trade also played an essential role in distributing food for humans and animals to increase per capita real GDP growth. The resulting vicious circle of population growth and the increasing use of innovative technology to expand agricultural output created a rising environmental wall, limiting further population growth unless a new, more sustainable solution is found out of this circle. Population growth in cities has worsened pollution, adversely impacting climate change, human health, and the widening spread of fires, floods, plagues, viruses, and sicknesses as the Earth's temperature and pollution has risen. These problems have been transported globally by human travels, migrations, wars, and other natural catastrophes.

Global Trade Supports a Healthier World

The exchange of goods between countries through international trade historically helped participating countries survive, grow, and develop. It was based on resource endowment, comparative advantages, and survival needs. For example, early sea and ocean shipping by the Chinese and Arabs helped sustain life with better food, clothes, tools, knowledge, and eventually printed books, innovative ideas, and inventions. Local and national wars were common as humans fought to expand the supply of food, clothing, and other raw materials – those who survived shared ideas and knowledge and depended on global trade for their needs.

Increasing international trade in goods and services and rapidly expanding financial flows reduced the significance of the 200 separate countries' political borders while elevating the realization that humans all share one planet. The average annual growth of global exports in goods and services since the mid-1800s has expanded 2–3 times faster than world growth in real GDP. Consequently, global exports of goods and services to GDP growth have risen to 25% today from 5% in the mid-1800s. At the same time, healthier humans began to live longer, with the average life span rising from less than 50 years in 1850 to 80+ years presently[ii] Population growth, increasing immigration, and better health with longer lives resulted in a massive increase in the demand for food, goods, and services, facilitating the expansion in global trade. Global trade supplying raw materials and finished products supported this continuous market growth and rise in per capita GDP.

Countries' increasing interlinkages and dependencies stimulate international commerce in goods, services, people, and capital despite periodic interruptions. Global trade also transmits knowledge and ideas between countries, promoting additional innovations and efficiently allocating resources. This exchange of knowledge, ideas, and discoveries, whether by labor migration or immigration, international trade in goods and services, or the movement of capital for financing between countries, is valuable for all nations. Global sharing of knowledge, culture, and values improves living standards and accelerates worldwide growth and per-capita living standards, furthering new linkages and interdependencies between economies. The speed and ease of this process are being amplified by the ever-expanding Internet and smartphone communication systems and the use of digital banking. We explore how knowledge exchange influences innovation, finance, economic development practices, institutions, procedures, and regulations that build the fertile foundation for future entrepreneurial activities.

Notes

All dates, innovators information, and events have been checked against information in the following sources: *Encyclopedia Britannica, Encyclopedia Americana, Collier's Encyclopedia, Compton's Encyclopedia, Investopedia, and Wikipedia.*

i A respiratory disease caused by corona virus infection that causes flu like symptoms.
ii NPT Reports: Aging Matters | Aging & the Workplace | Aging https://www.pbs.org/video/npt-reports-aging-maters-workplace/

2 First Industrial Revolution and Its Global Impact

Before the First Industrial Revolution, life in Europe and other regions was centered around agriculture and food production for survival. The population was increasing, and demand was outgrowing supply. When Henry VIII broke from the Catholic Church, agricultural production shifted toward responding to the growing market's demand for additional food. International trade and finance began to move northward to Amsterdam in the Netherlands, London in Britain, and Paris in France. As population density increased in the northern countries, so did agricultural productivity. Manufacturing activities, such as textiles and metallurgical handicraft industries, were on farms or in small villages. As population growth exceeded the food supply, food prices rose. Simultaneously, wages fell, and a series of bad harvests, the plague outbreak, and other diseases further complicated the demand–supply imbalance for food. Access to different continents for supplies was necessary but only available by wooden ships. As demand pressure mounted and prices increased, the return on improving shipments outweighed the development cost. Consequently, ship production technology changed toward larger (three, four, and five masts) wooden ships with bigger square sails because of increased investment to expand trade globally. Also, the hinged sternpost steering rudder replaced oared galleys to improve mobility in the rising number of ports.

More substantial ships were needed for ocean travel, transporting larger cargo to feed and supply the growing European population. Flemish, Dutch, and Portuguese ships became more extensive, manageable, and seaworthy, with greater cargo capacity for longer trips. Improved guidance was necessary to reduce time and costs, so the magnetic compass (from China) was adopted to improve navigation. Sailing maps improved as the African coast was explored, and shipping ports were established. Meanwhile, the shipbuilding industry shifted northwest from India to Britain, but as wood for more extensive and taller ships became exhausted, shipbuilding moved further northeast to Scandinavia.

Spanish and Portuguese ships started sailing south around Africa to India, China, and Japan, with the primary cargo being high-valued spices. A sizeable Muslim alliance fleet was destroyed in Diu, India, in 1509 by the Portuguese, which was the beginning of European dominance over Asian shipping. The

DOI: 10.4324/9781003024675-3

shipment of cotton, first from India and later from America, helped build one of Britain's and northern Europe's largest industries – the textile industry. Cotton textiles lowered clothing prices from expensive silk and uncomfortable wool material. Eventually, Portuguese and Spanish merchant ships turned to the Americas, searching for gold and silver instead of spices as both metals were recognized as a nation's source of wealth. This search helped to support the use of gold and silver coinage as a currency, and its increased use put upward pressure on prices in southern Europe.

The Spanish conquered the Aztec Empire in Mexico and the Inca Empire in Peru. To overcome the shortage of labor in the Americas, the Spanish brought enslaved people from Africa to Brazil and the northern part of South America to increase crop output shipped to Europe to feed their growing population. They brought new food products, including wheat, grains, sugar cane, coffee, cocoa, vegetables (potatoes, beans, squash, peppers, pumpkins, and corn), fruits, and turkey to feed the growing populations of Europe. As a result, food prices in Europe begin to fall, supporting further population growth. However, prices were volatile and under upward pressure from increasing the supply of gold and silver imports.

European population growth, particularly in Britain, Netherlands, and France, was heavily related and dependent on agricultural output and food supply in general. Agricultural output was heavily reliant on human power as the essential driver of production, and even the use of plows was heavily dependent on human energy to operate them. There were two significant needs to increase agricultural output: farm labor was not growing but gradually moving to cities, and farmers needed better production processes. Farming equipment and machinery were required to help increase production. As more land was brought into production, human resources were spread more thinly across more acres. In parts of Europe, agricultural serfdom working long hours daily and 6 days a week was insufficient to feed a growing population and caused periods of population stagnation with the decline in food output.

Expansion in Agricultural Output

The modernization of agriculture was related to Dutch commercial superiority. The key to changing agricultural output was specialization in high-value products such as livestock and dairy. More livestock produces more fertilizer, and the Dutch farmers also added other fertilizer sources, including pigeon dung and reclaiming sea and lake land. Urban merchants and investors funded the diking and draining required and sold or leased the reclaimed land to farmers to expand agricultural output. Most innovations involved minor improvements in farming production methods and only slowly increased output.

The exception came from the mechanization of agricultural farming, facilitated by the substantial amounts of open land available to European immigrants that moved to North America. Food production was a significant problem for new arrivals to America who used human and animal power to prepare the land to plant crops and harvest the matured crops. Most new immigrants relied on this process based on human and animal energy. Early attempts to introduce machinery to help with the plowing, planting, and harvesting were uncomfortable and unappealing to farmers. Farm owners did much of the work themselves as there was a limited amount of labor to help them, encouraging farmers to have large families. In this environment, **Cyrus McCormick (1809–1884, an American inventor and businessperson)** began to complete his father's efforts to develop a horse-drawn, wooden reaper for their farm in Virginia. McCormick began his experimentation with his knowledge of the few machines he had seen or heard about based on **Patrick Bell's (1799–1869, a Scottish minister and inventor of agricultural machinery**) design. McCormick demonstrated his first horse-drawn mechanical reaping machine in Virginia in 1831, but the machine had difficulty adjusting to the rough terrain. He continued improving the mechanism, but not until 1842 did he succeed in selling several devices. After that, sales continued to expand each year as farmers saw and heard what the machines could do. McCormick's mechanical reaper took fewer person-hours and increased harvesting productivity per person-hour worked. It was also well suited to the more extensive mid-western prairie farmlands. McCormick moved his production factory and company to Chicago, which had better rail and water transportation facilities to deliver his reaper and binder throughout the USA. The McCormick Harvesting Machine Company later became part of the International Harvester Company in 1902.

Case Study #2.1 Significant Disruptive Inventors and Innovations – Agriculture: Cutting and Harvesting Machinery

Key Disruptive Inventors	**Cyrus McCormick (1809–1884, an American inventor and businessperson)**
Location	**USA**
Disruptive Invention	The horse-drawn wood reaper was built in 1831 and patented in 1834. It was produced at his farm's blacksmith, and he developed innovative production, sales and financing methods, and product warranties. In 1847 patent of the iron wider cut reaper was named the "McCormick Patent Virginia Reaper."
Problem Resolved	More efficiently cutting and bundling ripe grain, managing, and delivering the grain than using a scythe took time and limited the number of workers hired.

(*Continued*)

(Continued)

Solution Impact	Faster harvesting with fewer person-hours of labor and increased harvesting per person-hour worked. It cut and managed the preliminary processing of grain faster. Grain had a limited harvest time of about 4–10 days. Continued improvements changed the reaper from a two-horse-drawn wood machine to an iron machine and widened the cutting path with a driver and the raker seat.
Economic Impact	The Midwest and West's flat western prairies were perfect for the McCormick reaper as they were too large for the farmer to cut by hand in the limited harvesting time. However, the machine could not be quickly shipped until railroads were built, so Cyrus set up regional warehouses for his products. McCormick also implemented a new management style of delegating decisions to his recruited specialists. His Chicago factory was one of the most significant and most up-to-date, managing all aspects of production and bundling for transport. McCormick also developed innovative marketing, sales, buyer financing programs, and warranty policies. He focused on analyzing longer-term strategies for his company as competition grew. The output capacity of his reaper began to move the country away from the threat of famine.
Cultural Impact	Farmers were skeptical and slow to accept innovation and doubtful the machine would be beneficial. However, he won their confidence by locating closer to farmers who needed his equipment, offering credit for purchasing it, and guaranteeing its performance with a refund if the machine failed. Once farmers began to be convinced, it developed into a herd effect – everyone needed one to become a major grain producer.
Inventors Education & Training	Local grammar school, but his father and mother provided a significant part of his training. His father trained him to use tools and simple mechanics and involved him in his business operations, and his mother exposed him to domestic manufacturing operations. At 18, he studied surveying, and he worked on the family farm where he had access to a blacksmith and a grain field for testing.
Innovation Environment	Favorable with profitable economic growth and the country expanding westward with farms expanding in size. For the gold rush, farmworkers began to take jobs in urban centers or moved westward to California. McCormick continually improved his product as farmers requested and introduced other products to enhance the farmers' output, such as a combination reaper-mower, traveling thresher, seed planters, and self-raking reaper. Chicago also began an expanding pace of growth competing with New York City. Railroads in

	Chicago expanded as they hauled farm equipment and other manufactured goods everywhere and brought wheat back into Chicago. The city became a major industrial and grain trading center. McCormick was able to extend his 1834 patent until 1865. Unfortunately, the outbreak of the Civil War (1861–1865) disrupted the innovation environment.
Financing	Family financed from farm income and friends, and it took nine years to sell the first reaper, so all reapers were built in the family farm blacksmith shop to control costs. In 1843 he finally sold 29 and 50 the following year for $100 each. McCormick licensed someone in Brockport, NY, and Cincinnati, OH, to make and sell reapers in specific areas, and in 1846 about 190 reapers were sold. In 1847 he moved production to Chicago, closer to the prairies and lakes. With limited financing available, McCormick had to find a business partner. He partnered with Gray, an earlier licensee, and began building a large factory to produce his reaper and assembled 500 machines for the 1848 harvest season. Gray sold his ownership share to William Ogden, a Chicago developer, and W.E. Jones. A total of 1,550 Reapers were sold for the 1850 harvest, and Cyrus ran his business without partners but recruited family members to join him in Chicago. He created a manufacturing system equipped with the best tools and a family members' marketing, sales, and distribution system. In 1848, he raised his reaper price to $120 and provided a written guarantee, with the farmer paying $30 at purchase and the rest in six months. The sale was conditional on the machine cutting 1.5 acres an hour with a full refund if the device failed. The following year, the price was raised to $125, with the farmer paying $35 cash plus freight from Chicago and the balance due after the harvest by December 1, along with 6% interest from July 1. McCormick established 19 agents and warehouses at specific high crop production customer locations to improve sales and increase access to reapers to ease delivery and provide better service. McCormick became a millionaire after relocating to Chicago, and during the Panic of 1857, the McCormick family invested heavily in Chicago real estate. In 1858 he married Nancy (Nettie) Fowler, and she was a good business partner and advisor to Cyrus. The Chicago fire in 1871 destroyed his factory, and he and his wife decided to rebuild a newer and larger factory at the original location with a production capacity of up to 15,000 machines per year. McCormick's engineers continued to improve the self-raking reaper, a self-binder machine, mowers, etc. Only one person was needed to operate this advanced reaper.

(*Continued*)

(Continued)

International Commerce	In 1850, McCormick began European marketing of his reaper and participated in the Great Exhibition in London. He also demonstrated his products in France and Germany. Since farm labor was cheap and plentiful, he had to explain to the wealthy landowners that even so, his reapers were more profitable, and sales to Europe began to grow. During the Civil War, the instability of farming, and the currency value in different States, he focused his attention on building his farm equipment in Europe. With his wife and family, he moved to London for two years. He began to sell his products in Europe and other countries worldwide and printed his companies' catalog in 20 languages. It is estimated that by the time he died in 1898, he had sold and exported more than 20,000 reapers to Europe from his Chicago factory.
Major Success Factors	Driven, persistent, tenacious, problem-solving, innovative, and analytical capacities with mechanical farming equipment, enjoyed competing, managerial, and marketing skills, and time was most valuable to him. He worked hard, listened to his customers, and took his sales and distribution to them. There were no unions or guilds.

During this period, enslaved African-Americans had several inventions that might have become innovations developed by the plantation or farm owner since enslaved people were denied ownership of inventions. One such invention was designed by **Henry Blair (1807–1860, an American farmer and inventor)** that helped make the farming industry more productive, and he was granted a patent in 1834. It was the second patent awarded to an African American, following the first patent awarded in 1821. Blair designed and built a mechanical corn planter that was animal-powered (cow or horse) that cut a trench with an iron plow at the front of an iron or wood frame followed by two large wheels carrying a seedbox. Corn seeds fell into a rotating hopper from the bottom of the seedbox and dropped to the ground 3–4 inches apart. Two fins followed behind the hopper to keep the seeds aligned in a row, followed by a V-shaped rake to cover the corn seed, followed by a farmer walking and guiding the planter. The corn planter allowed farmers to plant more corn using less labor in a shorter time. Blair's second invention was a cotton seed planter, for which he also was awarded a patent. US patent law allowed both freed and enslaved people to obtain patents. In 1857, a slave-owner challenged this law, claiming that he owned "all the fruits of the slave's labor," including his enslaved person's inventions. This action resulted in a law change in 1858, stating that enslaved people were not citizens and could not hold patents. After the Civil War ended, the law was reversed in 1871 to grant all men patent rights.

The first powered farm machinery was a steam engine on wheels with a leather belt used to power the mechanical farm machinery. **Richard Trevithick** developed a semi-portable stationary steam engine used to operate a corn threshing machine in 1812. The first tractor engine was built in 1859 by **Thomas Aveling (1824–1882, a British iron founder and agricultural engineer)**, later modified to be self-propelled. In 1962 Thomas Aveling and **Richard T. Porter (1835–1913, a British agricultural engine and steamroller manufacturer)** entered a partnership. They developed a steam engine to drive a steamroller. The Aveling and Porter Company had become the largest manufacturer of wide-wheeled iron steamrollers for roads producing one a day and selling to governments worldwide. The first gasoline-powered tractor with forward and reverse gears was invented in 1892 by **John Froelich (1849–1933, an American inventor).** Froelich started a Waterloo Gasoline Engine Company to build engines and tractors but was unsuccessful. About the same time, **John Deere (1804–1886, an American blacksmith, inventor, and entrepreneur)** invented the steel plow in 1837. He purchased the Waterloo Gasoline Engine Company and produced various tractors and agricultural machine tools in 1911. **Daniel Massey (1789–1856, an American blacksmith and businessperson)** began making labor-saving harvesting machinery. In 1847 he turned his business over to his son Hart to manage. Hart Massey grew the company's North American business and began producing and selling farm equipment in Germany and then Europe. In 1891, Hart merged with his competitor **Alanson Harris (1816–1894, a Canadian sawmill operator and farm implement manufacturer)** and formed Massey-Harris Company in Toronto. They produced the first self-propelled combine harvester in 1938. In 1953 Massey-Harris merged with the Ferguson company to become Massey Ferguson producing tractors and farm equipment and exporting and eventually manufacturing agricultural equipment worldwide.

Case Study #2.2 Significant Disruptive Inventors and Innovations – Agriculture: Tractor and Farm Equipment

Key Disruptive Inventors	**John Deere (1804–1886, an American blacksmith, inventor, and entrepreneur)** **Daniel Massey (1789–1856, an American-Canadian blacksmith, farm equipment, and entrepreneur)**
Location	**USA, US-Canadian**
Disruptive Invention	Deere built the steel plow in 1837 and gas-powered tractor and steel farm equipment pulled by tractors. He began producing harvesting machinery in 1847 in Ontario, Canada.

(*Continued*)

(Continued)

Problem Resolved	Deere saw a recurring trend in the wood and cast-iron plows he repaired that the design was meant for soft, sandy soil in the East and was not conducive to the thick, heavy prairie soil. Massey moved to Canada to take over his father's business and grew it to become a significant farm implement company.
Solution Impact	The gas-powered tractor was the beginning of the industrialization and mechanization of the agricultural industry worldwide with machinery and equipment designed for the local terrain in different world regions. Massey became known for building labor-saving farm machinery and repairing farm equipment.
Economic Impact	Deere and Massey were both responsible for expanding productivity in the agricultural industry with innovations in the farming and forestry industries. Farms grew through farmland ownership and leasing to accommodate more productive farm machinery and equipment. The result was the emergence of vast farms with increasingly efficient agricultural equipment. Massey also became an expert in clearing land to prepare them for farming.
Cultural Impact	While the percent of the labor force in agriculture has continued to decline, agricultural output per farmer has expanded dramatically, with products shipped and produced worldwide depending on demand soil type and weather conditions. As a result, food prices remained low and stable.
Inventors Education & Training	Deere attended Middlebury College, worked as a blacksmith apprentice, became a professional blacksmith, and moved to different cities to serve his customers' needs. Massey received his education in Watertown, New York, took over his family farm management when he was only 14 years old, and developed an understanding of farming equipment and its inefficiencies. He often traveled to the USA, brought back new farming equipment, and modified it for Canada.
Innovation Environment	Growing populations' demand for food required a significant increase in agricultural productivity. As a result, agricultural machinery has experienced many innovations in power source to diesel engines, specialized machinery for each crop and terrain, including driverless, GPS guidance systems, crawler-type tread tractor, and AI technology to control fertilizing, watering, and weed control.
Financing	Deere started with his blacksmith income and production of the steel plow. Deere repeatedly used partnerships with several funders and bought them out after the business grew. Today John Deere is one of the largest agricultural equipment producers and other tractors and machine tools with plants worldwide to adapt equipment to the local terrain.

	Massey used his blacksmith shop to launch his labor-efficient farm equipment manufacturing business and merged with Massey-Harris. Both were responsible for producing the self-propelled combine harvester. Its success led Massey to merge with the Ferguson Company to become Massey-Ferguson and joined harvesting machinery and tractor design to become a world leader in farm equipment. He had turned the management of his farm over to his son Hart to manage, which he did well so Daniel Massey could focus on his machine work developing new, more efficient farming equipment exported and produced worldwide.
International Commerce	The John Deere Company is the largest producer of farming, forestry, and construction equipment globally, with a revenue of $35.5 billion in 2019. Massey-Ferguson Company has become one of the world's largest farm equipment manufacturing providers.
Major Success Factors	Deere's principles are integrity, quality, commitment, and innovation. Deere wanted to make farmers' jobs a bit easier, and his motto was, "I will never put my name on a product that does not have the best in me." He produced creative innovations to help the world's farmers become more productive. Massey wanted to improve the efficiency of farm equipment to make life easier for the farmer.

Farming innovations at first were treated as minor changes in productivity, responding to market-driven demand, which increased overall income and growth of a local economy. They were made public gradually, becoming known only to the local farming community. Eventually, they became exported and then produced worldwide.

George W. Carver (1864–1943, an American agricultural scientist and inventor) promoted alternative crops to cotton and methods to prevent soil depletion. He introduced systematic crop rotation and new crops such as peanuts, sweet potatoes, soybeans, pecans, and other crops to restore nitrogen and improve the soil and farmers' quality of life.

Other innovations outside of agriculture were also barely recognized at the time of inventions, such as firearms and artillery, clock and watchmaking, and navigational equipment learned about from the Arabs who obtained it from the Chinese. Even in industry, any technological advance faced the opposition of authorities, monopolistic guilds, and public companies who feared unemployment would result from labor-saving inventions. Consequently, specific innovations that would significantly increase labor productivity and lower product costs and prices were legally forbidden to be adapted in Britain.

One notable exception was the British textile industry. Weaving advances produced more skilled labor than other innovations that modernized the cotton textile industry for lower-priced mass marketing. However, higher cotton industry profits promoted international trade with America and Africa, and Britain had already become the largest exporter in Europe's largest industry, textiles. The textile entrepreneur was a merchant-manufacturer who purchased the raw materials from overseas, provided them to small, local, home craft pieceworkers such as spinners, weavers, and other skilled artisans, and marketed the final product to distributors and independent marketers for worldwide sales. The **Medici's, Fugger's, and Rothchild's** fortunes created wealthy family merchant-manufactures and finance business empires built around international commerce and trade in textiles and other products. A significant impact on UK mercantilism was the Crown's grants of monopoly privilege and exclusive power to produce and sell domestic and foreign trade to public companies like the most famous **British East India Company.**

Expanding Global Commerce Changes the Shipbuilding Industry

Leading into the First Industrial Revolution, one industry that stands out is shipbuilding. Although there were no significant technological changes in shipping, one necessary change is ships became much more substantial. Many larger vessels were needed to meet the growing needs of international commerce. All ships were made of wood until after the First Industrial Revolution, and they had a short life span of about four years if they were built and used for ocean transportation. The leading shipbuilders were primarily in the Netherlands because of the rapid expansion of Dutch international commerce. The Dutch commercial merchant fleet grew tenfold and experienced an even more considerable increase in tonnage from the beginning of the 16th century to the middle of the 17th century. In responding to this rapid expansion and the demand from other countries, the Dutch Netherlands shipbuilding introduced basic mass-production techniques.

They concentrated its shipbuilding yards in Rotterdam directly north of Antwerp. The shipyards used mechanical saws and hoists powered by windmills, used interchangeable parts, and maintained an ample supply of parts on hand whenever possible. They led the world in shipbuilding efficiency, but they had to import all timber from the Baltic area. The great demand for sailcloth and cording ropes for these sail-powered ships stimulated supporting subsidiary industries in the surrounding areas. Vessels built for commerce in the Atlantic Ocean increased from 200 tons to 600 tons. Even larger ships were built for three-mast ships specialized for large cargo or tankers designed for bulky, low-value cargoes such as grain and timber. A minimal crew operated these large ships to help reduce costs for long ocean voyages. Construction by specialized shipyards using new tools and not convertible into a wartime vessel reduced its cost to half the competitor ships' price. These developments sharply lowered the cost of shipping bulk supplies for Dutch merchants, giving them a significant competitive advantage. The so-called *fluyt*, or large designated cargo vessel, contributed to the 17th-century rise of the Dutch seaborne empire.

Warfare was a significant part of the environment leading up to the First Industrial Revolution. Fiefdoms tried to extend their lands and agricultural output to ensure enough food for their soldiers and commoners who worked on the farms and operated the cottage industries producing textiles and other needs of their Lord. The growing importance of firearms and artillery in warfare resulted in Europe and Britain's metallurgical industries. Wrought iron had been the base metal for weapons, but it was slow and costly to produce and inaccurate. Blast furnaces with air injected by waterwheel-powered bellows, taller furnaces, and higher temperatures helped increase the charge's effectiveness yielding a more robust product. Simultaneously, charcoal ore and a flux added at the top of the furnace helped burn off more impurities strengthening the metal. Molten iron from the bottom was periodically removed to be cast directly into pots, hinges, brackets, or "pigs" or bars for further refining and processing. Heating the pigs and hammering them to remove the carbon produced wrought iron faster and more cheaply. However, it required additional capital to keep more extensive inventories of charcoal and ore for the gigantic furnace. Other improvements included wire-drawing machinery and waterwheel-powered rolling and slitting mills, which rolled and cut the heated pig bars into smaller bars. The iron industry was a heavy user of fuel even with the improvements. Eventually, the iron industry moved to Sweden with its higher-grade ore, plenty of timber, and water to drive the waterwheel. Sweden became the largest supplier of iron in Europe.

Silver mining and production improved in Europe by discovering the mercury amalgamation process for concentrating silver ores. German miners for other metals, including copper, lead, zinc, tin, were the foremost innovators of mining techniques involving deeper shafts, better ventilation, and water-removal pumping machinery. Germany's mining innovations were exported to other European countries to improve production before Watt's steam engine removed water from mines.

Large wood imports from the Baltic and later America began to satisfy the demand and replace the growing shortage of timber for construction, shipbuilding, and charcoal production. The need for coal continued to increase despite its undesirable air pollution. New industries began to emerge to accommodate the procession of new products from America, including sugar refining, tobacco processing, and porcelain dishware. Sugar cane provided the raw material for rum distilleries, and the Dutch invented gin for medicinal purposes, which eventually became an alcoholic drink. There was a gradual distribution throughout Europe of existing production technologies of printing presses for newspapers, books, and paper manufacturing. In Italy, glassware, optical instruments, and clocks became exported to other main population centers throughout Europe and Britain. Most workers in these new areas were part-time and continued to devote most of their energy and time to lower-productivity agricultural output.

The most robust area of persistent and expanding growth was international trade and commerce via Dutch and British sailing ships with Africa, India, China, Japan, and Russia. This expansion helped stimulate productivity and support economic development and technology transfer throughout Europe and Britain. The international trade centers shifted from Italy, Spain, and Portugal to the Dutch Netherlands, Britain, and France. The Dutch and British focused on developing commercial businesses and dominated international business growth between Europe with all the countries East of Europe to Japan. After the Spanish and Portuguese explored the Americas, the British, French, and Dutch established colonies, began business with the natives, and promoted international trade between these new territories and Europe. The shipping trade expanded across the oceans, but it also grew along the path of significant rivers throughout every country.

During the 18th century, the essential products shipped on British, Dutch, and French ships in international trade included timber, grain, fish, wine, metals, textile raw materials (cotton) and cloth, coal, salt and pepper, sugar, tobacco, and hides. In exchange for these products, gold and silver were paid to exporters in the eastern countries. Trade with countries to the west included firearms, knives, metal wares, gun powder, beads, cloth, and eventually enslaved people from Africa. International business practices involved double-entry bookkeeping and credit and bills of exchange. The **Fugger** family business, with headquarters in Augsburg, Germany, became known as one of the greatest and wealthiest business families with offices in major cities throughout Europe, including London, to facilitate international commerce.

Economic Disaster and Prevention of Economic Growth

Between 1500 and 1800, most countries of Europe followed policies that were politically motivated to maximize economic benefit resulting in wasteful wars. Policies included imposing increasingly higher taxes on the country's most productive sectors and industries and monopolistic restrictions supporting specific industries that would only benefit supporters of the monarchy. A mercantilist attitude and conditions were used to subsidize exports and restrict imports of raw materials, products, and new industries that might offer increased investment opportunities in emerging sectors supporting economic growth. Britain and Europe suffered from bad monarchies and politicians during this period, but not the Netherlands.

The Netherlands supported freedom, competition, self-government by towns and townspeople, and investment in productive industries. It did not heavily tax or regulate the productive companies and supported all peoples' independence and democracy, including accepting religious refugees and Jews from Spain and Portugal. No tariffs or subsidies encumbered exports or imports on raw materials or semi-finished goods, and any tariffs on consumer goods did not protect domestic industries. The Dutch also established a financial system in Amsterdam that included the Bank of Amsterdam, which primarily facilitated transactions rather than making loans. The Dutch had a stock exchange, a favorable balance of payments, and little foreign debt. There were no taxes on trade in precious metals like in other European nations, and it is estimated that between one-quarter to one-half of the annual imports of gold and silver from the Spanish Empire went to Amsterdam.

Significant Disruptive Revolution in Life

The industrial transformation in the 18th century represents the beginning of a dramatic change in the style, culture, and quality of life triggered by a period of significant disruptive innovations impacting every aspect of life. People were hungry and prone to illness and early death, while taxed and abused by their monarchies. People were unhappy and tired of being repeatedly abused by their local rulers. Many local rulers had exhausted their resources on wars. As they defaulted on their debts, political leadership became more centralized. Their focus shifted from conflict to gain more land for raw materials or agricultural output. They wanted change in all ways of living, including social, intellectual, political, commercial, financial, and farming. More books and articles became available, more children and adults learned to read. People became better educated and were exposed to the latest ideas and new ways of looking at things. They became curious and learned how to think, analyze, and ask "why" questions to expand understanding. Smaller farms were consolidated into much larger fenced farms, which helped increase agricultural output, provide healthier and taller bodies, and nourish healthier minds.

Scientific research methods such as "observation and experiment" became possible as people at all levels worried less about daily survival from wars, starvation, and sickness. Farmers experimented with new crops and different crop rotations, increasing livestock producing more fertilizer, dairy products, and meat for better diets. Farm enclosures existed privately for decades, but fencing gave farmers more control over their land and animals for experimentation. Gradually larger farms began to emerge, as did professional tenant farmers who rented larger land tracks to increase output more efficiently. Farm machinery appeared in horse-powered, then steam-powered plows, threshers, and harvesters. As farmers became more successful and wealthier, a growing market developed for consumer products, including cotton clothes. Improved iron tools and machinery further promoted the spread of industrialization in response to growing market demand.

The expansion and commercialization of agriculture promoted economic growth even though its share of national income and output declined. Meanwhile, economic development and the farmers growing purchasing power stimulated even faster growth in other sectors. Mining, manufacturing, and construction expanded, boosting its share contribution to national income. Improved trade and transportation methods experienced the most significant increases in their share of the expansion of national income. Goldsmiths began to function as bankers issuing deposit receipts that circulated as banknotes, further facilitating commerce. They made loans to creditable entrepreneurs, such as entrepreneurs involved in commercialization and transportation growth. Gradually, there was a growth of country banks to facilitate growing commercial transactions outside of London.

Over time, there was a reduction in the role and dependence on agriculture because of the increased productivity of farming, which comfortably fed a growing non-agricultural population. There was a shift from small single person or family shop production to larger groups of workers in factories producing much more than had been created by the sum of the individual shops' output. The causes and effects are difficult to separate as they feed on each other to multiply the impact on people's lives and lifestyles and economic growth and development. Craft-produced goods shifted to large factories managed by specialized production and human resource managers, engineers, accountants, inventors, investors, and owners. The movement into large factories came about because of the innovation of using coal instead of wood to power steam engines and blast furnaces. It worked better to remove water from mines to produce more iron and other minerals to make more extensive and more productive machines. The shift of an increasingly large segment of the population into manufacturing industries changed society's culture, but the change was not easy on people's lives. An even more considerable increase in the service industries emerged, especially in professional services that required a much higher level of education and training as science was beginning to blossom. Factory work became more specialized to accommodate lesser-educated workers and expand output.

Innovation and the First Industrial Revolution

During this enlightened period, innovations occurred in four areas: the use of mechanically powered machinery to replace human and animal power; the development of inanimate sources of energy such as fossil fuels; the increase in the use of materials that are created by scientists instead of by nature; and the introduction of new management skills for larger-scale businesses in most industries. The most significant advances in technology to power machinery were innovations related to the steam engine's development by **James Watt (1736–1819, a Scottish inventor, mechanical engineer, and chemist).** The steam engine became used in mining, manufacturing, and transportation powered by coal instead of wood.

Inventions in harvesting and the process of turning imported cotton into more comfortable clothing than more expensive wool expanded the output of the textile and clothing industries. Transportation was enhanced as roads were improved, canals and railroads expanded to transport larger loads over greater distances faster to satisfy growing consumer markets. Agricultural output experienced continuing innovations in production and harvesting methods, so canals and steam locomotives could feed a growing population throughout the USA. Unmet domestic needs increased import demand for food, clothing, and other goods and expanded international trade. The transition drew more workers to giant factories, raising income levels so people could purchase more goods. Increased company earnings from greater domestic and international demand helped finance a continuing growth cycle of expanding the labor force and productivity. Society shifted from being primarily agricultural to becoming more industrial and moving to urban manufacturing centers. The advances in steam power inspired people's imaginations to be creative in other areas.

The First Industrial Revolution started in Britain because of a confluence of these and other forces as living conditions improved due to advances in nutrition, hygiene, and medicine. The birth of industrial production created a larger urban workforce. Agricultural improvements started with laws passed in Britain that enclosed open fields and common lands and created more extensive and more profitable farms. Farmers began to use a crop rotation system so that no land remained unused nor became unproductive. With the introduction of new machinery, new crops, and fertilizers, the population had access to a healthier and more varied diet and continued to grow.

The rapid expansion of global commerce supported Great Britain's dominance of maritime trade through the East India Company and other similar monopoly companies. Britain's agriculture, textile, and international commercial activities provided the capital invested in industrialization. At the same time, domestic businesses also increased due to the greater worker demand for goods and services, and the resulting profits financed industrialization, economic development, and technological advancements in other significant areas. Britain allowed the middle class to participate in government and political decision-making. As a result, they promoted measures with laws to liberalize industrial production and provide a more favorable political and social environment, including legal patent protection for inventors.

What started in Britain then expanded to France, Germany, Italy, Austro-Hungary, Russia, the Netherlands, Scandinavian countries, Spain, and the Ottoman Empire. Finally, in the late 1700s, the US First Industrial Revolution started, aided by immigrants from Europe to gain access to almost unlimited resources and freedoms in the USA. The expansiveness and richness in America's land, lumber, natural resources, and precious metals further stimulated the new arrivals' imaginations and creativity, attracting others from various parts of Europe and other continents.

It was not long before the USA moved into a leadership role in innovation and economic growth. New innovations included the steam-powered ship, sewing machine, telegraph, sanitation plumbing drains and toilets, better and more productive farm equipment, electricity, automobiles, and ever-larger factories with more jobs. Factories promoted the workforce's specialization along a continuously moving assembly line and achieved more significant economies of scale. Factory production drove product prices lower while elevating the income and opportunities for the workers. The most important technological innovation was the introduction of machinery or capital. Each technical advance meant increased productivity and reduced costs. As products became cheaper, demand increased, resulting in higher profits. Innovations expanded productivity, which promoted economic growth and higher standards of living. Since the early 1800s, significant changes occurred in roads, railroads, steamships, ocean shipping, and cars, moving people and freight faster and cheaper. This improvement, combined with communication advancement in telegraph and telephone, connected people and eventually enabled the business community to communicate globally to conduct deals. Production, transportation, and communications innovations expanded productivity and promoted economic growth.

While humans learned to work with early machinery, the steam engine, invented by James Watt in 1769, became a symbol of the First Industrial Revolution. In the meantime, manufacturing systems were moved to ever-larger buildings with more workers divided by specializations under one roof. Each worker executed only a part of the production process. Business investment continued to increase as industries required more extensive money to finance new factories, more complex machinery, a constant inflow of raw materials and fuel. As a result, workers' wages gradually increased.

Transition From Wool to Cotton Textiles

The first sector to use machines in Britain in the 18th century was the textile industry with cotton production. Britain already had a well-developed wool-based textile industry. They imported massive quantities of cotton cloth from India since the climate was not suitable for cotton growing in England or Europe. The British government restricted finished cotton imports from India to stimulate its domestic cotton textile industry. The domestic consumer demand for cotton yarn and clothing rapidly increased because of its comfort and lower price than silk. A growing market with no competition because of import restrictions triggered two new inventions: the **flying shuttle** and the **spinning jenny machine**. These new machines were set up in rows in factories to enable substantial amounts of fabric to be made in less time and for less money, providing Britain's cotton textile industry a competitive advantage over India's cotton fabric. Quickly cotton output expanded tenfold, and factory-produced cotton textiles accounted for a quarter of British exports. British demand for raw cotton imports expanded beyond India to Egypt, the Caribbean, and the southern USA. Britain promoted cotton growth in the USA by exporting Africans to expand plantations as enslaved people to help pay for the cotton shipped back to Britain.

Development of Coal, Iron, and Steel Industries

A critical factor contributing to Britain's manufacturing industry development was its large coal and iron ore supply. Traditionally, the British had converted their iron ores to iron and steel by heating the raw material with charcoal made from burning wood. However, as wood became increasingly scarce and more expensive, **Abraham Darby (1678–1717, a British ironmaster**) began using coke (a solid fuel made by heating coal) in the blast furnaces in 1709. This more efficient process led to a significant development in the production of iron as a raw material. **Henry Bessemer's (1813–1898, a British inventor and engineer)** converter also allowed factories to produce much larger quantities of steel. The invention of the **Bessemer process** was the first inexpensive industrial operation for the mass production of steel from molten pig iron before developing the open-hearth furnace. The procedure removes impurities from the iron by oxidation with air being blown through the molten iron. This oxidation activity also raises the temperature of the iron mass, which keeps it molten. As charcoal's price continued to rise, **Henry Cort's (1741–1800, a British ironmaster)** invention of a **"puddling" and rolling process** in 1783–1784 reduced the iron production process's dependence on charcoal fuel. Cort's process melted bars of big iron in a **reverberatory furnace**, so it did not meet the fuel. The molten iron was then stirred or "puddled" with long rods to burn off the excess carbon and was then run through grooved rollers, which further squeezed out more impurities and provided the desired shape to the bars of wrought iron. This iron metal was then used to shape and construct cotton-weaving machinery.

Case Study #2.3 Significant Disruptive Inventors and Innovations – Construction: Iron and Steel[1]

Key Disruptive Inventors	**Abraham Darby (1678–1717, a British ironmaster)** **Henry Bessemer (1813–1898, a British inventor and engineer)** **Henry Cort (1741–1800, a British ironmaster)**
Location	**Britain**
Disruptive Invention	The Bessemer process was the first inexpensive industrial process for steel's mass production. Darby invented coke (a solid fuel made by heating coal) in the blast furnaces. The molten pig iron removed impurities from the iron by oxidation with air blown through the molten iron, as did Cort's invention of a "puddling" rolling process.
Problem Resolved	The rising cost of energy and impurities in iron weakened its product. The product required much forging to achieve the desired functional shape.
Solution Impact	The process reduced costs and strengthened iron and steel beams and rails for manufacturing, mining, and transportation.

(*Continued*)

(Continued)

Economic Impact	The construction industry emerged for taller and larger buildings and factories, longer bridges, stronger rails for railroads, and more robust machinery for every industry, including larger ships, trains, and eventually autos. Increased iron and steel production expanded economic growth and international trade.
Cultural Impact	People had to travel to factories for work at specific times. Workers began to be assigned specialized work activities and skills organized and guided by managers, while air and noise pollution became a more fundamental problem.
Inventors Education & Training	Darby was apprenticed to Jonathan Freeth, a fellow Quaker and a manufacturer of brass mills for grinding malt. Bessemer was taught and learned about iron production by working with and for his father. Cort learned ironmongery from his uncle working in the family ironmongery business, which supplied the navy with hundreds of different iron products.
Innovation Environment	The environment was robust and expanded growth and new employment opportunities in a new, creative, and transformational period.
Financing	The financial environment was undergoing dramatic changes. Bessemer worked in various mills for and with other investors until he could sell many licenses to use his process, and royalties for his approach generated more than a million pounds sterling. In addition, Cort worked as a Royal Navy pay agent. After leaving the position, Cort took over the family ironmongery business that supplied the navy with mooring chains, anchors, and hundreds of ironmongery items. Cort borrowed a substantial amount from the new chief clerk in the Royal Navy Pay Office to launch Titchfield Hammer. Later, Cort agreed with a South Wales ironmaster that all iron manufactured according to Cort's patents would result in 10 shillings per ton royalty.
International Commerce	Darby joined several Quakers to form the Bristol Brass Company and Cheese Lane Foundry to make brass and iron cooking pots and pans. He also built two blast furnaces to expand production. Bessemer built steelworks in Sheffield in a business partnership with others and Greenwich, London producing iron and steel prices below others. Cort began refining the iron from pig iron to wrought iron using innovative production systems he invented. They were adopted throughout Britain, with processed products exported to other countries.
Major Success Factors	These innovators and entrepreneurs were driven, persistent, tenacious, problem-solving, continuously innovative, and had solid analytical capacities with iron and steel manufacturing equipment. They enjoyed competing and time was most valuable to them.

To meet the increased demand for shipping manufactured textiles, the early part of the First Industrial Revolution saw improvements made to roads and canals in Britain. The first passenger railway line was built, joining Manchester and the shipping port of Liverpool in 1830. Over the next few decades, rail lines were built throughout continental Europe. Increased train speed, security, and hauling capacity reduced the cost of transporting goods on land. As a result, railways were constructed throughout Europe and later spread worldwide. The steam engine's use on trains and ships changed the transportation industry dynamics. The steam locomotive revolutionized transportation, supporting the delivery of manufactured machinery and products. A coal-fired steam engine powered the locomotive, and it pulled flatbeds or box cars for freight and carriages for passengers. The first steamboats began operating in the USA in 1807, and in 1847 steamships could cross the Atlantic in 15 days.

Sources of Energy

At the beginning of the 1800s in Britain, what industry there was, was primarily spread throughout rural areas and consisted of small family-run farms or cottage industries producing crops and cloth. The same was true for the rest of Europe also. This production process was because the primary power source was from wooden waterwheels near and driven by a river. The larger businesses consisted primarily of wool from local sheep farms. Urban-based entrepreneurial merchants supplied rural workers with natural materials and then marketed them locally and through international exports to British colonies overseas. In addition, prominent wealthy or royal landowner entrepreneurs were often engaged in the coal industry or mining other materials such as lead, copper, iron ore, or timber for homes, buildings, and ships.

During the mid-1800s, England and Scotland began experiencing a labor force productivity transformation with labor relocation to urban centers. The more rapid expansion in output from industrialization continually reduced the percent of GDP accounted for by agriculture output. Furthermore, the gradual transition of the population into large urban centers was triggered by growth in innovations and the early birth of giant factories to produce the first machinery and products of modern society's industrialization. This shift in the labor force created many challenges for humanity, such as increased pollution and deteriorating health conditions in the cities.

Urban Centers Emerge With Immigrations

The solutions that increased agricultural productivity were the rotation of field crops and pastures to feed more animals, improving soil fertility. Expanding and improving the food for animals produced more cattle, resulting in more fertilizer output to improve land output. The actual size of the average farm also began to expand to more than 300 acres. The enclosure of fields also led to selective breeding to increase meat, dairy, and wool output to satisfy growing urban demands. During the second half of the 1800s, farming mechanization expanded as farm machinery such as threshers and harvesters and eventually steam engine plows continued to improve animal and human food output per acre.

In the second half of the 1800s, with the growth in more densely populated cities, new concerns, needs, and bottlenecks emerged: how to transport an increasing demand for food into growing urban centers to feed people, how to store food to keep it from rotting, how to house the rising urban labor force population, and transport them to their workplace and back home at designated times, and how to train the new labor force for the changing technology of machinery and unique production processes of skill specializations and to work in large factories with much larger groups of people than on a farm. This period also emerged from a growing need for knowledge and education to keep up with the steadily changing occupations and new skills required to support industrialization. Workers and factory owners needed to learn how to read and communicate more complex production processes and commercialization. Britain was at the center of this process for changing economic infrastructure and applying the scientific method of observation and experimentation by self-taught engineers whose inventions came about from "trial and error experimentation."

Waterwheel Power Retires

The first reaction to growing production in urban areas was using existing energy sources such as the waterwheel, which originated in Persia, Egypt, India, and Greece before use in the Greek and Roman Empire periods. The waterwheel was used in most major industries, such as grain milling, textiles, mining, and lumber production. Significant innovations by **John Smeaton I (1724–1792, a British civil engineer and inventor)** in the 18th century to meet growing waterwheel efficiency needs were accomplished by adjusting where the flowing water was directed to strike the wheel. Research and testing alternative contact points for water powering the revolution focused on moving the river water contact point to the top of the waterwheel called backshot or overshot. Overshot added the force of gravity to the streamflow speed force and raised the waterwheel's efficiency from 50–60% to 80–90%. Varying the width and height of the waterwheel could also impact its power generation. The least efficient power generation occurred with stream undershot or breastshot.

The waterwheel's limitation as a source of power is the stream's location and the height the water can fall before striking the waterwheel. As a result, there was a growing need for power locations closer to labor sources in urban centers. There was also a need for increasing the amount of machine power produced to satisfy the needs of expanding industry, larger machines and factories, and the growing demands for iron and steel as forests were being depleted. Scarce wood for constructing housing and larger factories became too expensive and did not satisfy the required strength for taller buildings and longer strands. Consequently, the demand for steel beams expanded.

The expansion and diversification of the British economy required improvement in its infrastructure. The Romans had built a network of roads in Britain, all leading to London, strategically located along the Thames River to support its growth as a major shipping center for ocean-going ships. A series of canals and waterways were built in the 18th century to connect with navigable rivers and link all critical production and consumption centers with London as the center of economic activity since Parliament financed all acts. Roads built for horses and horse-drawn carriages were primarily funded by parishes who typically charged tolls, but most roads were not well maintained. By the early 1800s, more than 20,000 miles of major highways and turnpikes had been constructed throughout Britain.

Birth of Iron, Steel, and the Steam Engine

Historians of the First Industrial Revolution point to three innovations that triggered the drive to the mechanization of the industry: the process for smelting iron ore with coke instead of charcoal as charcoal was becoming increasingly expensive. The atmospheric (low pressure) steam engine became the primary power source for industrial machinery, replacing waterwheels and windmills as the primary energy source. And the rapid growth and mechanization of the cotton industry provided lower costs and more comfortable clothing.

In 1709, **Abraham Darby**, an ironmaster, had developed coke by heating coal in a closed container to remove the damaging impurities leaving coke or carbon, which was then used to fuel the blast furnace to make pig iron. Previously, the wood had been heated in a container to form charcoal, which was getting increasingly expensive as Britain's timber supply was depleted. Another innovation that enhanced the coke's acceptance and was used to make iron in 1783 by Henry Cort is the puddling and rolling process. When ironmasters combined all three of these processes in one continuous operation, significant economies of scale could be achieved, which improved Britain's competitiveness in making and exporting iron and iron products.

The increased demand for coal and metals caused mining companies to dig deeper mines, and flooding water in mines became an even more significant problem to increasing mine production. **Thomas Savery (1650–1715, a British inventor and engineer)** in 1698 obtained a patent for a steam pump, but it tended to explode because of the high steam pressure it generated that could not be contained in weak chambers. Therefore, it was not very efficient and had the negative side effect of polluting the local environment. In 1712 **Thomas Newcomen (1664–1729, a British inventor and military engineer)** designed an "atmospheric" or low-pressure steam pump for coal mines. The Newcomen steam pump was massive, and it burned significant amounts of coal to create enough steam in a cylinder to raise a large piston connected via a "T" shaped rocking beam to a pump. Cold water was then used to condense the steam creating a vacuum, and the weight of the atmosphere (or gravity) depressed the piston activating the rocking beam-driven pump to remove water from the mine. The Newcomen engines were used primarily to extract water in coal mines where coal was readily available and inexpensive because of their need to burn lots of coal. Therefore, it was not very efficient and had the negative side effect of polluting the local environment.

In 1769, **James Watt** experimented with the Newcomen steam engine and obtained a patent for adding a separate condenser to eliminate the piston cylinder's need for alternate heating and cooling. In 1774 he met **John Wilkinson (1728–1808, a British industrialist and ironmaster)** who had just received a new patent for making cannon barrels rounder and smoother. Watt and his partner and manufacturer **Matthew Boulton (1728–1809, a British industrialist and manufacturer)** used Wilkinson's technology to launch commercial production of mine water pumping steam engines, which Wilkinson adopted to use with his blast furnace. Since coal had become expensive, the Watt-Bolton steam engine became attractive because it was much less costly. Watt continued to improve his machine, adding a governor to regulate the engine's speed and a device that changed the reciprocating motion to a rotary motion, making the engine able to power grain milling and cotton spinning for cloth production. The Watt–Boulton steam engine was used widely in Britain as the primary power source for manufacturing and accelerated the First Industrial Revolution. By the end of the 1800s, Britain had become a major exporter of iron and iron wares.

Case Study #2.4 Significant Disruptive Inventors and Innovations – The Steam Engine Energy for Industry[2]

Key Disruptive Inventors	**James Watt (1736–1819, a Scottish inventor, mechanical engineer, and chemist)**
Location	**Scotland and Britain**
Disruptive Invention	Made significant, innovative improvements in the **Newcomen** steam engine that resulted in a steam engine that was an efficient power source for driving factory machinery and mine pumps to remove water. Watt's more powerful steam engine could be located anywhere and drove the industrial revolution.
Problem Resolved	Power from waterwheels or windmills was limited in strength and effectiveness and often in remote locations. They became increasingly unable to meet the demand for energy in the late 17th and 18th centuries as an industry with new technologies began to expand.
Solution Impact	More rapid growth in Britain meant its demand for wood for fuel in the form of charcoal and coke was deforesting the country and boosting the price of wood sharply. The result was an increase in the demand for coal, which increased sharply and needed additional minerals required by industry. The result was a growing need to remove water from mines, becoming a significant barrier to economic growth.

Economic Impact	As the supply of more efficient Watt steam engines increased and became more mobile, the energy cost declined. This also reduced the costs of the product. In addition, industrial production could be located nearer the raw material site or closer to transportation points for shipping. Factories could also be located close to lower-cost labor near the edges of the urban center.
Cultural Impact	There was a growing need for more well-educated workers to function in the more industrialized world. For lower-level workers, unions became essential to protect the standard of living of the working class. Time for enjoyment became increasingly scarce and more critical. Urban industrial centers were beginning to emerge in Europe and the USA, and better transportation systems became a concern for freight and people.
Inventors Education & Training	Watt grew up in Scotland, went to grammar school, and learned arithmetic. He had a high aptitude for math and geometry, like his grandfather. Watt's father was a successful small merchant and provided James with a workbench and tools in his workshop. He demonstrated his imagination, cheerful disposition, and creativity with his father's guidance. Watt worked persistently and analyzed and made accurate measurements to quantify his improvements. However, most of his more advanced education came from on-the-job learning and problem-solving.
Innovation Environment	It was an exciting time of change and an uncertain time with all the changes. The economic environment improved, and protecting inventions with a patent was necessary. Companies were beginning to make employees sign agreements that the company owned any creations or patents related to work. As a result, the number of innovations and patents grew more rapidly.
Financing	In 1754 James' mother and brother died, and his father suffered a financial loss from a shipwreck. At age 18, James took a position as an instrument maker apprentice and then took a job at the University of Glasgow as a "Mathematical Instrument Maker" in the physics department. He partnered with Chemistry Professor Joseph Black and made nautical instruments. In the early 1760s, he met Professor John Robinson, who introduced James to the Newcomen steam engine, which the University was studying why large machines used so much steam to operate. Watt's analysis suggested that it would rush into a vacuum cylinder and condense without cooling it since steam was elastic. So, he incorporated a condenser chamber in the steam engine into which the piston would move by steam force.

(*Continued*)

(Continued)

Watt worked to improve the Newcomen steam engine by removing atmospheric pressure. In Watt's steam engine, the piston's downstroke was caused by a vacuum in the cylinder below the piston as steam went from the cylinder into the condenser chamber. Watt improved the seal around the piston by using grease and lowered the condenser steam temperature to enhance the piston chamber's vacuum. Next, he located the steam chamber alongside but below the level of the piston cylinder. Finally, the steam chamber was attached to a pump with a piston operated by a thin rod connected to the main pumping beam, making the engine's operation automatic. The effect was to reduce the amount of heat used to drive the cylinder's pumping force, which helped to reduce the amount of coal needed by about 70%+/– of the Newcomen's engine, thereby significantly reducing the amount of coal required, lowering the operating cost and pollution of the Watt engine.

Watt's next challenge was to produce a full-scale model engine and commercialize his invention to meet the industry's needs. Watt had received financial support from his friend and associate at the University, Professor Joseph Black, who had supplied Watt with a significant loan. In 1769, Watt obtained a 14-year patent for his engine and his new friend John Roebuck was given two-thirds ownership of the patent to pay off Watt's loan from Professor Black. Black had earlier introduced Watt to John Roebuck, a part-owner of Carron Iron Works, and owned a coal mine with a water flooding problem. In 1768, Watt met Matthew Boulton, a successful manufacturer, and both became close friends. Watt had previously visited Boulton's Soho machinery factory, one of the largest at the time, and Boulton wanted to manufacture Watt's steam engine. However, Roebuck, who owned two-thirds of Watt's steam engine patent, only offered a license to sell the machines in a small, limited area. Boulton declined the offer because the area was too small to cover the production facilities' costs. Instead, Roebuck agreed to finance Watt to construct a full-size engine over his mineshaft, but Roebuck's men did not have the skills to complete the job. As a result, Roebuck eventually became bankrupt when credit availability collapsed in England.

Boulton was a significant creditor of Roebuck and, in settlement of the latter's debt, took Roebuck's share of Watt's steam engine patent in 1773, and Watt's partnership with Roebuck ended. Boulton's money came when he married a wealthy heir Mary Robinson who died in 1753 childless. Watt had taken a survey job for seven years to sustain his family. In 1774 at age 38, Watt quit the survey job and moved to Birmingham, where Boulton lived. Watt's steam engine's 1769 patent was to expire in 1783, so Boulton and Watt applied to Parliament for an extension, and in 1775 the patent was extended 25 years to 1800, covering both Scotland and England. Thus, the Boulton–Watt partnership to build steam engines began and significantly drove the Industrial Revolution. Watt was the inventor, and Boulton provided the commercialization, substantial capital, management expertise, business initiative, and capacity to influence Watt. Boulton made Watt's inventions a commercial success and excelled at marketing and negotiating deals with customers.

With the help of Boulton's highly skilled ironworkers, Watt made a series of improvements to the steam engine between 1774 and 1887. Watt knew that the piston and cylinder seal needed improvement for the machine to become an even more efficient energy producer. Watt arranged a meeting with John Wilkinson, who had developed a new water-powered, precision drilling mill that could bore a smooth, uniform barrel channel for the cannons. In 1775, after receiving Wilkinson's new iron cylinder and piston, Watt and Boulton rebuilt a much more efficient operating steam engine that used less than half the Newcomen engine's fuel. Wilkinson installed five-Watt steam engines in his foundries to power the blowers for blast furnaces and pumped water out of his coal mine. The word spread, and soon other foundries began to purchase Watt–Boulton engines. The Watt engines were large and had a 50-inch diameter piston for pumping water out of a mine. Wilkinson also used Watt–Boulton steam engines to power a tilt hammer pump in the waterworks in Paris and power a 70-foot steel barge. These sales of the various uses of the Watt engine began to attract more customers. Watt pursued additional patented inventions such as the rotating motion used by most machines in factories like the large cotton and textile industries to expand the Watt–Boulton steam engine's market and services. Wilkinson continued to be responsible for boring the cylinder holes for the pistons for Watt's engines for the next 20 years. Boulton and Watt developed a creative sales agreement to deliver and install the machine for their steam engine. The buyer would pay only an annual rent amount equal to one-third of the fuel saved by replacing the Newcomen engine with the Watt engine. Watt continued to improve his steam engine, including various instruments and devices.

(*Continued*)

(Continued)

	In 1781 Boulton saw new markets in corn, malt, and cotton mills and urged Watt to invent a steam engine's rotary motion. The following year he patented the double-acting steam engine, in which the piston was pushed and pulled by injecting steam above and below the piston. Watt pursued additional patented inventions, including the rotating motion drive shaft. To implement this change, Watt used his so-called "sun-and-planet gear" invention. An arm produced two revolutions for each steam engine cycle, converting reciprocating motion to rotary motion. This conversion was done by fixing a cogwheel at the end of the rod connected to the steam engine's main beam. With the main beam's motion, the cogwheel (planet) revolved around and turned the second cogwheel (the sun) a second rotating cog or gear fixed to the drive shaft generating a rotary motion. When both sun and planet have the same number of teeth, the drive shaft completes two revolutions for each double stroke of the main beam instead of one. The planet gear is fixed to the connecting rod and thus does not rotate around its axis.
International Commerce	Because the Watt steam engine was so large and heavy, it could not be quickly shipped or moved by wagon. However, the products it helped to produce became less expensive because they used less fuel. As a result, these products became more competitive in international commerce and created increased domestic demand. Also, as the steam engine became more refined by other inventors, they powered locomotives for railroads and steam-powered ships for ocean shipping, which helped promote international commerce for the USA. Britain refused to export to the USA of Watt's steam engine for fear of losing its competitiveness.
Major Success Factors	Curious, driven, persistent, tenacious, problem-solving, continuously innovative, and analytical capacities with steam energy producing equipment, enjoyed competing, and time was most valuable to them. Adopted the ideas of others and worked well with Boulton and his management and marketing talents.

Note

All dates, innovators information, and events have been checked against information in the following sources: *Encyclopedia Britannica, Encyclopedia Americana, Collier's Encyclopedia, Compton's Encyclopedia, Investopedia, and Wikipedia.*

3 Transitioning to the Second Industrial Revolution

Cotton Industry

The desire to reduce costs and improve productivity encouraged several labor-saving inventions that were more easily achieved in less regulated industries such as cotton. Cotton benefited from being a new product, unlike wool and linen, government and industry-regulated. For example, in 1733, a mechanic **John Kay (1704–1780, a British machinist and engineer)** invented the flying shuttle. As a result, the required number of workers fell from two to one, lowering the weaving machine's operating costs and increasing the demand for cotton yarn. In 1764, **James Hargreaves (1720–1778, a British weaver and carpenter)** invented the spinning jenny, the spinning wheel with several spindles instead of one, which enabled one person to complete the work of several. This further reduced cotton production costs and increased cotton cloth supply to meet growing demand. In 1768, **Richard Arkwright (1732–1792, a British inventor and entrepreneur)** invented the spinning machine. The giant machine was run by waterpower and, therefore, near streams and employed primarily women paid lower wages than men.

Case Study #3.1 Significant Disruptive Inventors and Innovations – Textiles: Cotton Spinning[1,2]

Key Disruptive Inventors	**Richard Arkwright (1732–1792, a British inventor and a leading entrepreneur)**
Location	**UK**
Disruptive Invention	In 1769, Arkwright patented the spinning frame, collaborating with John Kay, which produced twisted threads using wooden and metal cylinders rather than human fingers. In 1775 he received a patent for a new carding engine that converted raw cotton into a continuous thread before spinning. It could make cotton thread-thin and robust enough for the interwoven threads of cotton cloth. It significantly reduced cotton-spinning costs, resulting in significant textile industry changes.

(*Continued*)

DOI: 10.4324/9781003024675-4

(Continued)

Problem Resolved	Costly and time-consuming twisting of cotton became significantly faster and less expensive to produce.
Solution Impact	Britain's cotton textile competitiveness was improved by reducing its cost while improving its quality. He brought in workers from outside the locality, building a cluster of cottages near the mill to house them. Little training was required to operate the machinery making labor costs low.
Economic Impact	Arkwright's achievement was to combine power, machinery, semi-skilled labor, and the new raw material of cotton to create mass-produced yarn. His organizational skills earned him the accolade "father of the modern industrial factory system."
Cultural Impact	The development introduced families to significant factory life in a countryside location living in company housing with one week vacation.
Inventors Education & Training	Arkwright's parents could not afford to send him to school and instead arranged for his cousin Ellen to teach him to read and write.
Innovation Environment	Arkwright could patent his inventions, but efforts to enforce a Grand Patent failed because public opinion was hostile toward exclusive patents with so many competitors.
Financing	He began his working life as a barber and wig-maker. He invented a waterproof dye for use on the fashionable periwigs, the income from which he later funded his prototype cotton machinery. Next, Arkwright became interested in developing carding and spinning machinery to replace hand labor in converting raw cotton into the thread for weaving. In 1771, Arkwright and his partners built the world's first water-powered mill, covering both carding and spinning operations employing 200 people.
International Commerce	Arkwright's innovations enabled cotton textiles and clothing to be competitively exported from Britain to the world.
Major Success Factors	Arkwright's achievement was to combine power, machinery, semi-skilled labor, and the new raw material of cotton to create mass-produced yarn. His organizational skills earned him the "father of the modern industrial factory system." Aggressive and self-sufficient, Arkwright bought out all his partners and built factories at Manchester, Matlock Bath, New Lanark, etc.

Around 1779, **Samuel Compton (1753–1827, a British inventor)**, who learned how to spin yarn to support the family, experienced deficiencies. He invented the machine that combined the spinning jenny and the water frame (so-called "mule") to spin larger quantities of robust yarn. Around 1790 it was modified to use steam engine power. The "mule" became the predominant method of cotton spinning, and rows of "mules" were arranged in large factories built in cities with access to cheap coal and a concentration of workers. In 1785, a clergyman

Edmund Cartwright (1743–1823, a British inventor), with little experience in spinning and weaving, invented the power loom, which replaced the handloom weaving machines set up in large factories. The shift from small handicraft home production to large factories began labor specialization. Labor division led to the creation of managers to oversee all aspects of factory production.

Improved cloth production capability required an increased supply of cotton to be imported. Rising cotton demand was constrained by the high cost and slow process of hand removal of seeds. In 1793, **Eli Whitney (1765–1825, an American inventor)** invented a mechanical engine (gin) to remove seeds, and with continued modifications, the USA became the leading supplier of cotton to Britain's largest industry. The sharp price decline in cotton cloth and clothing and increased world demand gave US producers a competitive position. This development process became an essential model for facilitating other technological innovations. The process is also an example of how production innovations that require increased use of more significant amounts of raw material can stimulate international trade. Cotton grown in the US south was competitively priced and exported to satisfy Britain's growing demand. The finished cotton material was shipped worldwide to meet growing demand. Today the largest cotton-producing countries ranked are India, the USA, China, and Brazil.

Case Study #3.2 Significant Disruptive Inventors and Innovations – Clothing: Cotton Textiles[1–3]

Key Disruptive Inventors	**Eli Whitney (1765–1825, an American inventor)**
Location	**USA**
Disruptive Invention	Whitney invented the cotton gin, the machine to remove seeds from cotton. He was an advocate of interchangeable parts.
Problem Resolved	Removing seeds from cotton was a slow labor-intensive process yielding about a pound of seedless cotton per day. The cotton gin was a wooden drum stuck with hooks that pulled the cotton fibers through a mesh, but the cotton seeds would not fit and fell outside the mesh.
Solution Impact	A cotton gin generated up to 55 pounds of cleaned cotton daily, transforming Southern agriculture and the national economy.
Economic Impact	The cotton gin enabled a sharp increase in the output of washed cotton in the US south. The cotton was exported to Britain, significantly increasing the plantation owners' income, lowering the cost of cotton, and transforming Southern agriculture into the national economy.
Cultural Impact	Some historians suggest that this invention allowed African slavery to become more sustainable. Cotton became the most popular form of clothing throughout the world.

(*Continued*)

(Continued)

Inventors Education & Training	Whitney expected to study law but was short of funds, took a job, and never enrolled at Yale law school. His parents educated him. He attended Leicester Academy (now Becker College) in Connecticut and graduated Phi Beta Kappa in 1792.
Innovation Environment	Whitney spent substantial funds in legal battles over patent infringement for the cotton gin. The Whitney gin was easily duplicated, and he and his partner could not produce enough gins to meet demand. Whitney's invention was later improved upon and received a patent. However, Whitney and his partner lost most of their money trying to defend their patent.
Financing	Eli Whitney Sr. was a prosperous farmer. In 1780, Eli Jr., at age 14, operated a profitable nail manufacturing operation in his father's workshop during the Revolutionary War and then worked as a farm laborer and schoolteacher to save college money. Later Whitney went to visit a Georgia plantation, Mulberry Grove. The plantation manager became Whitney's business partner. Whitney did not make a fortune from his cotton gin after the expenses of patent violation lawsuits. So he tried securing contracts with the government to manufacture muskets for the newly formed US Army.
International Commerce	Southern states experienced a boom in cotton exports, and cotton became the USA's chief export, representing over half the value of total exports from 1820 to 1860.
Major Success Factors	Whitney had a very inventive mind that could visualize solutions

Dishware

International imports of delicate porcelain dishware from China by the wealthy as a substitute for gold- and silver-plated dishware created other domestic production opportunities. Pottery dishes became a domestic import-substitution industry for more expensive tableware from China. Several pottery artisans saw a chance to produce tableware domestically to compete with wooden or pewter dishes widely used by the middle-class in Britain. Also, at the same time in Britain, the demand for tea and coffee from America was beginning to expand as workers' incomes were rising with growing employment in large factories. The merger of these independent forces resulted in growth opportunities in small startup pottery shops. Individual shop artisans could produce different makes, styles, and tableware shapes for everyday use by the growing middle-class workforce.

Railroad and Steam Locomotives

The deforestation of Britain and Europe and the reduction in increasingly expensive wood supply caused the search for an alternative source of heat energy, resulting in the coal mining industry's growth. The need to remove water from mines resulted in the steam engine's invention, powered by wood and coal. Wood and then coal-fired steam engines were used to pump water out of the coal mines so that miners could dig coal, load it on a cart and transport it utilizing a shaft to ground level. The first railroads were used in coal mines on iron tracks to move coal and then above ground to transport coal to power steam engines located close to the coal mines. As the tunnels of coal mines grew, longer rails were used to move carts of coal to shafts lifted to the surface by human or animal power. At first, horses moved the carts over the rails, but later steam engines pulled cables to move coal carts. However, Watt's steam engines were too big, heavy, and lacked the power to move a locomotive.

The design and building of locomotive steam engines required more accurate and detailed machine tools. **John Wilkinson (1728–1808, a British industrialist and ironmaster)** had established some fundamental techniques for fabricating more precise machine tools with his accurate boring machine for cast-iron cannons. **John Smeaton**'s innovations significantly improved the efficiency of the atmospheric steam engine. **Henry Maudsley (1771–1831, a British machine tool engineer, tool and die maker, and inventor)** invented the slide-rest screw-cutting lathe in 1791, producing accurate metal parts. In 1801 **Richard Trevithick (1771–1833, a British mining engineer)** designed, constructed a high-pressure steam engine, and built the first locomotive to run on ordinary roads and mine rails. Still, neither could withstand the weight of the locomotive. **George Stephenson (1781–1848, British civil engineer and mechanical engineer, a self-taught engineer, and inventor)** in 1825 built and drove a steam engine locomotive to run on a railway between Liverpool and Manchester. George's son **Robert Stephenson (1803–1859, a British railway and civil engineer)** built on his father's achievements and was considered the most outstanding engineer of the 19th century. Robert was an apprenticed to the mining engineer **Nicholas Wood (1795–1865, a British colliery and steam locomotive engineer)**. Robert's father built the Liverpool and Manchester Railway, and Robert developed the steam locomotive *Rocket* that won the Rainhill Trials in 1829, in which five locomotive engines competed. Robert was appointed chief engineer of the London and Birmingham Railway in 1833 with a £1,500 per annum salary. By 1850 Robert had constructed a third of the country's railway system. He also designed the High-Level Bridge and Royal Border Bridge on the East Coast Main Line with **Eaton Hodgkinson (1789–1861, a British engineer and a pioneer applying mathematics to structural design problems).** Hodgkinson and Stephensen worked with **William Fairbairn (1789–1874, a Scottish civil engineer, structural engineer, and shipbuilder)** to develop wrought-iron tubular bridges. Hodgkinson built railways in France, Belgium, Norway, and Egypt.

Case Study #3.3 Significant Disruptive Inventors and Innovations – Transportation: Railroad and Steam Locomotive[4–8]

Key Disruptive Inventors	**Richard Trevithick (1771–1833, a British mining engineer)** **George Stephenson (1781–1848, British civil engineer and mechanical engineer, a self-taught engineer, and inventor) and son** **Robert Stephenson Jr. (1803–1859, a British railway and civil engineer)**
Location	**UK**
Disruptive Invention	Steam locomotive established reliable overland mass transportation for passengers and freight.
Problem Resolved	Complex, slow, and high-cost transportation became less expensive and faster for the movement of goods and people.
Solution Impact	Lower cost and faster passenger and freight mobility between cities and urban centers facilitated centralized production & consumption centers in larger cities. As a result, more workers had access to more varied jobs and incomes, and consumers had access to many more products at a lower cost and faster.
Economic Impact	The result was increased urbanization, greater individual mobility independence, concentration & specialization of industries & markets. There were economies of scale for producers and consumers, resulting in lower prices. The travel industry was launched and expanded over longer distances.
Cultural Impact	Factories could be located anywhere and were not constrained by transportation and distribution. Labor could be moved more easily if housing were provided or available. In addition, male workers were separated from families.
Inventors Education & Training	Few educational institutions, few books, learn from parents and experiment to solve problems.
Innovation Environment	There were improvements in free-market competition, a growing economy, supportive government, patent office to register but little enforcement protection to restrain violators.
Financing	Scarce with no traditional funding markets, financing came primarily from friends, family, and wealthy individuals who saw a significant income opportunity.
International Commerce	During the USA's formative years, the 13 colonies were prevented by Britain from importing any machinery or industrial equipment. Eventually, railroads and shipping would be linked to promoting international trade.

Major Success Factors	Curious, driven, persistent, tenacious, problem-solving, continuously innovative, and analytical capacities with steam energy producing equipment, enjoyed competing, and time was most valuable to them. Adopted the ideas of others and worked well with Boulton and his management and marketing talents.

Steamboat Transportation

In 1785, **John Fitch (1743–1798, an American inventor, clockmaker, entrepreneur, and engineer)** settled in Pennsylvania and worked on a steam-powered boat. Unable to raise funds from the Continental Congress, he persuaded various state legislatures to award him a 14-year monopoly for steamboat traffic on their inland waterways. With these monopolies, he secured funding from businesspeople in Philadelphia. Fitch had seen a drawing of an early British Newcomen atmospheric engine, and they were too massive for a boat. He had heard about the more efficient steam engine developed by James Watt in Scotland in the late 1770s. Britain restricted exports of any new technology to its former American colony. Fitch moved to Philadelphia and engaged the clockmaker and inventor **Henry Voigt (1783–1814, an American clockmaker, mathematical instrument maker, machine and steam engine builder, and Chief Coiner of the first US Mint)** to help him build a working model and place it on a boat. His steamboat *Perseverance's* first successful trial run was made on the Delaware River in 1787. It was propelled by a bank of oars on either side of the boat. Fitch and Voigt worked to develop better designs, and in 1790, they launched a 60-foot boat powered by a steam engine driving several stern-mounted oars that paddled like duck's feet.

Robert Fulton (1765–1815, an American engineer and inventor) is widely credited with developing a commercially successful steamboat, the *North River Steamboat* (renamed *Clermont*). In 1807 the *Clermont* traveled on the Hudson River with passengers, from New York City to Albany and back, a round trip of 300 miles in 62 hours. The success of this steamboat changed river traffic and trade on major American rivers. At 23, Fulton traveled to England to live for the next 20 years, where he began developing ideas for tugboat canals with inclined planes instead of locks. Fulton obtained a patent for his tugboat canal in 1794 and began working on ideas for steam-powered boats, published a pamphlet about canals, and patented the dredging machine and several other inventions. In 1794, Fulton moved to Manchester to gain practical knowledge of British canal engineering. He met **Robert Owen (1771–1858, a Welsh textile manufacturer, philanthropist, and social reformer)**, a cotton manufacturer. Owen agreed to finance the development and promotion of Fulton's designs for inclined planes and earth-digging machines. He introduced Fulton to a canal company, which awarded him a contract which he declined.

The first steamships with a steam engine moving oars were constructed by **Claude de Jouffroy (1751–1832, a French steamboat inventor)** in France called *Palmipède*. In 1783, de Jouffroy built *Phyroscaphe*, the first paddle steamer which sailed on the Saone River. **William Symington (1764–1831, a British engineer)** had successfully built steamboats in 1788, and Fulton was aware of these developments. In Britain, Fulton met the Duke of Bridgewater, **Francis Egerton (1736–1803, British nobility and founder of British inland navigation & canals),** whose canal was being constructed in the country used for trials of a steam tug. Fulton became very enthusiastic about the canals and wrote a 1796 treatise on their construction, suggesting improvements to locks and other features. Working for the Duke of Bridgewater between 1796 and 1799, Fulton had a boat constructed and christened the *Bonaparte* in honor of Fulton's service under Napoleon. In 1801, Egerton ordered eight vessels built by Symington. After expensive trials, the team feared the paddles might damage the canal's clay lining and eventually abandoned the experiment. In 1797 Fulton went to Paris and met **James Rumsey (1743–1792, an American mechanical engineer)**, an inventor from Virginia interested in steamboats. In 1786, he ran his first steamboat up the Potomac River. While living in France, Fulton designed the first working muscle-powered submarine, *Nautilus*, between 1793 and 1797 and experimented with torpedoes. When evaluated, his submarine operated underwater for 17 minutes in 25 feet of water, but the government declined to subsidize its construction. In 1800 the Minister of Marine granted permission to build it, and it sailed on the Seine River.

While in France, Fulton met **Robert R. Livingston (1746–1813, an American lawyer, politician, diplomat from New York),** the US Ambassador to France. They decided to build a steamboat to operate on the Seine. The ship was 66 feet long, had an 8-foot beam, and a speed of 3–4 miles per hour against the current. At the first trial, the boat ran perfectly, but in 1803, it sank on the River Seine. In 1804, Fulton moved to Britain as Prime Minister William Pitt the Younger requested him to build several weapons for the Royal Navy during Napoleon's invasion. His inventions were the world's first naval "torpedoes" or "mines." These were used in the 1804 raid on Boulogne with limited success. Fulton continued experimenting until 1806 when the British victory by Admiral Horatio Nelson at the Battle of Trafalgar reduced the risk of a French invasion.

From 1811 to 1812, Fulton, along with Livingston and **Nicholas Roosevelt (1767–1854, an American inventor),** worked together on a joint project to build a new steamboat called *New Orleans*, which was sturdy enough to be taken down the Ohio and Mississippi rivers to New Orleans. By proving the steamboat's ability to travel upstream against powerful river currents, Fulton changed the American heartland's river's total trade and transportation outlook. Fulton's final design was the first steam-driven warship built for the US Navy for the War of 1812. After Fulton's death, the heavy vessel was completed and named after him.

John Stevens (1749–1838, an American lawyer, engineer, and inventor) was born in New York City, the son of John Stevens Jr., a prominent state politician. His sister, Mary Stevens, married Robert R. Livingston, the first Chancellor of New York. His maternal grandparents were James Alexander, the Attorney General of New Jersey, and Mary Alexander, a prominent merchant in New York

City. The latter served as a delegate to the Continental Congress. Stevens graduated from King's College (Columbia University) in 1768, then studied law and was admitted to New York City's bar in 1771. He practiced law in New York and lived in New Jersey. Stevens built an estate at Castle Point, later becoming the Stevens Institute of Technology site. In 1790, Stevens petitioned Congress for a bill that would protect American inventors. His bill became law in 1790, enacting the US patent system. In 1802, he built a screw-driven steamboat *Phoenix* that sailed from Hoboken to Philadelphia in 1809 and became the first steamship to navigate the open ocean successfully. In 1811, Steven's ship, the *Juliana*, began operation as the first steam ferry service between New York City and Hoboken, NJ.

The first US railroad charter was given to Stevens and others in 1815 for the New Jersey Railroad. Through the Camden & Amboy Railroad, Stevens and his partners almost gained a monopoly on railroads in New Jersey. In 1825, he designed and built a steam locomotive, which he operated on a circle track at his estate in Hoboken.

Case Study #3.4 Significant Disruptive Inventors and Innovations – Transportation: Steamboat

Key Disruptive Inventors	**John Fitch (1743–1798, an American inventor, clockmaker, entrepreneur, and engineer)** **Robert Fulton (1765–1815, an American engineer and inventor)** **John Stevens (1749–1838, an American lawyer, engineer, and inventor)**
Location	**USA**
Disruptive Invention	Steam locomotive transportation replaces slower and more weather-vulnerable sailing ships
Problem Resolved	The complex, slow, and high-cost mobility of workers and consumers to production centers & markets was eased.
Solution Impact	More comfortable and safe long-distance travel in any weather conditions. Lower cost and faster Individual and product mobility between cities and urban centers facilitate centralized production & consumption centers in larger cities. More workers have more varied jobs and income, and consumers have access to a wider variety of goods. Shipping costs fall, and the delivery schedule is more dependable.
Economic Impact	Increased urbanization, greater individual mobility independence, concentration & specialization of industries & markets. Economies of scale for both producers and consumers result in lower prices for consumers: increased employment and increased marketing opportunities for businesses wherever they are located.

(*Continued*)

(Continued)

Cultural Impact	Factories could be located anywhere but were constrained by transportation and distribution. Labor could be moved more easily if housing were provided or available. Male workers were separated from families. Travel became more acceptable for marketing and service throughout the USA.
Inventors Education & Training	Few educational institutions, few books, learn by experimentation to solve a problem.
Innovation Environment	The environment increased free-market competition, a growing economy, supportive government, and patent office to register inventions but little enforcement protection to restrain violators.
Financing	Scarce with no traditional funding markets, primarily friends, family, and wealthy individuals saw an income and return opportunity. In addition, government support is beginning to become available for security reasons.
International Commerce	During the USA's formative years, the 13 colonies were prevented by England from importing any machinery or industrial equipment.
Major Success Factors	Curious, driven, persistent, tenacious, problem-solving, continuously innovative, and analytical capacities with steam energy producing equipment, enjoyed competing, and time was most valuable to them. Adopted the ideas of others and worked well with Boulton and his management and marketing talents.

Chemistry Innovations

The chemical industry experienced significant expansion and diversification resulting from the progress of chemical science by **Antoine Lavoisier (1743–1794, a French chemist)**. Advances resulted from the empirical experiments of manufacturers of soap, paper, glass, paints, dyes, and textiles. For example, sulfuric acid, a versatile and widely used chemical, was expensive and dangerous to produce, and it was used primarily in the textile industry as a bleaching agent. **John Roebuck (1718–1794, a British inventor and industrialist)** invented an economical production process using lead chambers. **Samuel Garbett (1717–1803, a British industrialist)** began producing sulfuric acid on a commercial scale. In 1749 Roebuck and Garbett invested in a manufacturing center for sulfuric acid, and in 1760 they each had invested in a 25% share in the Carron Iron Works in Scotland. They partnered again to set up a laboratory in Birmingham where precious metals would be refined and assayed.

In 1799, **Alessandro Volta (1745–1827, an Italian physicist, chemist, and pioneer of electricity and power)** invented the electric battery and discovered methane. Volta proved that electricity could be generated chemically using two electrodes, zinc, and copper, in diluted sulfuric acid used as an electrolyte. Zinc is oxidized, creating negative electrons that move to the positive copper electrode yielding electricity. This discovery disproved the prevalent theory that electricity was generated solely by living beings. Volta's invention sparked a significant amount of scientific excitement and led to the development of electrochemistry.

In the 1790s sulfuric acid was replaced by Scottish firms introducing the chlorine gas discovery of **Claude Berthollet (1748–1822, a French chemist),** who was the first to demonstrate the bleaching action of chlorine gas and was first to develop a solution of sodium hypochlorite as a modern bleaching agent.

Another group of chemicals widely used in industrial processes is alkalis like caustic soda and potash produced by burning kelp and barilla. Still, the supplies of these seaweeds were limited and expensive. Then, in 1791, **Nicholas LeBlanc (1742–1806, a French chemist)** discovered a process for producing alkalis using sodium chloride or salt, which was first used commercially in Britain. The new alkalis had many industrial uses in soap, glass, paper, paint, pottery, and another valuable by-product was hydrochloric acid.

Construction Cement

The emergence of urban centers and increased demand for all types of construction using bricks and stones spurred the development of cement in Britain. **John Smeaton (1724–1792, a British civil engineer and designer of bridges, canals, harbors, and lighthouses)** pioneered hydraulic lime[i] in concrete, pebbles, and powdered brick as aggregate. **Louis Vicat (1786–1861, a French engineer)** developed a similar approach. Vicat combined chalk and clay and heated it to produce a mortar cement in 1817. **Egor G. Cheliev (1771–1839, a Russian surveyor and builder)** in early 1800 went to Moscow to help plan and rebuild the city after the fire of 1812. He invented a hydraulic binder like portland cement by mixing lime and clay. **William Aspdin (1815–1864, a British cement manufacturer and a pioneer of the Portland cement industry)** is considered the inventor of **Portland cement**. Today, Portland cement is still the most common type of cement worldwide as a primary ingredient of concrete, mortar, stucco, and grout. Aspdin increased the limestone content in the mixture and burned it at much higher temperature, resulting in it setting slowly and developing strength quickly. In the early 1840s, Aspdin developed the first cement to contain alite (alite is an impure form of tricalcium silicate) called "modern" Portland cement. Aspdin built and acquired several plants to grow his cement company but eventually went bankrupt due to financial mismanagement. Portland cement concrete used in construction increased from 1850 onward and was soon the dominant cement in Britain and the USA. In the USA, the first large-scale use of cement was Rosendale cement. A natural cement mined from a massive deposit of dolomite discovered in 1875 near Rosendale, New York. The rapid growth in construction in the US also triggered the development in 1852 by **Richard VerValen (1817–1892, an American brick manufacturer)** of a brickmaking machine connected to a steam-powered drive shaft. It provided perfect duplicates of the rectangular shape of the brick. This innovation significantly improved the process of bricklaying and the appearance of buildings.

Food Preservation and Refrigeration

In 1795, the French army offered 12,000 francs to preserve food to feed its troops when fighting distant wars. **Nicolas F. Appert (1749–1841, a French inventor of food preservation)** immediately began experimenting with ways to preserve foodstuffs, succeeding with soups, vegetables, juices, dairy products, jellies, jams, and syrups. His process was to place the food in glass jars, seal them with cork and sealing wax, and put them in boiling water (he switched to using an autoclave). Although some homemakers may have used this technique, Appert was the first to do this on an industrial scale. In 1804, Appert established near Paris the first food bottling factory globally and built a business selling various foods preserved in sealed thick glass bottles. He found this type of glass bottle container able to withstand being dunked in boiling water for a period before tightly sealing the wide-mouth bottle with a cork. It was so simple that it quickly became widely used by families. In 1810, the French Bureau of Arts and Manufactures of the Interior's Ministry paid Appert 12,000 francs to publish a book describing his process. However, Appert's high production costs and product pricing limited local sales, and he declared bankruptcy in 1806.

Case Study #3.5 Significant Disruptive Inventors and Innovations – Agricultural: Food Preservation[5]

Key Disruptive Inventors	**Nicolas F. Appert (1749–1841, a French inventor of food preservation)** **Peter Durand (1766–1822, a British merchant)** **Bryan Donkin (1768–1855, a British industrialist)**
Location	**France and Britain, Britain, Britain**
Disruptive Invention	In 1804, Appert used only fresh food uncooked, put it in a glass jar that was loosely corked, and then immersed it in boiling water for several hours depending on the type of food. He then stored the jar at hot temperatures under pressure for a time, and, when removed, he immediately secured the cork, sealed it with a retaining wire, covered it with wax, and wrapped it in a canvas bag. He developed an autoclave or a pressure chamber to support his process, which is used today to conduct industrial and scientific operations requiring elevated temperatures and pressures. Durand and Donkin introduced the use of tin cans for preserving food. The canning food makes it available any time of the year and for the military fighting in large armies or navies at sea or on land in distant locations.
Problem Resolved	Focused on preserving meats, vegetables, and fruits for winter use, they lasted several decades. However, the transport of fresh foods was slow and did not last long after purchase, so people frequented the food market often.

Solution Impact	People could store food at home or travel long distances by sea and other means without worrying about healthy food for nourishment. Appert food preservation was the only safe method for canning and preserving most foods, including meats, poultry, seafood, and dairy goods. Durand and Donkin introduced tin cans instead of glass bottles and successfully marketed their canned food.
Economic Impact	The French government offered a large reward to anyone who could develop a food processing system and produce easily transportable items – storing food reduced the need to go to the market daily, making time more manageable. Housing began to include more kitchen storage facilities or pantries, and there was growth in the need for refrigeration for food storage, particularly in urban areas. Two industries emerged: a container fabrication industry and an accurate machinery industry to fabricate airtight cans using safe metals and soldering. Eventually, production cost considerations introduced glass and plastic containers to replace metal containers to see the food inside.
Cultural Impact	Gradually there was an acceptance and trust in canned and bottled foods as safe and tasty substitutes for fresh food products, stored without refrigeration and transported on travels. Wars during the 19th century increased the demand for canned foods. In addition, canned and bottled foods could be stored for many months to reserve for unforeseen events.
Inventors Education & Training	Appert was the son of an innkeeper and restaurant operator, a self-taught cook, and learned how to pickle foods – through curiosity and experimentation. He knew how to preserve foods in bottles for extended periods.
Innovation Environment	Appert did not patent his food preserving processes and depended on Napoleon and the French government's support. Competitors grew overseas after reading his book describing his process. Donkin successfully developed preserved canned foods, and Donkin and his brother-in-law John Hall (who founded the Dartford Iron Works) launched the preserved canning industry.
Financing	Napoleon and the Government of France offered a reward of 12,000 francs in 1810 to anyone who could provide a food preserving system that produced easily transportable items for economic and military purposes for a traveling army and navy forces. Appert received the prize and published a book describing his making preserved juices, dairy products, jams, syrups, and whole fruits. Appert used the award money to build and develop a canning factory with bottled foods, but his business eventually failed because of high-cost machinery.

(*Continued*)

(Continued)

	Donkin and Hall purchased the Appert patent, created a profitable preserved food canning business, and launched a new industry. In 1801–1802, Donkin was contracted to construct a prototype of a paper-making machine based on the Fourdrinier machine that had problems. In 1802, Donkin started the enterprise that became the Bryan Donkin Company, which continued to do business into the early 21st century. In 1804 he succeeded in producing a working printing machine. A second, improved printer was made the following year, and in 1810 eighteen of the complex machines had been installed at various firms.
International Commerce	Donkin's company continued to make printing machines and by 1851 had produced 200 machines for use across the world. By 1847, Donkin's company had designed its first products for the emerging gas industry. The name Donkin has become a generic name for individual gas valves, and Bryan Donkin RMG Gas Controls Limited remains a going concern in Europe. Today, Donkin's gas valves can still be purchased on Amazon, and AVK and Howden Blowers also continue manufacturing Bryan Donkin equipment.
Major Success Factors	All three inventors had logical, analytical minds for solving mechanical engineering problems. Curious, driven, persistent, tenacious, problem-solving, continuously innovative, and analytical capacities cover many subjects and challenging issues. Donkin turned out to be the most significant entrepreneur.

In 1810, British inventor and merchant **Peter Durand (1766–1822, a British merchant)** is widely credited with receiving the first British patent to preserve food using tin cans creating the modern-day process of canning foods. In 1812 **Bryan Donkin (1768–1855, a British industrialist)** and **John Hall (1764–1836, an American businessperson)** purchased both patents and began producing preserves. Donkin established a factory to can vegetable soups and preserved meats for the British Navy. Donkin also developed the first paper-making machine and created a printing machine as a forerunner of the rotary press and a composition printing roller. These machines replaced the much slower old flatbed press that moved back and forth, which could not print fast enough to produce prominent newspapers. Although this machine eventually failed, composition rollers were widely adopted.

Clarence Birdseye (1886–1956, an American biologist) developed freezing food preservation and set up his own Birdseye Seafoods. It failed, and he developed a new company with his patents for a quick freezing process named **General Seafood Corporation**. He expanded his quick-freezing operation to meat, poultry, fruit, and vegetables as the refrigerator was developed with a freezing compartment for storage. After a long series of M&A, **Birds Eye Frozen Foods** was reconstituted in 2003 and is sold in most major markets today.

William Cullen (1710–1790, a Scottish physician, chemist, and agriculturalist) demonstrated the first artificial refrigerator in 1748 at Glasgow. He understood the concept of a refrigerator and what it could do but did not put his findings to any practical use. **Oliver Evans (1755–1819, an American inventor, engineer, and businessperson)** made the first design for the refrigerator in 1804, but until 1834 no one was interested until **Jacob Perkins (1766–1849, an American inventor, mechanical engineer, and physicist)** built the first refrigeration machine. It created cool temperatures using a vapor compression cycle. Unfortunately, refrigerators from the late 1800s until 1929 used toxic gases such as ammonia, methyl chloride, and sulfur dioxide as refrigerants, which led to several fatal accidents because of methyl chloride leaking out of refrigerators. In 1844, a physician **John Gorrie (1803–1855, an American physician, scientist, inventor of mechanical cooling)** built a working unit based on Oliver's designs and used it to cool yellow fever patients' air. Gorrie was also granted a patent for a machine to make ice. In Australia, the first practical refrigeration system was built in 1854 and patented in 1855 by **James Harrison (1816–1893, a British-Australian newspaper printer, journalist, politician, and pioneer in mechanical refrigeration)**.

Three American corporations: **Frigidaire, General Motors, and DuPont**, launched collaborative research to develop a less dangerous refrigeration method. In 1928, **Thomas Midgley, Jr. (1889–1944, an American mechanical and chemical engineer)**, aided by **Charles F. Kettering (1876–1958, an American inventor, engineer, and businessperson)**, invented non-toxic Freon, and compressor refrigerators using Freon became the standard for all home kitchens. Midgley also played a significant role in developing leaded gasoline, and both products were later banned due to their adverse impact on human health and the environment. Midgley was granted more than 100 patents throughout his career. Kettering, the holder of 186 patents, was a founder of Delco and head of research at General Motors from 1920 to 1947. His automotive developments were the electrical starting motor and leaded gasoline. He was co-inventor of Freon for refrigeration and air conditioning systems with the DuPont Chemical Company. Kettering developed Duco lacquers and enamels as colored paints for mass-produced automobiles at DuPont. At the Dayton-Wright Company, he invented the "Bug" aerial torpedo, considered the world's first aerial missile. He also helped develop lightweight two-stroke diesel engines, revolutionizing the locomotive and heavy equipment industries.

Case Study #3.6 Significant Disruptive Inventors and Innovations – Refrigeration[5]

Key Disruptive Inventors	**Thomas Midgley, Jr. (1889–1944, an American mechanical and chemical engineer)** **Charles F. Kettering (1876–1958, an American inventor, engineer, and businessperson)**
Location	**USA**
Disruptive Invention	Midgley and Kettering invented some of the first chlorofluorocarbons (CFCs), better known as Freon, and compressor refrigerators that became the kitchen standard. They also played a significant role in developing leaded gasoline (Tetraethyllead) or anti-knock leaded gasoline, which is no longer sold because of the risk of lead poisoning. Kettering's most widely used automotive inventions were the electrical starting motor for autos.
Problem Resolved	Previously dangerous cooling chemicals were toxic, flammable, or explosive, causing deaths when gas escaped. In 1916, Midgley began working at General Motors under Charles Kettering at the GM Dayton Research Laboratories in Ohio, which led to the development of Freon.
Solution Impact	Freon enabled the development of safe advanced refrigerators in households and eventually air conditioning in autos and homes.
Economic Impact	Cars ran more smoothly on leaded gas. With the discovery of Freon, sales increased, and every household with electricity had a refrigerator. Three decades later, both products were replaced with more environmentally friendly products.
Cultural Impact	Both products made life more comfortable for people. Midgley died three decades before the ozone-depleting and greenhouse gas effects of CFCs in the atmosphere became widely known. In addition, leaded gasoline and Freon have been found damaging to humans and the environment resulting in both no longer being produced and sold.
Inventors Education & Training	Midgley was born in a family with a history of inventions and graduated from Cornell University with a mechanical engineering degree. Before transferring to The Ohio State University, Kettering attended The College of Wooster and graduated from OSU in 1904 with an electrical engineering degree.

Innovation Environment	Innovations were transferred to corporations by establishing Research & Development (R&D) departments or centers where the inventors were recognized. For example, Midgley and Kettering were hired by three American corporations: Frigidaire, General Motors, and DuPont, to conduct collaborative research on a safe cooling gas for refrigerators while at the GM R&D Center in Detroit. The sponsoring company received revenues from the innovation.
Financing	Delco Electronics Corporation was the automotive electronics design and manufacturing subsidiary of General Motors based in Kokomo, Indiana, which manufactured Delco radios and other electric products found in GM cars. In 1972, General Motors merged it with the AC Electronics division, and it continued to operate as part of the Delco Electronics Division of General Motors. Delco's name came from the Dayton Engineering Laboratories Co., founded in 1909 in Dayton, Ohio, by Charles Kettering and Edward A. Deeds. Delco was responsible for several automobile electric systems innovations, including the first reliable battery ignition system.
International Commerce	All their inventions were exported worldwide, which helped create US jobs and economic growth.
Major Success Factors	Midgley was born in a family with a history of invention, and Kettering was a good leader and head of GM R&D Research Center and a creative, analytical person. Both men had hundreds of patents in their names.

Thomas Moore (1802–1864, an American farmer, engineer, and cabinet maker) invented the icebox, an early refrigeration device for food storage. An icehouse is a building used to store ice throughout the year and used before the refrigerator's invention to keep food fresh. Moore used the icebox to transport butter from his farm to the markets and sold solid brick butter instead of melted tubs like other merchants. Several years later, larger icehouses began to provide cold storage for most of the year and became very common near freshwater lakes used to pack the icehouse with snow and ice during the winter.

Carl von Linde (1842–1934, a German scientist, engineer, and businessperson) discovered a refrigeration gas cycle and invented the first industrial-scale air separation and gas liquefaction processes, which led to the first dependable and efficient compressed-ammonia refrigerator in 1876. Linde was also the founder of what is now known as Linde plc, the world's most significant industrial gas company, and ushered in creating the industrial gases' supply chain as a profitable business line.

Case Study #3.7 Significant Disruptive Inventors and Innovations – Chemicals: Industrial and Medical Gases[5,9–11]

Key Disruptive Inventors	**Carl von Linde (1842–1934, a German scientist, engineer, and businessperson)**
Location	**German/American**
Disruptive Invention	He discovered a refrigeration cycle and invented the first industrial-scale air separation and gas liquefaction processes, which led to the first dependable and efficient compressed-ammonia refrigerator in 1876. In addition to plants for air separation, in 1906, Linde engineers separated water gas constituents. This work developed into capabilities in recovering hydrogen, carbon monoxide, and other critical feedstocks for the emerging chemicals industry.
Problem Resolved	The founder of what is now known as Linde plc, the world's most significant industrial gas company, ushered in creating the industrial gases' supply chain as a profitable business line.
Solution Impact	In 1895 he liquefied air by first compressing it and then expanding it rapidly, cooling it. He then obtained oxygen and nitrogen from the liquid perspective by slow warming. In the early days of oxygen production, the most prominent use by far for the gas was the oxyacetylene torch, which revolutionized metal cutting and welding to construct ships, skyscrapers, and other iron and steel structures. Linde is the founder of what is now known as Linde plc, initially in New York, now the world's most significant industrial gases company Linde Plc. and the world's first supply chain.
Economic Impact	Carl von Linde was a business-minded engineer. He was the first to extract oxygen gas from the air, making it a commercially viable product and commoditizing it, thus launching the industrial gas industry and developing modern refrigeration. In addition, he created the industrial gas supply chain. The company's primary business is manufacturing and distributing atmospheric gases, including oxygen, nitrogen, argon, rare gases, and process gases, including carbon dioxide, helium, hydrogen, electronic gases, specialty gases, and acetylene used to cut steel beams for skyscrapers. By 2019, Linde consolidated the three companies he had initially started to sell his products globally.

Cultural Impact	Changed the medical and construction industries and established a global supply chain. Urban life was made much more comfortable with refrigerators and not shopping for food daily. Refrigeration rapidly displaced ice in food handling and was introduced into many industrial processes and medical treatments.
Inventors Education & Training	He was educated in science and engineering at the Federal Polytechnic in Zurich, Switzerland. After leaving university, he worked for short periods in several industries before joining The Technical University of Munich and becoming a professor. He became a full mechanical engineering professor in 1872 and set up an engineering lab to continue his research.
Innovation Environment	The innovation environment was well established when he submitted his patent applications. In addition, the demand for his research and contributions was robust in several industries and the medical field, which kept the environment receptive to his innovations.
Financing	After his education, he was a professor and worked in various industries. Finally, he established Linde plc. which generated income to support further research, which resulted in new patents. He worked effectively to exploit the value of his patents and knowledge through licensing arrangements – Linde Gas supplies industrial, medical, specialty, refrigerants, and other chemicals. Depending on the gas and the quantity required, these may be provided in portable high-pressure gas cylinders, liquefied by road tanker, on-site gas generators, or gaseous via pipeline to large customers. As a result, he became a very wealthy person.
International Commerce	Linde plc is an American-Anglo-German multinational chemical company and is the largest industrial gas company by market share and revenue. It serves customers in the healthcare, petroleum refining, manufacturing, food, beverage carbonation, fiber-optics, steel making, aerospace, chemicals, electronics, and water treatment industries. He established one of the first global supply chains and delivered his products worldwide to industrial and medical companies.
Major Success Factors	Curious, driven, persistent, tenacious, problem-solving, continuously innovative, and analytical capacities with steam energy producing equipment, enjoyed competing, and time was most valuable to them. Adopted the ideas of others and worked well with Boulton and his management and marketing talents.

The Second Industrial Revolution (Electricity, Steel, Telephone, Auto) 1850–1914 The Second Industrial Revolution, also known as the **Technological Revolution**, was driven by a more mobile and flexible energy source – electricity. It included rapid standardization and industrialization between **1850 and 1914** when WWI occurred. There were advances in manufacturing and production technology and a new source of a more flexible and environmentally cleaner power source called electricity. Advances in the need to produce more robust metal for the transportation and construction industries resulted in the development and expansion of steel production. Communication innovations resulted in the emergence of the telephone. Transportation became increasingly important in expanding urban centers resulting in the invention of the automobile. It was a rapid industrial development period in the USA, Canada, Britain, Germany, France, Italy, and Japan.

Much of what happened originated in the First Industrial Revolution, beginning in 1750 in Britain. As described in Chapter 2, the concept of interchangeable parts mass production, primarily powered by waterwheels, began to shift to a steam engine-powered economy. Meanwhile, having moved from human to animal power, the agricultural sector turned to mechanized energy. Simultaneously, the wrought iron making shifted from wood-fired to coal-fired, less expensive production furnaces. The falling costs for making iron coincided with the growing need for rail supporting railroad transportation expansion. The economic externality of coal was the beginning of a deteriorating environment by the most extensive users, including China, India, Britain, the USA, several remaining OECD countries, and gradually many developing economies. Global trade continued to expand rapidly to satisfy population growth in urban centers.

Steel Production Innovations Drive Ocean and Land Transportation Growth

Ironmaking had several difficulties because iron ore had impurities to be removed to make the product more robust. After several major iron bridges collapsed, there was increased interest in improving steel production. Second, the fire transforming iron ore into finished product needed to be consistently hotter. Steel is an alloy composed of between 0.2% and 2.0% carbon, with the balance being iron. Making steel involves adding carbon to iron in a forge or cementation. The introduction of the blast furnace reversed the problem. From prehistory through the blast furnace's creation, iron was produced from iron ore as wrought iron. A blast furnace produces pig iron, 90% iron, and carbon alloy. When steelmaking is started with pig iron, instead of wrought iron, a small amount of up to 2% of carbon must be removed to produce the stronger steel. Before 1860, steel was an expensive product, made in small quantities and used primarily for swords, tools, and cutlery, and all large metal structures were wrought or cast iron. Steelmaking began in Britain and was exported to European and American markets. The

Bessemer and the Open Hearth processes, two technological advances made in Britain, significantly reduced the cost of steel production.

James B. Neilson (1792–1865, a Scottish inventor) developed a coke-driven hot-blast process with hot flue gas from the blast furnace reused to preheat air blown into the blast furnace. This process increased the heat efficiency of smelting iron. The development in 1857 by **Edward A. Cowper (1819–1893, a British mechanical engineer)** of the regenerative hot blast stove known as the Cowper stove improved the hot blast process's economy. The Cowper stove used firebrick[ii] as a heat storage medium to produce a hotter burning furnace preventing the iron cracking problem, increasing output, and lowering costs. **Henry Bessemer (1813–1898, a British inventor)** developed a steelmaking process that became the essential steelmaking technique from 1856 to 1950. He invented the **Bessemer process,** which blew air through the molten iron to remove excess carbon and other impurities by oxidation. By 1870 Bessemer steel was widely used for ship plates. In the 1850s, the speed, weight, and quantity of railway traffic were limited by the strength of wrought iron rails. The solution was to use steel rails, and the Bessemer process made steel price competitive by increasing the scale and speed for the mass production of steel, thereby lowering the cost for railroad expansion. Steel had much greater strength and durability for rail and safer and longer bridges and could accommodate the increasingly heavy and faster trains.

In Europe, iron ore came with phosphorus, an impurity, and **Sidney G. Thomas (1850–1885, a British inventor)** and **Percy Gilchrist (1851–1935, a British chemist and metallurgist)** developed a way to remove the phosphorus in the production of steel. The **Siemens-Martin Process**[iii] of making steel further enhanced the **Bessemer process** by controlling nitrogen exposure, which would cause the steel to become brittle. It also allowed the smelting and refining of scrap steel, which helped to further lower costs. The Bessemer process was gradually replaced by **Open-Hearth** steelmaking in the 1860s in Germany and France. The open-hearth process used pig iron, ore, and scrap and became known as the **Siemens–Martin process**. The process was invented by **Charles (or Carl) W. Siemens (1823–1883, a German-British electrical engineer and businessperson**). It was a more efficient high-temperature furnace regenerative preheating fuel and air combustion chamber in an open-hearth furnace to melt steel. **Pierre-Emile Martin (1824–1915, a French industrial engineer)** applied the hot gas recovery in an open hearth furnace invented by Siemens. Refining steel in a hearth consists of smelting a mixture of cast iron and scrap or ore, refining it by decarburization, desulfurization, and dephosphorization. This method made it possible to produce fine and alloy steels by adding desired elements. Siemens–Martin's low-cost process allowed building more robust bridges, extended rail for railroads, taller buildings into skyscrapers, and larger ships carrying more cargo.

Case Study #3.8 Significant Disruptive Inventors and Innovations – Construction: Steel Production[4,6,7,8]

Key Disruptive Inventors	**Charles (or Carl) W. Siemens (1823–1883, a German-British electrical & mechanical engineer and businessperson)** **Pierre-Emile Martin (1824–1915, a French industrial engineer)**
Location	**German/United Kingdom and France**
Disruptive Invention	Steel's improved strength and durability were obtained with Siemens–Martin Process and electric arc furnace.
Problem Resolved	An open-hearth furnace produced a more efficient higher-temperature regenerative preheating fuel and air and hot gas recovery. Its main advantages over the Bessemer Process were that it did not expose the steel to excessive nitrogen (which would cause the steel to become brittle). It was easier to control and permitted substantial scrap iron and steel refining. The process took longer than the Bessemer converter and was easier to manage and sample for quality assessment.
Solution Impact	Siemens–Martin's low-cost process allowed the building of larger bridges, more extended rail for railroads, taller buildings into skyscrapers, and larger ships carrying more cargo.
Economic Impact	New infrastructure construction expanded job opportunities and productivity in many fields, supporting GDP growth of countries worldwide.
Cultural Impact	Construction and transportation changed the way people lived in urban centers, expanding their freedom & mobility.
Inventors Education & Training	In Magdeburg, Siemens went to the School of Trade and Commerce and then to the University of Göttingen, where he took physical geography and technology classes, higher mathematics, theoretical chemistry, and practical chemistry and physics.
Innovation Environment	There was a strong need for new technology to strengthen steel and lower its price by reducing production costs. Martin implemented the process that bears his name for producing steel in a hearth by remelting scrap steel with cast iron to reduce impurities.
Financing	Family financing, and in 1850 he established the London sales office of Siemens & Halske, the engineering company that produced telegraph cables, which his brother Werner had founded in 1847 in Berlin. He started selling such devices to the wire rope producer RS Newall and Company in Dundee, of which his friend (and uncle of his later wife) Lewis Gordon was the co-owner. Newall & Co also outsourced test jobs

	for cables to Siemens, enabling the new company to enter the ocean cable-laying business. The branch office became Siemens Brothers in 1858. In the 1850s, they participated in building long-distance telegraph networks in Russia. In 1855, a company branch headed by another brother, Carl Heinrich von Siemens, opened in St Petersburg, Russia. In 1867, Siemens completed the Indo-European (Calcutta to London) telegraph line. Siemens received revenue from fees generated from users of the Siemens–Martin Process.
International Commerce	The Siemens–Martin process gave Britain and Germany a competitive advantage in steel production, better quality control, and lowered steel cost.
Major Success Factors	Siemens drew on his knowledge in two areas electricity and metallurgy. The electric pyrometer is the most important and original of all William Siemens's inventions.

Steel proved superior strength and durability and facilitated more extensive and faster machines. New and more robust steel products appeared, such as steel cables and rods, sheet steel, high-pressure boilers, and high-tensile strength steel for machinery. The open-hearth steel process made more powerful engines, gears, axles, and more potent military weapons for land and sea. The crucible process was used for making high-quality alloy steel in the late 1900s. In 1900, the **electric arc furnace** was adapted to steelmaking, and by the 1920s, the falling cost of electricity allowed it to supplant the crucible process for specialty steels. The electric arc furnace uses high-current electric arcs to melt steel scrap and convert it into liquid steel of specified chemical composition and temperature. In 1878–1879 **Charles Siemens** took out patents for electric furnaces of the arc type. Electric arc furnaces benefit from being built to any size – very small or large. This flexibility allows inexpensive production of very specialized steel in short custom production runs.

Railroad Expansion and Domestic and International Commerce

The decline in the cost of producing steel rail resulted in replacing iron, which was not as strong or durable as steel. Steel rails were found to last ten times longer than iron rail, and heavier and stronger locomotives could pull longer trains and larger freight cars. The first person to make steel rails was **Robert F. Mushet (1811–1891, a British metallurgist and businessperson)** in the **Darkhill Ironworks** in the UK. In 1857 Mushet was the first to make durable steel rails, providing the basis for rail transportation worldwide. Also, rail maintenance costs fell as they were needed less often with fewer repairs, reducing delaying train traffic. Longer lengths of heavier-weight rail[iv] meant less deterioration at rail joints and reduced train wheel wear, which allowed average train speed to be increased. Railroads became the dominant form of low-cost land transportation for passengers, especially for industrial revolution products and machinery freight distribution in Europe and the USA. In 1861, Mushet also invented a clay cone or sleeve, heated white-hot, inserted into the top of the ingot mold near the end of the pour, and then filled with molten steel. It provided a reservoir of molten steel, which drained down and filled the pipe as the casting cooled.

Innovation and Economic Growth Stimulant of Electric Power

Benjamin Franklin (1700–1774, an American polymath and one of the USA's founding fathers) was the first to discover electricity. Still, his experiments only established the relationship between lightning and electricity. **Joseph Swan (1828–1914, a British physicist, chemist, and inventor)** began working with carbonized paper filaments in the evacuated glass bulb to develop an incandescent lightbulb in 1850. With the help of **Charles Stearn (1848–1941, an American expert on vacuum pumps**) in 1878, Swan developed a processing method that avoided the early incandescent bulb blackening by removing the air from the bulb. However, the lights were not commercially practical as the bulb only lasted about 40 hours. Stearn and Swan developed the continuous filament spinning process and the machinery needed to wash and collect the viscose yarns for filaments. In the early 1880s, Stearn began installing light bulbs in homes and landmark buildings in England. The **Stearn Electric Lamp Company** began manufacturing lightbulbs in 1907 and became a key supplier to the Electrical Wholesale industry.

Thomas A. Edison (1847–1931, an American inventor and businessperson) is America's greatest inventor based on the number of patents awarded. He developed many devices for electric power generation, mass communication, sound recording, and motion pictures. These inventions included the phonograph, the motion picture camera, and early versions of the electric light bulb. They had a widespread impact on the modern industrialized world. Edison began in-depth research into developing a practical incandescent lamp in 1878 and filed his first patent application. The first successful test was in 1879 and lasted 13.5 hours. Edison continued to improve his design and, in 1879, filed for a US patent for an electric lamp using a carbon filament or strip coiled and connected to an alloy of platinum and several other metals contact wires. Edison and his team later discovered a carbonized bamboo filament could last more than 1,200 hours. In 1880, the *Oregon Railroad* and the steamer *Columbia* became the first application for Edison's incandescent electric lamps (it was also the first ship to use a dynamo[v]). Electric lighting improved working conditions and did not produce fire, pollution like gaslighting, or carbon monoxide poisoning. Edison was one of the first inventors to apply organized science and teamwork to the invention process. He established the first industrial research laboratory with many researchers and employees working in teams to conduct experiments.

Case Study #3.9 Significant Disruptive Inventors and Innovations – Electricity as a Source of Power[12]

Key Disruptive Inventors	**Thomas A. Edison (1847–1931, an American inventor and businessperson)**
Location	**USA**
Disruptive Invention	Edison developed many devices in electric power generation, mass communication, sound recording, and motion pictures, including the phonograph, the motion picture camera, and early versions of the electric light bulb.
Problem Resolved	Oil and gas lamps were dirty and dangerous.
Solution Impact	Society quickly adopted the use of electricity for lighting electric bulbs.
Economic Impact	Electric lighting extended the number of working shifts available in factories, which helped expand output, generate more jobs, and support economic growth. Electricity was a more environmentally friendly light source than oil or gas lanterns.
Cultural Impact	Societies' needs were significant for additional learning, family life, relaxation, and access to electricity extended a day's useful life. It also resulted in crime reduction and improved safety in urban cities.
Inventors Education & Training	His mother educated him at home in reading, writing, and arithmetic. He enrolled in a four-year chemistry course at The Cooper Union for the Advancement of Science and Art in 1875 at age 28.
Innovation Environment	The general environment was blooming with innovation opportunities to satisfy the country's needs and people's desire to improve the quality of life. It was a continually active entrepreneurial period with many options and a need for innovations.
Financing	Edison obtained an exclusive right to sell newspapers that began a long streak of entrepreneurial ventures and developed his business skills, which inspired his 14 companies, including General Electric. One of his early mentors was a fellow telegrapher and inventor named Franklin Pope, who invited Edison to live and work in his home's basement. Pope and Edison founded their own company in 1869, working as electrical engineers and inventors. Edison's major innovation was the establishment of an industrial research lab in 1876. It was built in Menlo Park, NJ, with the $10,000 from Edison's

(*Continued*)

(Continued)

	quadruplex telegraph (allows the sending of four messages on one line). Edison had created Menlo Park to be the first industrial laboratory focused on developing knowledge and then controlling its application. Edison Lamp Works, in its first year, turned out 50,000 lamps. His phonograph patent was the first device to record and reproduce sounds. Edison began work to improve the microphone for telephones by developing a carbon microphone that modulates a direct current and uses a transformer to transfer the telephone line and create an improved telephone for Western Union. In 1880 Edison applied for a patent for an electric lamp (light bulb) using a carbon filament or strip coiled and connected to platina contact wire. Later, the filament was replaced with a carbonized bamboo filament that lasted over 1,200 hours. In 1878, Edison formed the Edison Electric Light Company in New York City with several financiers, including J. P. Morgan, the Vanderbilt family, and venture capitalist Spencer Trask, Now Edison was equipped to develop an electric "utility" to compete with the existing gas light utilities, and in 1880 he founded the Edison Illuminating Company, and patented a system for electricity distribution. Before WWI, Edison became concerned with America's reliance on foreign rubber supply and tried to find a domestic supply working in his new laboratory in Fort Myers, Florida. Thomas Edison, Henry Ford, and Harvey Firestone pulled together $75,000 to form the Edison Botanical Research Corporation for the Fort Myers laboratory. After reviewing all plants, he chose Leavenworth's Goldenrod with a 5% latex yield which Edison modified through cross-breeding to produce plants twice the size and with a latex yield of 12%. Next, Edison designed and created the first commercially available fluoroscope or X-ray machine and discovered that calcium tungstate fluoroscopy screens made brighter images. Edison's next venture was a patent for the motion picture camera, and he built a Kinetoscope, a viewer installed in penny arcades for viewing short films in 1891. In 1896, Thomas Armat's Vitascope, manufactured by the Edison factory and marketed in Edison's name, was used to project motion pictures in New York City. Edison later added a mechanically synchronized voice soundtrack to the movie. In the late 1890s, Edison developed a lighter, more efficient

	rechargeable battery and obtained the US and European patent for his nickel-iron battery in 1901 and founded the Edison Storage Battery Company in 1904 and hired 450 employees. They produced the first rechargeable batteries for electric cars and refined them until 1910, when he developed a very efficient and durable nickel-iron battery with lye as the electrolyte. The nickel-iron battery was never successful and was replaced with the lead-acid battery for turning over gas-powered car starter motors. Edison's last project was during WW I, when most chemicals were imported from Europe. There was an immediate shortage of imported chemicals, and Edison responded by building two plants with six tons of phenol per day. Production began one month after the war started in Europe. He made two plants to produce benzene in Pennsylvania and Alabama, replacing supplies previously imported from Germany. Edison also manufactured aniline dyes, previously supplied by the German dye trust. Other wartime products include xylene, p-phenylenediamine, shellac, and Pyrex. Wartime shortages made these ventures profitable, and by mid-1915, his production capacity was fully committed.
International Commerce	Many of Edison's products were exported worldwide, and he learned much from innovations in Europe.
Major Success Factors	Edison was a very inquiring child who learned most things by reading independently. He became fascinated with technology and spent hours working on experiments at home as a child. He established two industrial research laboratories with many researchers to work on profitable projects under his supervision. Edison was hard of hearing and believed this enabled him to concentrate easier.

The fundamental principles of electricity generation were discovered in the late 1820s and early 1830s by **Michael Faraday (1791–1867, a British scientist).** He researched electromagnetism and electrochemistry and developed the principles of electromagnetic induction, diamagnetism, and electrolysis. He had minimal formal education, but he was one of the most influential scientists and discovered that electricity could be generated by a loop of wire between a magnet's poles. Previously the only way to produce electricity was by chemical reactions or using battery cells, and the sole practical use of electricity was for the telegraph. Faraday showed that central power stations are economically beneficial by developing alternating current (AC) power transmission, using power transformers to send power at high voltage.

Four scientists made several significant contributions to the use of electricity. **Sebastian de Ferranti (1864–1930, a British electrical engineer and**

inventor) built the first modern power station in 1891. His contribution was to discover that electricity could be made on a large scale in one place and then distributed to all those who needed it. To make this work, he invented the power station, cables to carry high voltage electricity, the transformer to reduce the voltage for use, and the voltmeter to measure its use by a home or business. Commercial electricity production began in 1870 with the generator's coupling to the hydraulic turbine. **George Westinghouse Jr. (1846–1914, an American entrepreneur and engineer)** saw the potential of using alternating current (AC) for electric power distribution in the early 1880s and focused his resources on developing and marketing it. This development put Westinghouse's business in direct competition with Thomas Edison, who sold direct current (DC) electric power distribution. In 1884, Westinghouse started developing his own DC domestic lighting system and hired **William Stanley Jr. (1858–1916, an American physicist)** to work on it. Westinghouse became aware of the new European alternating current (AC) systems in 1885.

AC could be "stepped up" in voltage by a transformer for distribution and then "stepped down" with a transformer for consumer use. This flexibility allowed centralized power plants to supply electricity long distances in cities with more dispersed populations. This ability was advantageous over the low voltage DC systems being marketed by Thomas Edison's electric utility, which had a limited range due to the low voltages. Westinghouse saw AC's potential to achieve more significant economies of scale than a DC lighting system, and he used patents simply different enough to get around the Edison patents. In 1886, Stanley installed the first multiple-voltage AC power system with Westinghouse's backing, and Westinghouse formed the **Westinghouse Electric & Manufacturing Company**, which he renamed the **Westinghouse Electric Corporation** in 1889. In the early to mid-1890s, General Electric, backed by financier J. P. Morgan, participated in costly takeover attempts and patent battles with Westinghouse Electric. In 1896 a patent-sharing agreement was signed between the two companies orchestrated by the financiers, pushing Edison Electric toward AC and replacing Thomas Edison as chair.

William Stanley Jr., who Westinghouse hired, obtained 129 patents covering various electric devices. In 1890, Stanley founded the **Stanley Electric Manufacturing Company** in Massachusetts, and in 1903 the **General Electric Corporation** purchased a controlling interest in the firm. In 1886, Stanley demonstrated the first complete high voltage AC transmission system, consisting of generators, transformers, and high-voltage transmission lines. His approach allowed the distribution of electrical power over significant areas and his transformer design became a prototype for future transformers. Staley's AC distribution system formed the basis of today's electrical power distribution.

Nikola Tesla (1856–1943, a Serbian-American inventor, electrical engineer, mechanical engineer, and futurist) was best known for his innovative contributions to the modern alternating current (AC) electricity supply system. He experimented with mechanical oscillators/generators, a wireless lighting system, and an electric power distribution system. Tesla founded the

Niagara Falls Hydraulic Power and Manufacturing Company and the American Institute of Electrical Engineers.

Electric motors also significantly impacted transportation after **Frank J. Sprague (1857–1934, an American naval officer and inventor)** developed the first **DC motor**. Sprague also contributed to the development of **electric railways** and **electric elevators**. His contributions were significant in promoting urban development by increasing cities' size and allowing greater business concentration in commercial sections. By 1889 more than 100 electric street railways used their urban centers to take people to work, go shopping, and visit friends. The AC motor began to be used in the electrification of cities in the 1890s. Henry Ford believed that mass production would not have been possible without electricity because it allowed machine tools and other equipment to be placed close to individual workers.

In the USA, electricity generation at central power stations started in 1882. A steam engine driving a dynamo or generator at Pearl Street Station produced a direct current (DC) powered public lighting on Pearl Street in New York City. Many cities worldwide quickly adopted modern technology, and they modified their gas-fueled streetlights to electric power. Electric lighting spread to public buildings, businesses, and shared power transport, including trams and trains. The first power plants used waterpower or coal. Various energy sources are used today, including coal, nuclear, natural gas, hydroelectric, wind, oil, solar energy, tidal power, and geothermal. Electricity generation and distribution were seen as a "natural monopoly" and only efficient if a restricted number of organizations participated in the market. By the middle of the 20th century, vertically integrated companies provided all stages from generation to delivery, and governmental supervision regulated the rate of return and cost structure.

Notes

All dates, innovators information, and events have been checked against information in the following sources: *Encyclopedia Britannica, Encyclopedia Americana, Collier's Encyclopedia, Compton's Encyclopedia, Investopedia, and Wikipedia.*

i Hydraulic lime is a general term for varieties of lime, which set through hydration. Thi- contrasts with varieties of air lime or slaked lime, used to make lime mortar, the other common types of lime mortar, which set through carbonation. Hydraulic lime provides a faster initial set and higher compressive strength than air lime and hydraulic lime will set in more extreme conditions including under water.

ii A fire brick, firebrick, or refractory is a block of ceramic material used in lining furnaces, kilns, fireboxes, and fireplaces. A refractory brick is built primarily to withstand high temperature but will also usually have a low thermal conductivity for greater energy efficiency.

iii https://encyclopedia.thefreedictionary.com/Open+hearth+furnace (accessed February 2021).

iv Length of 50 kg/m rail or above is 25 m, 50 m, 100 m. The standard and most seen lengths are 12.5 m and 25 m.

v Dynamos were the first electrical generators capable of delivering power for industry and the foundation upon which many other later electric-power conversion devices were based, including the electric motor. The discovery of the dynamo principle made industrial-scale electric power generation technically and economically feasible.

4 The Second Revolution (1850–1914)

Specialized Machine Tools

The need for machine tools became apparent during the First Industrial Revolution as mechanization required more specialized metal parts, and hand tools were too slow and inaccurate. **John Wilkinson's** cannon boring machine was the beginning of specialized machine tools as it bored a precise hole for James Watt's steam engine cylinder. More customized machine tools began to be developed by **Henry Maudslay (1771–1831, an English machine tool innovator, mechanism and die maker, and inventor).** He is considered a founding father of machine tool technology by refining and standardizing screw threads and developing the screw-cutting lathe, making v-thread machine metal screws standardized and interchangeable. **Joseph Whitworth (1803–1887, an English engineer, entrepreneur, inventor, and philanthropist)** refined standardization in developing the first national machine tool standard, the **British Standard Whitworth**. Whitworth developed a method of producing accurate flat surfaces during the 1830s. In 1841 Whitworth devised a standard for screw threads with a fixed thread angle of 55° and having a standard pitch for a given diameter. This method soon became the first nationally standardized system, and the railway companies adopted it. It later became a British Standard, "British Standard Whitworth" for screw threads. He also designed and produced the Whitworth rifle, which was more accurate than existing British rifles. The importance of machine tools for mass production and industrialization is illustrated by the production of the Ford Model T, which used 32,000 machine tools.

Growing Paper Demand

Papermaking is 2000+ years old and started in China, but the five-step process was slow and costly. In the 1800s, steam-driven machinery was invented, making paper with fibers from wood pulp known as the **Fourdrinier Machine** after its two inventors. **Henry Fourdrinier (1766–1854, a British papermaking entrepreneur)** was a paper and stationery maker and grandson of the engraver Paul Fourdrinier. And **Sealy Fourdrinier (1773–1847, a British**

DOI: 10.4324/9781003024675-5

papermaking entrepreneur) commissioned the Fourdrinier Machine's development to make paper. The machine used a moving woven mesh to create a continuous paper web filtering out the fibers held in a paper stock and producing a continuously moving wet fiber mat. They were then dried in the machine to create a strong paper web. The device is an industrialized version of the historical hand papermaking method, which could not satisfy the demands of a rapidly developing modern society. In the 1840s, **Charles Fenerty (1821–1892, a Canadian inventor)** invented the **wood pulp process** for papermaking, first adapted to newsprint production. At the same time, **Friedrich G. Keller (1816–1895, a German machinist and inventor)** also invented the wood pulp process for papermaking and his **wood-cut machine**. Unlike Fenerty, Keller took out a patent for his wood-cut invention. Both invented the machine that extracted fibers from wood to make paper and started a new papermaking industry with lower costs than rag-based paper. Simultaneously, the fountain pen and massed produced pencils were created. The steam-driven rotary printing press and cheaper wood-based paper triggered an expansion in schoolbooks, fiction and non-fiction books, and the development of newspapers in 1900. This proliferation encouraged everyone to learn how to read.

Petroleum and Portable Power Generation[12–14]

Since ancient times, petroleum has been used for lighting in China, where well drilling was developed. The production and refining of oil began in 1848 in Scotland by **James Young (1811–1883, a Scottish chemist)**. He experimented with the refining or distillation of petroleum into several useful products. Young built his first commercial refinery in 1850 and used locally mined coal shale to produce naphtha (a flammable oil containing various hydrocarbons) and lubricating oils, which he began selling in 1856. In 1859, **Edwin Drake (1819–1880, an American businessperson)** became the first American to drill for oil in Pennsylvania, which launched US oil production. Oil was used to produce kerosene for lighting because of its low cost and brighter light until the gas mantle was invented. **Carl Auer von Welsbach (1858–1929, an Austrian chemist)** developed the modern gas mantle. Welsbach studied rare-earth elements to create the **Welsbach Mantle** for gaslighting. In 1891 he perfected a new mixture of 99% thorium dioxide and 1% cerium dioxide that gave off a much whiter light and produced a more substantial mantle. He began selling this new mantle commercially in 1892, and it quickly spread throughout Europe and became an essential part of street lighting. Kerosene and gas mantles were replaced by electricity in the 1890s for street lighting and home and building lighting in the 1920s.

The mass production of automobiles beginning in 1914 resulted in a new need for gasoline, a byproduct of oil refining. The **Burton Process** is a thermal cracking procedure invented by **William M. Burton (1865–1954, an**

American chemist). The method uses the destructive distillation of crude oil heated in a still under pressure, which produced assorted products appearing from a bubble tower at different temperatures and pressures. The process more than doubled gasoline production from most kinds of oil, lowering its cost. In 1937 the Burton process was superseded by catalytic cracking, but the Burton process is still used today to produce diesel fuel.

Fluid catalytic cracking (FCC) is one of the most important conversion processes used in petroleum refineries. It converts crude petroleum oil's high-boiling, high-molecular-weight hydrocarbon fractions into more valuable gasoline, olefinic gases, and other products. Chemical engineering professor **Warren K. Lewis (1882–1975, an American MIT professor & father of modern chemical engineering)** co-developed the **Houdry Process** under contract to **The Standard Oil Company of New Jersey** into the current **fluid catalytic cracking system** with Edwin R. Gilliland. **Edwin R. Gilliland (1909–1973, an American chemical engineer and Professor at MIT)** received his Sc.D. from MIT in 1933 for work on a wetted-wall column technique used in mass transfer. Lewis and Gilliland developed mathematical analyses of fractional distillation columns and discovered fluidized catalytic cracking methods. Gilliland consulted extensively with Exxon, Merck, Goodyear, General Electric, and Nestle and served as the President and CEO of Ionics, Inc. between 1946 and 1971. Gilliland also discovered that a low-velocity gas flowing through a powder might "lift" it enough to cause it to flow like a liquid. Using the idea of a fluidized catalyst, chemical engineering researchers **Donald L. Campbell (1904–2002, an American chemical engineer), Homer Martin, Eger V. Murphree (1898–1962, an American chemist), and Charles Tyson** together at **The Standard Oil Company of New Jersey** developed the first economically practical fluidized catalytic cracking unit. It provided a more efficient method for petroleum refiners to obtain high-octane gasoline by converting crude oil. Based on their work M. W. Kellogg Company constructed a large pilot plant in Louisiana. The process produces more gasoline with a higher octane rating and gases with more carbon-carbon double bonds (i.e., more olefins) and more economic value. Today, this technique is widely used and produces 500 million US gallons of gasoline per day, half the world's demand.

Other Chemical Discoveries

In 1856, **William H. Pekin (1838–1907, a British chemist)** discovered synthetic dye by removing aniline with alcohol, producing a vibrant purple color called mauveine. He also found other artificial colors in his research, which became among the first chemical dyes mass-produced. By 1914 the German chemical industry became the research and development leader. By the beginning of the 20th century, it dominated the world market for synthetic dyes. BASF, Bayer, and Hoechst, three significant firms, produced several hundred different hues.

Technological Advance in Shipping

The key innovation that made ocean-going steamers practical was changing from the paddle wheel to the screw-propeller. In 1835, **Francis P. Smith (1808–1874, a British inventor)** accidentally discovered the new ship propeller when the screw propeller broke, accelerating its speed. The first sea-going steamboat was Richard Wright's *Experiment* in 1813. The first iron steamship to go to sea was the 116-ton *Aaron Manby*, built in 1821 with an oscillating engine by **Aaron Manby (1776–1850, a British Shipbuilder).** It became the first iron-built vessel to cross the English Channel in 1822, carrying passengers and freight to Paris averaging 8 knots.

John Penn (1805–1878, a British marine engine engineer), invented the *lignum vitae* (water/self-lubricated hardwood) bearing for propellor shafts. He improved the oscillating engine and introduced the **Royal Navy trunk engine**, the first mass-produced, high-pressure, and high-revolution marine engine perfected for battleship use in the 1870s. In 1938, the RMS *Queen Elizabeth* was the largest passenger steamship ever built powered by Penn's engines. In 1969, RMS *Queen Elizabeth 2* (QE2) was the last passenger steamship to cross the Atlantic Ocean on a scheduled liner voyage before converting to diesel engines in 1986.

Rudolf C. K. Diesel (1858–1913, a German inventor and mechanical engineer) was famous for his engine invention. Diesel intended to design an internal combustion engine that could approach the maximum theoretical thermal efficiency. In 1892 he completed his task and received a German patent in 1893. Diesel understood thermodynamics and the theoretical and practical constraints on fuel efficiency and knew that 90% of the fuel's energy is wasted in a steam engine. Much higher efficiency ratios drove his engine design work. In Diesel's machine, fuel was injected at the end of the compression stroke ignited by the hot temperature resulting from the compression. The Diesel engine benefits from running more fuel-efficiently than gasoline engines due to much higher compression ratios and longer combustion duration. The temperature rises more slowly, allowing more heat to be converted to mechanical work. The Diesel engine was used in many other applications, such as stationary engines, agricultural machines, off-highway machinery in general, submarines, ships, locomotives, trucks, and automobiles.

Automobile and Mobility

Karl F. Benz (1844–1929, a German engine designer and automotive engineer) motorcar patent in 1885 is considered the first automobile with a four-stroke engine between the two rear wheels. It had evaporative cooling and a coil ignition with power connected by two roller chains to the rear axle. The vehicle was financed by his wife Bertha Benz's dowry. Benz developed a plant to produce the three bicycle-wheeled tires, and it became commercially available in the fall of 1888. **Gottlieb Daimler (1834–1900, a German engineer, industrial designer, and industrialist)** and **Wilhelm Maybach**

(1846–1929, a German engine designer and industrialist) converted a stagecoach by adding a petrol engine later that year. The **Mercedes** automobile was first marketed in 1901 by **Daimler-Motoren-Gesellschaft (DMG)**. **DMG and Benz & Cie**. a joint venture launched in 1924, focusing on remaining competitive through coordinated designs, production techniques, purchasing strategies, sales, and advertising. The **Mercedes-Benz Automobil GmbH** initially managed the joint marketing activities of the "Mercedes" and "Benz" brands. In 1926, the two oldest automotive manufacturers joined forces establishing **Daimler-Benz AG** launching their product line at the 1926 Berlin Motor Show. Together with Mercedes, they became known as the world's leader in designing and constructing quality autos with exceptional performance.

Henry Ford (1863–1947, an American industrialist and business magnate) built his first car in 1896, founded the **Ford Motor Company** in 1903, and was the chief developer of the mass production assembly line. He created the first automobile that middle-class Americans could afford. Ford's assembly line mass production of the Model T automobile revolutionized transportation and American industry. Ford was against labor unions and paid his assembly line workers $5 per day, more than doubled most similar workers. This salary enabled his employees to purchase Ford cars, helped reduce constant turnover, and attracted Ford's best mechanics to Detroit. By developing their human capital and knowledge, Ford raised productivity, lowering training costs. Profit-sharing was offered to employees who had worked at the company for six months or longer and conducted their lives responsibly, no heavy drinking or gambling, and serving as a good father and head of the household. In 1926 Ford introduced a reduced workweek of five 8-hour days and a 40-hour week. Ford promoted consumerism by systematically lowering costs. He established the franchise system to put Ford Motor car dealerships in North America and major cities overseas. Ford left most of his substantial wealth to the Ford Foundation, permanently controlled by his family.

Case Study #4.1 Significant Disruptive Inventors and Innovations – Transportation: Automobile[1–8]

Key Disruptive Inventors	**Karl F. Benz (1844–1929, a German engine designer and automotive engineer)** **Henry Ford (1863–1947, an American industrialist and business magnate)**
Location	**Germany and USA**
Disruptive Invention	Karl Benz led in the development of new engines, and in 1878, began creating a dependable two-stroke gas engine, and in 1886 he patented his new car. Ford founded the Ford Motor Company and was the chief developer of the assembly line technique of mass production, creating the first automobile that middle-class Americans could afford.

Problem Resolved	The auto provided freedom from public transportation and its time schedules, and people gained more control of what and when to travel to various places.
Solution Impact	Highway and bridge infrastructure expands to support auto travel with fuel stations along every road. Cars create many jobs for manufacturing, repair, travel, gas stations, and policing of roads.
Economic Impact	The most visible impact cars have on the economy is creating jobs at automakers, car dealers, repair centers, and gas stations. Although the major auto industry producers have been declining for several decades, thousands of people still make a good living designing, building, servicing, and selling cars. Investment in new plants in foreign countries also creates jobs in these communities. Transporting new cars to dealerships and marketing them to consumers are additional employment opportunities created by cars. For the car-buying public, cars represent a significant purchase decision. A new car may cost the equivalent of a year's wages or more. Beyond the initial purchase, a car has a broader economic impact. Cars require fuel, regular maintenance, and repair following an accident. Cars also require a driver's license, car registration, car insurance and are additional costs to the owner. Cars that create more pollution – particularly older cars may be more affordable, forcing buyers to decide between their budget and the environment. Consequently, more propane and electric autos are now being produced.
Cultural Impact	Increase individual freedom to drive if the road rules are followed. The driver must have a license and insurance to cover an accident. A car and supporting costs take a sizable portion of a person's income.
Inventors Education & Training	In 1853 Benz started at the scientifically oriented Lyceum, studied at the Poly-Technical University, and took mechanical engineering at the University of Karlsruhe, followed by seven years of professional training in several companies. In 1871 Benz joined August Ritter in launching the Iron Foundry and Mechanical Workshop in Mannheim, later renamed Factory for Machines for Sheet-metal Working.
	In 1879, Ford left home to work as an apprentice machinist in Detroit, first with James F. Flower & Bros., and later with the Detroit Dry Dock Co. In 1882, he returned to Dearborn to work on the family farm, where he became adept at operating the Westinghouse portable steam engine. Westinghouse later hired him to service their steam engines. Ford also studied bookkeeping at Goldsmith, Bryant & Stratton Business College in Detroit. Ford built a "steam wagon or tractor" and a steam car on the family farm but thought "steam was not suitable for light vehicles" and in 1892, he completed his first motor car, powered by a two-cylinder four horsepower engine.

(*Continued*)

(Continued)

Innovation Environment	The USA and Europe were experiencing a highly creative period of innovation in many areas until WWI.
Financing	Benz's lifelong hobby brought him to a bicycle repair shop. In 1883, he founded a new company producing industrial machines: Benz & Companie Rheinische Gasmotoren-Fabrik, usually called Benz & Cie. Soon, stationary gas engines were well. Its success allowed Benz to indulge in designing a horseless carriage featuring wire wheels with a four-stroke engine of between the rear wheels, an advanced coil ignition, and evaporative cooling. Power was transmitted using two roller chains to the rear axle. Karl Benz finished his creation in 1885, and it was the first automobile entirely designed to generate its power, and it was patented in 1886. The following year Benz created the Motorwagen Model 2, which had several modifications, and in 1889, the definitive Model 3 with wooden wheels was introduced. Benz began to sell the vehicle (advertising it as "Benz Patent Motorwagen") in the late summer of 1888, making it the first commercially available automobile in history sold in Germany and France. The early 1888 version of the Motorwagen had only two gears and could not climb hills unaided. This limitation was rectified after Bertha Benz made her trip driving one of the vehicles a great distance and suggested to her husband to add third gear for climbing hills. She also invented brake pads when she ordered a shoemaker to nail leather onto the brake blocks for going downhills. In 1893, Benz created the Victoria, which could reach the top speed of 18 km/h (11 mph) and had a pivotal front axle operated by a roller-chained tiller for steering, and it was successful with 85 units sold. Eventually, competition with Daimler Motoren Gesellschaft (DMG) in Stuttgart began to challenge the leadership of Benz & Cie. Benz announced his retirement from design management in 1903 but remained as a director on the Board of Management through its merger with DMG in 1926. He remained on the board of the new Daimler-Benz Corporation until he died in 1929. That year, Benz & Cie. sales reached 3,480 automobiles, and the company remained the leading manufacturer of cars. While a director of Benz & Cie., Karl Benz started another company, C. Benz Söhne (with his son Eugen and closely held within the family), a privately held company for manufacturing automobiles solely funded with their capital. In 1906, their new company produced cars and gas engines. The Benz Sons automobiles were of excellent quality and became popular in London as taxis. In 1923, the last production year of the Benz Sons company, 350 units were built. The German economic

crisis worsened. In 1923 Benz & Cie. produced only 1,382 units in Mannheim, and DMG made only 1,020 in Stuttgart, and the average cost of an automobile rose to 25 million marks because of rapid inflation. Negotiations between the two companies resulted in an "Agreement of Mutual Interest" in 1924, valid until 2000. Both enterprises standardized design, production, purchasing, sales, and advertising – jointly marketing their automobile models, keeping their respective brands. In June 1926, Benz & Cie. and DMG merged as the Daimler-Benz company, branding its automobiles Mercedes-Benz.

In 1891, Ford became an engineer with the Edison Illuminating Company of Detroit. Encouraged by Edison, Ford designed and built a second vehicle, completing it in 1898. Backed by Detroit lumber baron William H. Murphy, Ford founded the Detroit Automobile Company in 1899. However, the automobiles produced were of lower quality and higher price than Ford wanted. The company was dissolved in 1901. With the help of C. Harold Wills, an American engineer and businessperson, Ford designed, built, and successfully raced a 26-horsepower automobile in 1901. With this success, Murphy and other stockholders in the Detroit Automobile Company formed the Henry Ford Company in 1901, with Ford as chief engineer, but in 1902 Ford left the company. Teaming up with former racing cyclist Tom Cooper, Ford produced the 80+ horsepower racer, which Barney Oldfield was to drive to victory in a race in October 1902. Ford received the backing of a friend Alexander Y. Malcomson, a Detroit-area coal dealer, and they formed a partnership, Ford & Malcomson, Ltd., to manufacture automobiles. Ford designed an inexpensive car, leased a factory, and contracted with a machine shop to supply over $160,000 in parts, but sales were slow. So Malcomson brought in another group of investors and convinced the Dodge Brothers to accept a portion of the new company. Ford & Malcomson was reincorporated as the Ford Motor Company in 1903, with $28,000 capital. The original investors included Ford and Malcomson, the Dodge brothers, Malcomson's uncle John S. Gray, Malcolmson's secretary James Couzens, and two of Malcomson's lawyers.

Ford then demonstrated a newly designed car on the ice of Lake St. Clair, driving 1 mile in 39.4 seconds and setting a new land speed record at 91.3 miles per hour. Convinced by this success, Barney Oldfield took the car around the country, marketing the Ford brand throughout the USA. The Model T debuted in 1908 with the steering wheel on the left, the entire engine and transmission were

(*Continued*)

(Continued)

	enclosed, the four cylinders were cast in a solid block, and the suspension used two semi-elliptic springs. The car was straightforward and cheap to repair and sold for $825 in 1908. Model T sales passed 250,000 in 1914, and by 1916 the price dropped to $360 for the essential touring car, and sales hit 472,000 for $170 million in revenue. Over the next 27 years to 1927, Ford sold more than 15 million Model Ts. Ford's sales began falling because of competition in color, style, and car quality for every price range from General Motors, run by Alfred Sloan. Ford constructed a massive new assembly plant for the new Model A launched in 1927.
International Commerce	Ford and Benz cars were exported and sold worldwide and represented a significant new export category, and both manufacturers eventually established production facilities worldwide.
Major Success Factors	Benz built quality cars and participated in all engineering aspects until his son became old enough to take on the marketing and design of the vehicle. Ford built quality cars, paid his workers well, and hired top engineers but paid less attention to style.

Ford opposed US entry into World War II, believing that international business and free trade could generate the prosperity that would head off wars. Like other automobile companies, he entered the aviation business, building Liberty engines during WWI. After the war, Ford bought the **Stout Metal Airplane Company**. Its most successful plane was the **Ford 4AT Trimotor** with corrugated metal construction using a new alloy Alclad that combined the corrosion resistance of aluminum with aluminum duralumin's strength. The Trimotor plane flew in 1926 and was the first successful US passenger airliner accommodating 12 passengers. The US Army purchased 200 planes before production was discontinued in 1933. The Ford Airplane Division shut down during the Great Depression.

Before the USA entered WWII, responding to President Roosevelt's December 1940 for the "Great Arsenal of Democracy," Ford constructed a massive new aircraft factory in Willow Run near Detroit. In 1941, he began producing the **B-24,** with the first plane completed in October 1942. At 3.5 million sq ft, it was the most extensive assembly line globally, and in 1944, the plant produced 650 B-24s per month, and by 1945 was completing a B-24 in 18 hours, with one rolling off the assembly line every 58 minutes. Ford produced 9,000 B-24 bombers, half of the total made.

Better Roads Needed

Asphalt, or bitumen, is a sticky, black, highly viscous liquid or semi-solid form of petroleum found in natural deposits or is a refined product. Natural bitumen has been used for waterproofing and as an adhesive and mortar for stones and bricks dates years BC. In 1837, **Richard T. Claridge (1797–1857, a prominent asphalt contractor)** patented **Seyssel asphalt pavement**. He had seen it employed in France and Belgium. **Claridge's Patent Asphalte Company**, formed in 1838, laid one of the first asphalt pavements on the footway in Whitehall and at Knightsbridge Barracks stable. He led the development of a British asphalt industry. Asphalt could also be used for flooring, building damp proofing, and waterproofing for pools and baths. Claridge's asphalt was most used in the 1840s and 1850s. Today the primary use of asphalt is in road construction, as the glue or binder mixed with aggregate particles to create asphalt concrete. Its other uses are bituminous waterproofing products, including roofing felt and sealing flat roofs. In the USA, asphalt was first used to pave streets in the 1870s.

Airplane Development[9]

Toward the end of the Second Industrial Revolution, the brothers **Orville Wright (1871–1948, an American printer/publisher, bicycle manufacture, and airplane manufacturer)** and **Wilbur Wright (1867–1912, an American printer/publisher, bicycle manufacture, and airplane manufacturer)** invented the airplane. Self-funded, they designed, built, and flew the world's first motor-operated airplane and trained others to pilot and fly. Between 1900 and 1902 the Wrights gained experience testing gliders at Kitty Hawk. Their last glider in 1902 led directly to the design of the **Wright Flyer**. Between 1903 and 1905 they refined their flying machine to make longer, more aerodynamic flights with their fixed-wing plane. The Wrights were the first to invent aircraft controls that made fixed-wing powered flight possible using a three-axis control system to balance or keep the aircraft in equilibrium. This technique was adopted from learning to ride a bicycle. They also developed a wind tunnel to evaluate their airplane control balancing system. The Flyer was a canard[i] biplane configuration. Like gliders, the pilot flew lying on the lower wing, head toward the front of the craft to reduce drag. The pilot steered the plane by moving a cradle attached to their hips which pulled wires that warped the wings and turned the rudder simultaneously. Considerable progress toward a fully controlled flight was achieved with a third Flyer biplane (wingspan: 40 ft 4 in, empty weight: 605 lb) in fall 1905 when Wilbur made the fourth attempt, a 39-minute, 24-mile nonstop circling flight.

Wright's team member **Charlie Taylor (1868–1956, an American inventor, mechanic, and machinist)** became a significant contributor in building the first airplane engine. He designed and built the lightweight cast aluminum-copper water-cooled gasoline-fueled internal combustion engine. A sprocket chain drive, using bicycle technology, powered the handmade twin propellers. One drive chain was crossed over so that the propellers rotated in opposite directions to avoid the impact of torque on aircraft handling.

Fertilizer Growth Energizer

Justus F. von Liebig (1803–1873, a German scientist) discovered the importance of ammonia in fertilizer and made significant contributions to organic chemistry's agricultural and biological principles. Described as the "father of the fertilizer industry," he emphasized nitrogen and trace minerals as essential plant nutrients. Liebigs "**minimum law**" defines how plant growth relies on the scarcest nutrient resource rather than the total resources available. Liebig also developed a manufacturing process for beef extracts, starting the **Liebig Extract of Meat Company** to exploit the minimum law concept and later introduced the **Oxoid** brand beef bouillon cube. The Liebig Extract of Meat Company was acquired by the Vestey Group in 1924 and renamed Frigorífico Anglo del Uruguay (El Anglo). The company's assets included 2–3 million hectares of farmland and large cattle herds in Argentina, Uruguay, Paraguay, Rhodesia, Kenya, and South Africa. El Anglo merged with Brooke Bond in 1968, which was then acquired by Unilever in 1984 and then by Campbells Soup, who sold the UK operation to Premier Foods in 2006. Oxoid also was purchased by Unilever and joined their Medical Products group as Unipath. Unipath was purchased by Fisher Scientific, which merged with Thermo Electron Corporation in 2006 and became the Microbiology Division of Thermo Fisher Scientific.

John B. Lawes (1814–1900, a British entrepreneur and agricultural scientist) founded an experimental farm at his home that eventually became **Rothamsted Research**. Lawes developed superphosphate which marked the beginnings of the chemical fertilizer industry. By treating phosphates with sulfuric acid, he produced artificial manure. In 1842, Lawes experimented in raising crops and feeding animals for more than half a century, rendering Rothamsted famous as a scientific agriculturist. In 1889, Lawes took measures to ensure the continued existence of the Rothamsted experimental farm financially by constituting the **Lawes Agricultural Trust**. It is the oldest agricultural research facility in the world.

Edward Packard, Sr. (1819–1899, a British businessperson) founded and developed one of the first large-scale commercial fertilize plants in Britain in the 1850s. **Edward Packard, Jr. (1843–1932, a British chemist and businessperson)** further expanded and developed a primary artificial fertilizer industry. He was influential in rationalizing the fertilizer industry in the 1880s and imposing higher quality standards. As a significant artificial fertilizer industry emerged in the UK, Packard senior became a very wealthy and prominent figure. In 1919 he oversaw negotiations leading to the Packard's merger with **James Fison**, another well-known British artificial fertilizer company leading to **Packard and James Fison Ltd's** formation, and he became Chair. The new company was one of the largest fertilizer manufacturing businesses in the UK, and in the 1870s, both plants shipped superphosphates worldwide. In 1942 the company name was changed to **Fisons Ltd**. During the 1950s, Fisons promoted the spraying of crops with helicopters. In 1982, Fisons decided to focus on pharmaceutical products. Its fertilizer activities were sold to Norsk Hydro in 1982. Fisons became a British multinational pharmaceutical, scientific instrument, and horticultural chemicals company and was acquired by Rhone-Poulenc in 1995.

Case Study #4.2 Significant Disruptive Inventors and Innovations – Agriculture: Fertilizer

Key Disruptive Inventors	**Justus F. von Liebig (1803–1873, a German scientist)** **John B. Lawes (1814–1900, a British entrepreneur and agricultural scientist)** **Edward Packard, Sr. (1819–1899, a British businessman), Edward Packard, Jr. (1843–1932, a British chemist and businessperson)**
Location	**Germany and Britain**
Disruptive Invention	Liebig and Lawes developed superphosphate marking the beginnings of the chemical fertilizer industry. The Packards' developed and expanded the first large-scale commercial artificial fertilize plants and industry in Britain and expanded production at low cost.
Problem Resolved	Animal fertilizer is in limited supply and costly if available.
Solution Impact	Food production per acre increased, lowering food costs.
Economic Impact	The result was healthier diets, increased food output, and control of crop-destroying pests and crop disease.
Cultural Impact	Food availability is no longer a constant problem.
Inventors Education & Training	Liebig attended the University of Bonn and Erlangen, received a doctorate, and taught and researched at Giessen. Lawes was educated at Eton College and Brasenose College, Oxford, and afterward, he began growing medicinal plants on the Rothamsted estates. Edward Packard jr. was educated at King's College, London, and the Royal Agricultural College at Cirencester. He inherited the artificial fertilizer plant from his father, Edward Packard, sr., in 1822 and built a fertilizer industry.
Innovation Environment	This period was a time of creative innovations, the emergence of university research, and innovations in many different areas. The development of the artificial fertilizer industry was critical to expanding agricultural production.
Financing	Liebig developed an experimental research farm and discovered that nitrogen and trace minerals are essential agricultural nutrients and formulated the minimum law, which described how plant growth relied on the scarcest nutrient resource. In 1825 Liebig was given a full professorship and appointed an endowed chair in chemistry, receiving an increased salary and a laboratory allowance.

(*Continued*)

(Continued)

	The laboratory became renowned as a model institution for teaching practical chemistry. It was also significant for emphasizing applying fundamental research discoveries to develop specific chemical processes and products. In 1839, he obtained government funds to build a lecture theatre and two separate laboratories at the University of Giessen. In 1865, Liebig partnered with Belgian engineer George C. Gilbert and was named scientific director of Liebig's Extract of Meat Company, located in Fray Bentos, Uruguay. In 1852, Liebig accepted an appointment from King Maximilian II of Bavaria to the Ludwig Maximilian University of Munich, including a house, lecture hall, and laboratory.
	Lawes patented a manure formed by treating phosphates with sulfuric acid in 1842 and thus initiated the artificial manure industry while continuing his agricultural plant research on the Rothamsted Research Estate. Lawes took measures to ensure the continued existence of the Rothamsted experimental farm by setting aside money solely for that purpose and constituting the Lawes Agricultural Trust.
	Packard sr. built the E. Packard & Co. business in artificial fertilizers with his first factory set up in an old flour mill in 1847. It became a coprolite (animal feces) warehouse when he relocated closer to rail freight and away from the town. The company became successful financially. Packard established one of the largest fertilizer manufacturing businesses in Britain. His son continued to build this successful fertilizer production and export industry. In 1872 Packard patented a new type of highly concentrated superphosphate. The works covered four acres of land with a surrounding village of houses for employees, and 800 tons of superphosphates and other manures were being produced every week. About half of the 882 vessels leaving the Port of Ipswich in 1871 were loaded with his Packard's fertilizer.
International Commerce	Packard's company exported concentrated super fertilizer to Europe and many other international markets.
Major Success Factors	Packard senior was well educated in chemistry to create new fertilized production facilities and be an excellent entrepreneur. His son followed him and further expanded the business worldwide while contributing to the local development and growth of music and the arts.

Carl Bosch (1874–1940, a German chemist and engineer) was a pioneer in high-pressure industrial chemistry and the founder of **IG Farben.** Working with **Fritz Haber (1868–1934, a Polish/Russian-German chemist),** they developed the more efficient **Haber–Bosch** process to synthesize ammonia from nitrogen gas and hydrogen gas. Most producers currently use this process for the large-scale synthesis of fertilizers and explosives. Bosch received the Nobel Prize in Chemistry in 1918 for the **Haber–Bosch** process. Haber and **Max Born (1882–1970, a German physicist and mathematician)** were instrumental in quantum mechanics.[ii] Born won the 1954 Nobel Prize in Physics for his fundamental research in quantum mechanics, especially in the statistical interpretation of the wave function named the **Born–Haber Cycle**. He also made contributions to solid-state physics and optics. Born and Haber used molecular nitrogen and methane gas with ammonia as the primary raw material to produce nitric acid used as an essential industrial chemical to manufacture fertilizers and explosives.

Case Study #4.3 Significant Disruptive Inventors and Innovations – Agriculture/Industry – Chemicals/Fertilizer

Key Disruptive Inventors	**Carl Bosch (1874–1940, a German chemist and engineer)** **Fritz Haber (1868–1934, a Polish/Russian-German chemist)**
Location	**Germany and Polish/Russian**
Disruptive Invention	Bosch was a pioneer in high-pressure industrial chemistry and founder of IG Farben, which at one point was the world's largest chemical company and became part of BASF. The chemical industry comprises the companies producing and converting raw materials (oil, natural gas, air, water, metals, and minerals) into thousands of products supporting industrialization. Haber's development of the Haber–Bosch process synthesizes ammonia from nitrogen gas and hydrogen gas, essential for the large-scale synthesis of fertilizers and explosives. The Haber–Bosch process is a more efficient and lower-cost production process. Approximately two-thirds of annual global food production uses nitrogen from the Haber–Bosch process, supporting half of the world population.
Problem Resolved	The rising need to increase food production at a lower cost to support the growing population in cities.
Solution Impact	Improve people's access to more nutritious foods, resulting in healthier, stronger, and longer, more healthy lives.
Economic Impact	Labor productivity expanded with more people working and GDP growth increasing more rapidly.

(*Continued*)

(Continued)

Cultural Impact	The impact of Bosch and Haber was to change farming from a family business into a significant industry.
Inventors Education & Training	Bosch completed his studies in mechanical engineering and metallurgy at the Technical University of Charlottenburg in 1896. Haber received his doctorate cum laude from Friedrich Wilhelm University in May 1891.
Innovation Environment	Despite the interruption of WWI, the environment was exceptionally favorable as there were many opportunities for improvements.
Financing	Bosch was born in Cologne, the first of seven children of Carl Bosch senior (1843–1904), co-owner of the installation company Bosch & Haag in Cologne. Bosch gradually created a large-scale industry around the high-pressure synthesis of ammonia and made ammonia available for industry. After the First World War, Bosch participated in the 1918 armistice negotiations in Spa and Versailles as an economic advisor. At the instigation of Bosch, BASF resumed its efforts to merge the primary chemical industry after WWI in the 1920s. While Duisberg, Chairman of the Board of Management of Bayer AG, advocated a holding structure, Bosch sought to merge the companies. Haber's father, Siegfried, was a well-known merchant who had founded his own business in dye pigments, paints, and pharmaceuticals. During his time at the University of Karlsruhe from 1894 to 1911, son Haber invented the Haber–Bosch process, which is the catalytic formation of ammonia from hydrogen and atmospheric nitrogen under high-temperature conditions and pressure.
International Commerce	BASF founded IG Farben with Hoechst, Bayer, and three other companies. BASF was the nominal survivor, as all shares were exchanged for BASF shares before the merger. Rubber, fuels, and coatings were added to the range of products. BASF SE is a German multinational chemical company and the largest chemical producer globally. The BASF Group comprises subsidiaries and joint ventures in more than 80 countries and operates six integrated production sites and 390 other production sites in Europe, Asia, Australia, the Americas, and Africa. The allies dissolved IG Farben in November 1945. In the 1960s, BASF production abroad was expanded, and plants were built in Argentina, Australia,

	Belgium, Brazil, France, India, Italy, Japan, Mexico, Spain, the UK, and the USA. More recently, a large plant was built in China. Following a change in corporate strategy in 1965, greater emphasis was placed on higher-value products such as coatings, pharmaceuticals, pesticides, and fertilizers. Its headquarters is in Ludwigshafen, Germany. BASF has customers in over 190 countries and supplies products to various industries.
Major Success Factors	Both men were well-educated and highly-respected chemical engineers and focused on lower-cost fertilizer for improved agricultural production.

Engines and Turbines

In 1884 **Charles A. Parsons (1854–1931, an American-Irish engineer)** invented the compound steam turbine and launched the **C. A. Parsons and Company**. He worked as an engineer on generators, turbine design, and power generation, influencing naval and electrical engineering. Parson's steam turbine, developed in 1903, made cheap and plentiful electricity possible, and by the 1930s, his turbine was adopted for all major world power stations. The turbine produced rotary power rather than reciprocating power like early steam engines. The substantial number of fins of the turbine allowed for high efficiency and reduced size by 90%. Today, Parson's turbine design generates about 80% of the world's electric power, primarily using the combustion of fossil fuels. Parson's company was merged with Clarke Chapman to form Northern Engineering Industries in 1977 and became part of Rolls-Royce plc in 1989. Siemens Energy acquired the Parson Company in 1997 from Rolls-Royce. Several nuclear power stations use Parson's steam turbines in Britain and Scotland. Parsons also developed optical equipment for searchlights and telescopes, which revolutionized marine transport and naval warfare.

Case Study #4.4 Significant Disruptive Inventors and Innovations – Electric Power Generation

Key Disruptive Inventors	**Charles A. Parsons (1854–1931, an American-Irish engineer)**
Location	**USA – Irish**
Disruptive Invention	Compound steam turbine to generate electricity efficiently and inexpensively.

(*Continued*)

(Continued)

Problem Resolved	Electrical power generation was prohibitive cost and limited in supply.
Solution Impact	Less expensive cost of energy.
Economic Impact	In 1889, he founded C.A. Parsons and Company in Newcastle to produce turbo generators according to his design. In the same year, Parsons set up the Newcastle and District Electric Lighting Company (DisCO). And in 1890, DisCo opened Forth Banks Power Station, the first power station to generate electricity using turbo generators. Although his first turbine was only 1.6% efficient and generated a mere 7.5 kilowatts, rapid incremental improvements in a few years led to his first-megawatt turbine built in 1899 for a generating plant at Elberfeld, Germany.
Cultural Impact	Helped to lower the cost of electricity for consumers.
Inventors Education & Training	Parsons was educated at home in Ireland by private tutors who were well-versed in the sciences and functioned as a practical assistant to the Earl in his astronomical work. Parsons majored in mathematics at Trinity College, Dublin, and St. John's College, Cambridge, graduating in 1877 with a first-class honors degree. He joined the Newcastle-based engineering firm of W.G. Armstrong as an apprentice.
Innovation Environment	It was a competitive innovation environment with increasing patent lawsuits.
Financing	Parson's father was an Earl and well off. The Parsons turbine company survives near Newcastle and is now part of Siemens, the German conglomerate. Sometimes referred to as Siemens Parsons, the company completed a major redevelopment program, reducing the size of its site by around three-quarters and installing the latest manufacturing technology for steam turbines. In 1925 Charles Parsons acquired the Grubb Telescope Company and renamed it, Grubb Parsons. That company survived in the Newcastle area until 1985. Parsons was also interested in marine applications and founded the Parsons Marine Steam Turbine Company in Newcastle. In 1897, his turbine-powered yacht, Turbinia, was exhibited moving at 34 kn/39 mph.
International Commerce	Strong interest in electrical power generation and globally promoted international trade in electricity generating systems.
Major Success Factors	Parsons had a solid educational background and good analytical skills, persistence, and determination.

Internal Combustion Engines

Nicolaus A. Otto (1832–1891, a German engineer), in 1861, developed the **compressed charge internal combustion engine**, which ran on petroleum gas and led to the modern internal combustion engine. In 1864, Otto needed financing and partnered with **Eugen Langen**, a sugar industrialist, who started **NA Otto & Cie** in Cologne and later changed to **Deutz AG.** Deutz was the world's first company focused entirely on stationery, internal combustion engines' design, and production. The 1864 Otto & Langen engine was a free-piston atmospheric engine. It consumed less than half the gas of other (**Lenoir and Hugon**) atmospheric engines and was a commercial success selling over 50,000 in the next 17 years. Their company also made engines for agricultural machines such as combine harvesters and tractors and commercial vehicles such as trucks and buses.

Case Study #4.5 Significant Disruptive Inventors and Innovations – Power: Internal Combustion Engine

Key Disruptive Inventors	**Nicolaus A. Otto (1832–1891, a German engineer)**
Location	**Germany**
Disruptive Invention	Developed the compressed charge internal combustion engine, which ran on petroleum gas and led to the modern internal combustion engine.
Problem Resolved	There was a need for a more powerful engine for automobiles. The ignition of the compressed fuel-air mixture was initiated by a timed spark powerful enough to move a heavy vehicle at a reasonable speed up an incline.
Solution Impact	The transportation industry for automobiles and trucks was born, which provided many workers with a job and livelihood. Otto did not want to build engines for transportation, but one of Otto's employees, **Gottlieb Daimler**, did and was able to get around Otto's patent, assemble engines, and build cars.
Economic Impact	A significant new industry was born, providing people with an accessible power source for work and pleasure.
Cultural Impact	The engine was used in many ways in agriculture and industry to provide power for different professions and was copied by Daimler for use in automobile transportation.
Inventors Education & Training	He went to elementary school for 6 years and then to high school, which he did not complete but performed well in science and technology. He studied the engines produced by others and built a two-stroke engine before building his four-stroke internal combustion engine.

(*Continued*)

(Continued)

Innovation Environment	Several inventors were developing diverse types of atmospheric engines. Even though Otto received a patent for his four-stroke machine, an earlier patent was by a French engineer who never built his engine, allowing Daimler to produce the engine for cars.
Financing	Otto worked odd jobs after leaving school to support himself and experimented with a four-stroke engine in 1861. He looked for investors and found **Eugen Langen**, a sugar merchant's father. Otto and Langen became partners establishing a company, NA Otto & Cie, in Cologne, focusing on the design and production of internal combustion engines. Otto worked on a Four Stroke stationary compressed charge engine that became immediately successful when it appeared in 1876. The company produced 634 engines a year by 1875, producing three hp and was over 10 feet long.
International Commerce	Otto's engines were sold throughout Europe and eventually exported globally, and as the machines were further developed for use in cars, they were exported even more widely worldwide. The engine provided an alternative to the larger steam engine and was a reliable power source for farms and industry.
Major Success Factors	Otto's engine was immediately successful because of its reliability, efficiency, and relative quietness. The Otto engine was the first practical alternative to the steam engine as a power source.

Globalized Telecommunications

Sir William F. Cooke (1806–1899, a British inventor) and **Charles Wheatstone (1802–1875, a British scientist and inventor)** were the co-inventors of the **Cooke–Wheatstone** electrical telegraph. They developed the first commercial telegraph system operating between Camden Town London and Euston Railway Station in 1837. Cooke and **John L. Ricardo (1812–1862, a British businessperson and politician)** founded the **Electric Telegraph Company**, the world's first public telegraph company, in 1846. Wheatstone was the inventor of many scientific breakthroughs but is best known for his contributions to telegraphy development. **Samuel H. Christie (1784–1865, a British scientist, physicist, and mathematician)** invented the Wheatstone bridge, which is used to measure an unknown electrical resistance. **John W. Brett (1805–1863, a British telegraph engineer)** built the first undersea cable between France and England. In 1856 Brett with **Charles T. Bright (1832–1888, a British electrical engineer)** and **Cyrus W. Field (1819–1892, an American businessperson and financier)** founded the **Atlantic Telegraph Company**, which laid a commercial telegraph cable across the Atlantic Ocean.

Alexander G. Bell (1847–1922, a Scottish-born American inventor, scientist, and engineer) invented and patented the first practical telephone in 1876, which helped speed business communications. He also co-founded the **American Telephone and Telegraph Company (AT&T)** in 1885. **James C. Maxwell (1831–1879, a Scottish scientist in mathematical physics)** who, with the publication of "A Dynamical Theory of the Electromagnetic Field" in 1865, demonstrated that electric and magnetic fields travel through space waves moving at the speed of light. He proposed that light is an undulation in the same medium that is the cause of electric and magnetic phenomena. The unification of light and electrical phenomena led to his prediction of the existence of radio waves. Maxwell's electromagnetic waves theory was confirmed by **David E. Hughes (1831–1879, a British-American inventor, practical experimenter, and music professor)** known for his work on the microphone's printing telegraph. And **Heinrich Hertz (1857–1894, a German physicist)** first conclusively proved the electromagnetic waves predicted by James C. Maxwell's electromagnetism equations. In his honor, the unit of frequency, cycle per second, was named "hertz."

Case Study #4.6 Significant Disruptive Inventors and Innovations – Communications: The Telephone

Key Disruptive Inventors	**Alexander G. Bell (1847–1922, a Scottish-born, American inventor, scientist, and engineer)**
Location	**Scottish/Canadian/US**
Disruptive Invention	Bell is credited with inventing and patenting the first practical telephone in 1876.
Problem Resolved	The phone replaced the telegraph, which was not the most robust form of communication.
Solution Impact	Growth in demand for telephones and people who had phones could more easily stay in touch and communicate for business and pleasure. The cost and convenience of calling someone improved and provided a better idea of their feelings in the tone of their voice. Better informed people were able to make better decisions.
Economic Impact	The communications industry began to expand dramatically, stimulating growth in marketing and advertising.
Cultural Impact	The telephone provided a feeling of a closer relationship between friends and family.
Inventors Education & Training	Bell received his early schooling at home from his father, and at 17, he attended the University of Edinburgh. In 1868 Bell completed his matriculation exams and was accepted for admission to University College in London
Innovation Environment	The innovation environment was favorable, with friends and family providing financing and wealthy people looking for opportunities.

(*Continued*)

(Continued)

Financing	In 1872, Bell became Vocal Physiology and Elocution professor at the Boston University School of Oratory. In 1876 Bell shared a laboratory with **Meucci**, filed a patent for a telephone, became a celebrity, and made a lucrative deal with Western Union. Meucci sued and was nearing victory when he died in 1889, ending the legal action. When Bell mentioned to **Gardiner Hubbard** and **Thomas Sanders** that he was sending multiple tones on a telegraph wire using a multi-reed device, the two wealthy patrons began to support Bell's experiments financially. Hubbard's patent attorney submitted the patent. In 1876, Bell focused on improving the electromagnetic telephone, and the first two-way conversation over a 2.5-mile line took place between Cambridge and Boston in 1876. The Bell Telephone Company was created in 1877, and by 1886, more than 150,000 people in the USA owned telephones. Bell Company engineers made numerous other improvements to the telephone, which emerged as one of the most successful products. In 1879, the Bell company acquired Edison's patents for the carbon microphone from Western Union. This microphone made the telephone practical for longer distances, and it was no longer necessary to shout to be heard at the receiving telephone. In 1915, Bell made the first ceremonial transcontinental telephone call from the AT&T head office in New York City to his associate Thomas Watson in San Francisco. In 1880, Bell's assistant transmitted a wireless voice telephone message to Bell. Bell received many awards, and in 1880 he received the Volta Prize with a purse of 50,000 French francs from the French Government for the invention of the telephone. The Bell Telephone Company was organized in Massachusetts in 1877 by Bell's father-in-law **Gardiner G. Hubbard**, who also helped organize a sister company – the New England Telephone and Telegraph Company. The two companies merged in 1879 to form two new entities, the National Bell Telephone Company of Boston, and the International Bell Telephone Company, headquartered in Belgium. The National Bell Telephone Company merged with the American Speaking Telephone Company in 1880 to form the American Bell Telephone Company in Massachusetts. The Bell Telephone Company was organized with **Hubbard** as "trustee," although he was also its de facto president. He also controlled his daughter's shares by power of attorney and with **Thomas Sanders**, its principal financial backer, as treasurer. The American Bell Telephone Company evolved into the American Telephone & Telegraph Company (AT&T), which at times has been the world's largest telephone company.

International Commerce	Better international communications helped to increase global exports and imports.
Major Success Factors	Bell received strong family support, had wealthy friends, persistence, and a long-term vision of the importance of his invention.

Guglielmo Marconi (1874–1937, an Italian inventor and electrical engineer) is known for his pioneering work on long-distance radio transmission, Marconi's law, and a radio telegraph system. He is credited as the radio and wireless telegraphy development inventor and founded **The Wireless Telegraph & Signal Company** in Britain in 1897. He sent the first wireless communication over the open sea and, in 1901, made the first transatlantic transmission from Cornwall to Newfoundland. High-powered sending and receiving stations were built on both sides of the Atlantic, and, in 1904, he began a nightly commercial news service to subscribing ships.

Case Study #4.7 Significant Disruptive Inventors and Innovations – Communications: Telegraph and Wireless Radio Communications

Key Disruptive Inventors	**Samuel F. B. Morse (1791–1872, an American inventor and painter)** **Guglielmo Marconi (1874–1937, an Italian inventor and electrical engineer)**
Location	**USA and Italy**
Disruptive Invention	Morse developed the telegraph using electromagnetic technology. Marconi established the foundation for wireless radio communications systems employing electromagnetic waves, known for his pioneering work on long-distance radio transmission and a radio telegraph system. He is credited as the inventor of the radio and was the first to manufacture and commercialize equipment for wireless communication worldwide.
Problem Resolved	The problem was communicating faster than pony express over a long distance. Morse was introduced to **Joseph Henry**, a scientist at Princeton and known expert in electromagnetism. In 1835 Henry invented the electrical relay, and with an endless chain of circuits, it was possible to send a message of electrical pulses at any distance, which was the telegraph. This discovery solved Morse's problem for distance. At a presentation

(*Continued*)

(Continued)

	at New York University, a wealthy ironworks owner **Steven Vail** offered Morse workspace and $2,000 to hire his son, **Alfred Vail**, as an assistant. Vail made an improved receiver for creating dots and dashes, and Morse completed his word and number dictionary, which began the Morse code. Vail changed the transmission from numbers to letters. Vail also introduced the key to replacing Morse's lead composing strip, reduced the receiving machine's size, and later invented the printing telegraph patented in Morse's name. Morse presented his electromagnetic system to Congress in 1837.
Solution Impact	As the world's population, business, and international trade expanded, global news and communication increased the need for global radio communications as a primary source of reliable information and knowledge for domestic and international business.
Economic Impact	More information became available to everyone. Price differential became more apparent and moved toward the lowest level except for perceived quality differences. People began to make better-informed decisions. International trade expanded.
Cultural Impact	The telegraph made it much easier to communicate with friends and business associates. Wireless radio communication enables news and events to be heard by others more quickly.
Inventors Education & Training	Morse was born in Massachusetts, attended Phillips Academy at Andover, entered Yale in 1805, and graduated in 1810, where he studied religious philosophy and attended lectures on electricity. He was interested in art and painting. He worked in a bookstore to learn about business, went to London to study art, won awards, and returned to the USA. In 1815 he became a leading American artist for painting portraits of well-known people. While returning from Europe in 1832, Morse met **Charles T. Jackson** of Boston, who understood electromagnetism. Witnessing various experiments with Jackson's electromagnet, he became interested in electricity and magnetism and drew sparks from a magnet. At age 43, Morse began formulating the concept of a single-wire telegraph which he developed. In May 1845, the Magnetic Telegraph Company was formed to build telegraph lines from New York City toward Philadelphia, Boston, and Buffalo. Eventually, 12,000 miles of telegraphic lines rapidly spread throughout the US by 1850. Marconi was born in Italy to a wealthy Italian business family whose mother was Scotch-Irish and

taught Marconi to speak and write English. He was privately educated in Bologna and studied college-level physics under several well-known professors. Marconi was interested in science and knowledgeable of the works by Maxwell, Hertz, Lodge, and Righi in electromagnetic waves. **Righi** was a neighbor and friend of the Marconi's and familiarized Guglielmo with Hertzian electromagnetic waves, which Marconi reproduced using Lodge's coherer device (radio wave detector) began experiments in generating and receiving wireless signals at home. Marconi continued to expand the distance of the signal by using antennas and location reflectors to obtain a directional beam that could travel over hills and beyond sight. Because the Italian government showed little interest, Marconi went to England and found the British postal system highly interested in his work and filled for a patent in 1896 in London.

He returned to Italy to give demonstrations to the Navy of land to ships at sea communications. His British patent was approved, and he applied for an Italian patent and established the Wireless Telegraph & Signal Company (later, he changed the word Wireless to Marconi). Marconi returned to England to perform a transmission test for Lloyds over 18 miles, and the newspaper *Daily Express* obtained news using Marconi's system. In 1898 Marconi began to commercialize and market his wireless communication system. Reporting on events like yacht racing helped Queen Victoria receive radio messages about the health of the Prince of Wales from the royal yacht at sea. SOS help signals sent from a sinking lightship enabled lifeboats to rescue the ship's crew, and news of the event triggered increased sales of Marconi's wireless system. Marconi continued to expand the distance of wireless signals reaching 75 miles in 1899, and he began having permanent transmission/receiving stations built in several locations. In New York the same year, Marconi's communication equipment broadcast Admiral Dewey's victory in the Spanish-American war. Newspapers began praising Marconi's accomplishments and used his equipment to broadcast America's Cup yacht races with the US defeat of England. Marconi formed his American Marconi Company and, the following year, his Marconi Internal Marine Communications Company for installing land-to-ship communication systems.

(*Continued*)

(Continued)

	He applied for another US and British patent for a tunable type of continuous-wave transmitter and receiver machines that could communicate at distinctly different frequencies to overcome the interference between several transmitters and receivers. Marconi continued to do research and experiments to demonstrate greater distances over which wireless communication signals could be transmitted using new patented inventions for sending and receiving. He continued building his companies' businesses by commercializing his new technology, including microwave and beam technology.
Innovation Environment	Many European inventors worked on the use of electromagnetic waves for communication systems. Still, none had proven technically and commercially successful. US Government established a $30,000 prize in the early 1800s for a communication telegraph that would extend a thousand miles. Marconi received a US Patent issued in 1849. Marconi was also an entrepreneur, businessperson, and founder of The Wireless Telegraph & Signal Company in the United Kingdom in 1897, which became the Marconi Company. Numerous investigators and inventors explored wireless telegraph technologies and even building systems using electric conduction, electromagnetic induction, and optical (light) signaling for over 50 years. There was significant litigation for both inventors over telegraph patents during this period.
Financing	Morse supported himself by painting portraits but had no significant savings or extra funds in his early years. In 1835 he accepted a literature professor of arts and design but was paid little. He developed a working prototype telegraph instrument in which led strips were the core of the transmitter. An electromagnet that pulled against the mid-region of a lever was the core of the receiver. One end of the lever was fixed, and the other held a pencil that marked a variable or intermittent line on a strip of paper drawn by a wooden clock mechanism. Long and short pencil marks corresponded to a code for numbers that represented words. Morse lived in poverty until 1843. Congress awarded $30,000 to Morse to build a test line between Washington DC and Baltimore. However, Francis Smith, Chairman of the House Committee on Commerce, awarded himself a $20,000 contract for the first 13 miles, full of short circuits. Finally, a bare wireline was put atop poles and completed in 1844,

	and on May 24, the line was activated using new instruments constructed by Vail of a single activated key. Congress became preoccupied with trouble in Mexico in 1845, and Morse found partners and formed the Magnetic Telegraph Company to license the patent in various parts of the country. Trains, newspapers, and sea captains began using it heavily. Meanwhile, Morse became disinterested in his company, expanded the telegraph, and became involved in patent lawsuits. He won, ending his poverty days and becoming an affluent celebrity and philanthropist.
International Commerce	In 1856, **Hiram Sibley** organized Western Union and began buying up all the improvements and control of most lines, keeping each system's best features using the Morse code system. In Europe, the Morse code was adapted to foreign languages and became the International Morse code used in most developed and more advanced developing countries.
Major Success Factors	Morse had a problem getting a telegraphic signal to carry over more than a few hundred yards of wire when **Professor Leonard Gale** helped Morse introduce extra circuits or relays at frequent intervals, enabling Morse to send a message over ten miles of wire.
	Marconi was focused on the transmission of telegraph signals by radio waves. He succeeded in making an engineering and commercial success of radio by innovating and building on the work of previous experimenters. Marconi also had a strong entrepreneurial and persistent nature.

In 1904 **Sir John A. Fleming (1849–1945, a British electrical engineer and physicist)** invented the first thermionic valve or **vacuum tube** and designed the radio transmitter to make the first transatlantic radio transmission. He set the foundation for the development of modern electronics and radio broadcasting. **Lee De Forest (1873–1961, an American inventor)** self-described "Father of Radio" and a pioneer in developing sound-on-film recording used for motion pictures. He had over 180 patents. His most famous invention, in 1906, was the **three-element Audion vacuum tube**, the first practical amplification of electronic signals device. It was the foundation of electronics, making radio broadcasting, long-distance telephone lines, and talking motion pictures, among many other applications. The grid **Audion**, which de Forest called "my greatest invention," and the vacuum tubes developed from it, dominated the field of electronics for 40 years. They made long-distance telephone service, radio broadcasting, television, and many other applications possible. It could also be used as an electronic switching element and was later used in early digital electronics, including the first electronic computers. However, the 1948 invention of the transistor would lead to microchips that eventually replaced vacuum-tube technology.

Modern Business Emerges[4,10]

During the Second Industrial Revolution, transportation had a significant impact on changing how business was managed. This change resulted from the shift from the cottage or home-based business to factories, focusing on labor specialization, time, efficiency, and labor productivity. The steam engine was still the primary energy source for industries running in larger factories as investment focused on scale production. The opening of railroads and their expansion westward supplied the means to deliver farm machinery and food supplies. There was growing demand as immigrants from Europe and China developed their farms and used railroads to ship their crops to the growing urban markets.

Railroads were complex operations and employed substantial capital, which had to be tracked, supported, and delivered to the correct location on time. As railroads expanded westward and suffered severe accidents, managers were recruited to reduce overlapping responsibilities and concentrate functions into departments' responsibility centers. Bookkeeping and accounting became increasingly important to improve the tracking of costs and management of parts inventories for regular maintenance and repairs. Railroad accounting systems were later adopted by the steel and other industries.

Economic growth from 1870 to 1890 expanded rapidly, and living conditions improved with the decline in the price of goods as the cost of living fell with productivity increases. Machines and factories replaced labor, and unemployment increased and was also hurt by replacing outdated, more labor-intensive machinery. There were also widespread improvements in public health sanitation and water treatment to regulate its minimum quality standards implemented by local governments. The increased efficiency of steam engines helped expand international trade volume and value. The telegraph improved order placement, tracking, changes, and prompt deliveries along rail lines and shipping ports. The Suez Canal opening in 1868 also eased the growth in less expensive and faster international shipping of goods. The Suez Canal is an artificial sea-level waterway in Egypt, connecting the Mediterranean Sea to the Red Sea through the Isthmus of Suez, which opened new and faster shipping of products between Europe and Asia.

The shift in economic activity and employment from agriculture to industry continued as the factory system expanded, urban centers grew, and workers became more skilled and specialized. The increasingly professional middle-class helped set the stage for developing a more consumer-based culture with rising spending power. The increase in their standard of living helped improve their health and reduce worries.

Corporate Management Innovations[4,10]

Adam Smith (1723–1790, a Scottish economist, philosopher, pioneer of political economy) developed the concept of "division of labor" and how rational self-interest and competition can lead to economic prosperity. He argued that the cause of national wealth was labor, not gold or silver, in 1776. As more significant and complex corporations emerged with hundreds and thousands of employees with each Industrial Revolution, the environment and challenges of management changed. **Henry Ford** was one of the first to deal with this management problem. Ford focused on mass production, efficiency, mechanization, worker specialization, and simplifying each worker's task. At first, he tried to pressure workers to work harder, but labor unions pushed back. He then tried providing incentives by doubling wages, creating a five-day workweek of 40 hours, and introducing different worker shifts for groups of assembly line workers.

Ford also hired **Frederick W. Taylor (1856–1915, an American mechanical engineer and founder of scientific management theory)** to improve industrial efficiency. Taylor made his name in scientific management and his fortune patenting steel-process improvements. He was one of the first management consultants and was one of the **Efficiency Movement's** intellectual leaders. In 1911, Taylor presented his efficiency techniques in **The Principles of Scientific Management**. His pioneering work in applying engineering principles to work on the factory floor was instrumental in creating and developing the engineering branch known as industrial engineering. Work tasks became specific, and training and development were provided for each job function. Micro-management, instruction, and supervision became the norm, and management principles were used to plan the work required and ensure the necessary tasks were completed based on scientific principles. Time and motion studies were analyzed to improve each worker task's efficiency, and new, more specific engineering fields were developed like industrial engineering, manufacturing engineering, and business management. Taylor believed management and labor had a common goal in increasing productivity, which was used to restructure the entire operations of factories. He introduced production-line time and motion studies to identify the best-performing tasks to set work standards and compensation. Other contributors to scientific management theory were **Henry L. Gantt (1861–1919, an American mechanical engineer and management consultant)** and **Frank Gilbreth (1868–1924, an American engineer, consultant, and author)** and **Lillian Gilbreth (1878–1972, an American psychologist, industrial engineer, consultant, and educator)**. Scientific performance measurement tools include Gantt Charts, Critical Path Method (CPM) from DuPont, and Program Evaluation and Review (PERT) used by the US Navy.

Four management schools emerged: scientific, organizational, behavioral, and management science. Under the organizational school, **Henri Fayol (1841–1925, a French mining engineer, mining executive, author, and**

director of mines) was responsible for systematizing total organizational functions. He developed 14 Principles of management and believed management was a skill that could be taught based on his set of underlying principles. **Max Weber (1864–1920, a German sociologist, historian, jurist, and political economist)** developed a bureaucratic approach to management where activities and objectives were thought out and whose divisions of labor were clearly defined. Performance was to be based on merit in an environment where operations are predictable and productive. **Mary P. Follett (1868–1933, an American social worker, management consultant, philosopher, and pioneer in organizational theory and organizational behavior)** believed that humans grew through relationships with others in organizations. Her management theory included a broader set of relationships inside the organization and outside impacted by environmental factors, including politics, economics, and biology, which needed to be considered. **Chester I. Barnard (1886–1961, an American business executive and public administrator)** found that a corporation can operate efficiently only when the companies' goals are kept in balance with the individuals' objectives. His identification of this informal organization of groups or teams was his significant contribution. **Walter Flanders (1871–1923, an American industrialist in the machine tool and automotive industries)** was an expert in mass production and thought breaking down each worker's function into smaller units would speed production and efficiency. **Charles Sorenson (1881–1968, a Danish-American principal of the Ford Motor Company**) used technology by installing a conveyer belt to improve efficiency and accelerate production significantly.

The behavioral management innovators emphasized that the organization is people and should include sociology and psychology. Hence, managers need to focus on human relations resulting in a series of studies at the **Western Electric Company**. **The Hawthorne Experiments** from 1924 to 1933 divided workers into test groups to determine what influenced workers' performance. **Elton Mayo (1880–1949, an Australian psychologist, industrial researcher, and academic organizational management scientist)** determined that a complex chain of attitudes determined worker productivity. Sympathetic management supervision resulted in group motivation and pride, and the social environment of workers also had a positive impact on productivity. Total quality leadership, which provided training and improvement processes for employees and empowered them to facilitate restructuring to enhance productivity and profits, was recognized as key to their success. Outsourcing support was provided to employees determined to be redundant, which helped build worker morale. **Abraham Maslow (1908–1970, an American psychologist)** identified that workers led complex lives, and those organizational relationships needed to recognize that complexity to boost productivity. He developed **Maslow's hierarchy of needs**, a theory of psychological health predicated on fulfilling innate human needs in priority, culminating in self-actualization. At the top of the list is the need for respect, and lower-level needs (e.g., survival or safety) must be satisfied before higher-level needs can be met, resulting in increased stages of work engagement. Behavioral scientists' innovation was that no two people are alike, so management must tailor motivational approaches to everyone's needs. Managers should realize that the order of the hierarchy differs significantly based on nationality values.

Douglas M. McGregor (1906–1964, an American management professor at the MIT Sloan School of Management) has contributed to developing management and motivational **Theory X and Theory Y**, which take opposite views of people's commitment to work. McGregor proposed that managers' individual assumptions about human nature and behavior determined how individuals manage their employees. McGregor believed his idea would lead managers to investigate the two sets of beliefs, invent others, evaluate the assumptions underlying them, and develop managerial strategies that made sense in those tested views of reality. Theory X assumes people must be constantly coaxed, while Theory Y thinks people relish work and see it as an opportunity to develop their creative abilities.

Management science provides an objective basis for decision-making but does not consider people's importance and relationships based on assumptions. Management science starts with recruiting a mixed team of specialists from relevant disciplines to solve a problem and propose a solution. Computers are used to construct a statistical model of the company and simulate the impact of various management decisions to evaluate solutions to the problem and their potential impact on the corporation.[iii]

Notes

All dates, innovators' information, and events have been checked against information in the following sources: *Encyclopedia Britannica, Encyclopedia Americana, Collier's Encyclopedia, Compton's Encyclopedia, Investopedia, and Wikipedia.*

i A canard is an aeronautical arrangement with a small wing is placed in front of the main wing of a fixed-wing aircraft.

ii Quantum mechanics is the study of trivial things and explains the behavior of matter and its interactions with energy on the scale of atomic and subatomic particles. Classical physics explains matter and energy only on a scale familiar to human experience, including the behavior of astronomical bodies such as the Earth, Sun, and Moon.

iii http://polaris.umuc.edu/~tgrodsky/admn601/managethought.html (accessed September 17, 2021).

5 Shifting From Peace to the Impact of War

Pre-War Issues and Why WWII

On September 1, 1939, WWII began in Europe when Germany invaded Poland. Great Britain and France responded by declaring war on Germany on September 3. The conflict between the USSR and Germany started in June 1941, with Germany's invasion of the Soviet Union. The War in the Pacific began in late 1941, when Japan attacked the American naval base at Pearl Harbor and other American, Dutch, and British military installations throughout Asia. On June 6, 1944, the war ended in Europe with the Allied Forces landing on Normandy, opening a second front in Europe. The final German offensive to the West at Ardennes in 1944–1945 failed and was aborted. Simultaneously, the Russian Red Army advanced from the East, with the Soviets claiming all the territory along its path. The Allied Army converged on Berlin, and Hitler committed suicide on April 30, 1945, and the War in Europe ended on May 8, 1945. After that, the American military destroyed Japanese military bases throughout the Pacific and then bombed significant cities throughout Japan. The war ended in August 1945 after the USA dropped two atomic bombs on Hiroshima and Nagasaki.

WWII was caused by German aggression to a perceived lack of resistance in Europe, which allowed the Nazi Party in Germany to build its military strength to take on the Ally Alliance. Fundamentally, the war has its roots in the political philosophies of two men. Adolf Hitler believed the Arian race was superior to the rest of the world and the less well-known Sadao Araki, the premier right-wing theorist in Imperial Japan and a top general in Japan's Army.

The Great Depression in 1929–1931 and the yen's appreciation with the Gold Standard's return caused abrupt deflation and severe contraction in global economic activity and international trade. These events hit Japan particularly hard because Japan has few natural resources and had problems obtaining support. Natural resources around the Pacific were under the control of Western colonial powers. The Japanese were cut off from trade, exasperating Japan's economic struggle for recovery and causing considerable civil discontent.

Deep anger arose in Weimar Germany of retaliating after the Treaty of Versailles to punish Germany for causing WWI in 1918. The German takeover

DOI: 10.4324/9781003024675-6

promoted an aggressive foreign policy in violation of the Versailles Treaty of 1919 and Germany's success in forming an agreement with the Soviet Union in August 1939 to divide Eastern Europe. The Treaty focused on three issues: Germany's Rhineland demilitarization, the prohibition of reunification with Austria, and the loss of some German-speaking territories.

Fighting Wars Overseas

Many needs materialize when a country must fight and win a war on foreign soil. It took time to find out what those needs were for the USA. WWII was a significantly different fight than WWI. In WWI, the USA declared war on Germany on April 6, 1917, more than two years after the war's start. Following a slow start in mobilizing the economy and labor force, by spring 1918, the USA was poised to play a role in the conflict. A ceasefire and Armistice were announced on November 11, 1918. Before entering the war, the USA had remained neutral but was an essential supplier to the UK, France, and the other Allied powers. The USA made significant contributions in supplies, raw materials, and money, beginning in 1917. Under **General John Pershing**, Commander-in-Chief of the American Expeditionary Force (AEF), American soldiers arrived at 10,000 men a day on the Western Front in the summer of 1918. The USA mobilized over 4 million military personnel and suffered more than 110,000 deaths, including around 45,000 deaths due to the 1918 Spanish influenza outbreak. WWII was a significantly different fought war than the US brief experience in WWI. The war saw a dramatic expansion of the US government to harness the war effort and a significant increase in the Armed Forces' size.

Computer, a Major Advantage[1]

During WWII, the most disruptive innovation was the computer development in England by **Alan Turing (1912–1954, a British mathematician, computer scientist, logician, cryptanalyst, philosopher, and theoretical biologist).** The Allied forces knew the German military was using a so-called "Enigma" machine to encrypt its planned activities. If the code could be broken, this would significantly advantage the Allied Forces in winning the war and saving lives and property. Turing developed the **Turing Machine, the first computer**, and it was used to decode the German Enigma encrypted message system.

Before WWII, **Charles Babbage (1791–1871, a British mathematician, philosopher, inventor, and mechanical engineer)** launched the **digital programmable computer**. Babbage developed a mechanical automated computer called an Analytical Engine for calculating mathematical and astronomical tables since hand-calculated tables had errors. His idea was to use machinery to compute all tabular functions to avoid errors and be done more quickly. In 1822 he began with a "difference" engine to calculate the value of polynomial functions. His improved second design was constructed in 1989–1991 as a fully-fledged general-purpose computational machine with punched cards to control a mechanical calculator. Babbage's design was the same logical structure as electronic computers. **Ada Lovelace (1815–1852, Augusta Ada King, Countess of Lovelace was an English mathematician and writer)** was the first to recognize that the machine had applications beyond pure calculation. She published the **first algorithm** intended to be conducted by such a machine and is regarded as one of the **first computer programmers**.

The language used to conduct processor instructions originated in the 1600s in a binary numerical system developed by **Gottfried W. Leibniz (1646–1716, a German philosopher, mathematician, scientist, diplomat, and polymath).** He refined the binary number system, the foundation of all digital computers, including the **Von Neumann architecture**, the standard design paradigm, or "**computer architecture**," followed from the second half of the 20th century to the 21st century. In 1847 **George Boole (1815–1864, a self-taught British mathematician, philosopher, and logician)** worked in differential equations and algebraic logic and was best known as the author of *The Laws of Thought*, which contains **Boolean algebra**. This algebra is a logic system in mathematical equations that employs a **binary approach** in which the relationship between different mathematical quantities would be either true or false, 1 or 0. Boolean logic is credited with laying the foundations for the information age. In 1886, **Charles S. Pierce (1839–1914, an American philosopher, logician, mathematician, and scientist)** determined that **electrical switching circuits** could solve the equations.

In 1936, Alan Turing published a paper, "On Computational Numbers, with an Application to the *Entscheidungs* problem." This paper was a unified theory on what constitutes a general-purpose computer, then called a "Turing Machine" with a limitless memory, reads data, writes results, and stores a program of instructions. At about the same time, **Konrad Zuse's (1910–1995, a German civil engineer, pioneering computer scientist, inventor, and businessperson)** most outstanding achievement was the world's **first programmable computer, the Z3**, in 1941. Zuse worked independently and was not aware of the functional program-controlled Turing machine. Zuse has often been regarded as the inventor of the "modern computer." During the same period, **John V. Atanasoff (1903–1995, an American physicist)** invented the first **electronic digital computer** at Iowa State College.

In 1943, Britain's computing prototype *Colossus* was announced. The IBM-funded *Harvard Mark I* was activated in 1944. The first fully operational electronic digital general-purpose computer became functional at the University of Pennsylvania (the center for wartime computing) in 1946. The ENIAC and the EDVAC, BINAC, and UNIVAC I computers were designed by **John W. Mauchly (1907–1980, an American physicist),** who assumed responsibility for programming, coding, and applications, and **J. Presper Eckert (1919–1955, an American electrical engineer and computer pioneer)** who designed the computer's electronics. They also started the first computer company **Eckert–Mauchly Computer Corporation** and pioneered stored programs, subroutines, and programming languages. **Remington Rand** later purchased the company. **John von Neumann (1903–1957, a Hungarian-American mathematician, physicist, computer scientist, engineer, and polymath)** provided a feasible architecture for **stored-program computing**. Von Neumann was regarded as the foremost mathematician of his time and "the last representative of the great mathematicians" who integrated pure and applied sciences. The first computer to operate on a stored program using the von Neumann architecture was the *Manchester Mark I*. These machines were slow, ran on many bulky vacuum tubes occupying large rooms, and used enormous energy.

In 1947, **John Bardeen, Walter Brattain, and William Shockley** at Bell Telephone Laboratories developed an innovative technology called **point-contact transistors**. Transistors, which replaced vacuum tubes, amplify electrical current, can be used as switches, are small, more dependable, and use less power. Shockley eventually alienated Bardeen and Brattain and blocked the two from working on the junction transistor. Bardeen began pursuing a theory for superconductivity and left Bell Labs in 1951. Brattain refused to work with Shockley and was assigned to another group. In 1956 Shockley moved to California to start **Shockley Semiconductor Laboratory** and live closer to his ailing mother. The company, a division of **Beckman Instruments, Inc.**, was the first establishment working on **silicon semiconductor devices** in what came to be known as Silicon Valley. Shockley hired an electrical engineer **Robert N. Noyce (1927–1990, an American physicist).** Noyce co-founded **Fairchild Semiconductor** in 1957 and **Intel Corporation** in 1968. In late 1957, eight of Shockley's researchers, including Noyce, resigned after Shockley decided not to continue researching silicon-based semiconductors. They formed **Fairchild Semiconductor**, a Fairchild Camera and Instruments division, a loss that devastated Shockley Semiconductor. Noyce continued to explore integrating the transistor and other components into an integrated circuit. In 1958 **Jack Kilby (1923–2005, an American electrical engineer)** invented the first **hybrid integrated circuit** made of germanium while working at **Texas Instruments**. Kilby also was the co-inventor of the hand-held calculator and the thermal printer.

Meanwhile, Noyce independently invented a new type of integrated circuit, the **monolithic integrated circuit** made of silicon, and it was widely adopted. Noyce put all components on the chip and connected them with copper wires using the planar process. **Jean Hoerni (1924–1997, a Swiss-American engineer)** developed the **planar process** as an essential technology for reliably fabricating and manufacturing semiconductor devices, such as transistors and integrated circuits based on Mohamed Atalla's methods developed in 1957. Noyce and **Gordon Moore (1929–, an American businessperson engineer)** left Fairfield Semiconductor and founded **Intel** in 1968. Moore became chairperson of **Intel Corporation** and the author of **Moore's law**.[i] Noyce oversaw **Marcian "Ted" Hoff (1937–, an American electrical engineer)** credited with creating the first **microprocessor**. While working for Intel in 1969, Hoff developed the architecture with **Stanley Mazor (1941–, an American microelectronics engineer)** for the world's first microprocessor, the **Intel 4004**. It was a single-chip **Central Processing Unit (CPU)** 1/16-by-1/8-inch in size and could run the computer's programs, remember information, and manage data by itself. This **microprocessor** is one of the most important inventions and paved the way for the personal computer (PC) revolutions and made it cheaper and easier to produce computers.

Case Study #5.1 Significant Disruptive Inventors and Innovations – Computers: Hardware and Software[1–3]

Key Disruptive Inventors	**Robert Noyce (1927–1990, an American physicist and entrepreneur)** **Gordon E. Moore (1029–, an American chemical engineer, physicist, and businessperson)**
Location	**Both USA**
Disruptive Invention	In 1959 Noyce invented the monolithic integrated circuit chip (IC) made of silicon. Moore developed pioneering technical roles in integrated circuit processing, leadership in the development of MOS memory, the microprocessor computer, and the semiconductor industry.
Problem Resolved	Noyce Integrated Circuit mass production capability, reliability, and building-block approach to integrated circuit design have ensured the rapid adoption of standardized ICs in place of designs using discrete transistors. Moore's innovations in microelectronics – large-scale integrated memory and the microprocessor – have fueled the information revolution.
Solution Impact	The monolithic integrated chip is a set of electronic circuits on one small flat piece (or "chip") of semiconductor silicon. Large numbers of tiny MOSFETs (metal – oxide – semiconductor field-effect transistors) integrate into a small chip. This results in circuits that are orders of magnitude smaller, faster, and less expensive than those constructed of discrete electronic components. ICs are now used in all electronic equipment and have revolutionized the world of electronics.
Economic Impact	Rapid advances in the sophistication, speed, and power of the laptop computer made it priced for everyone. More sophisticated research and analysis can be done by everyone, saving time for everyone. Moore's Law stated that the number of components (transistors, resistors, diodes, capacitors) in a dense integrated circuit would double every two years.

Cultural Impact	The individual gains more control over their lives and performs at a higher level in school, work, and home life.
Inventors Education and Training	Noyce received a BA from Grinnell College and a Ph.D. in Physics from MIT in 1953 and took a job at Philco Corporation in Philadelphia and left in 1956 to join William Shockley at Shockley Semiconductor Lab. He co-founded with Gordon Moore the **Fairchild Semiconductor Corporation**. In 1968 Noyce and Moore left Fairfield and founded NM Electronics which later became **Intel**. At Intel Noyce treated employees as family and was active in research projects with employees. He shunned executive perks, promoted a relaxed working environment, and oversaw Ted Hoff's development of the microprocessor. A microprocessor is a computer processor where the data processing logic and control is included on a single integrated circuit, or a small number of integrated circuits. The microprocessor contains the arithmetic, logic, and control circuitry required to perform the functions of a computer's central processing unit. The integrated circuit is capable of interpreting and executing program instructions and performing arithmetic operations. Moore started at San Jose State University and after 2 years went to the University of California Berkely and received a BS in Chemistry in 1950. He then went to the California Institute of Technology where he minored in physics and received a PH.D. in Chemistry in 1954. Between 1953 to 1956 he did post-doctoral research at the Applied Physics Laboratory at Johns Hopkins University. Moore then joined Shockley at Shockley Semiconductor Laboratory. He left Shockley with the "traitorous eight" with Noyes and joined Fairchild Semiconductor as Director of Research. Then in July 1968 Noyce and Moore founded NM Electronics which became Intel Corporation. Moore was executive vice president of Intel until 1975 when he became President and in 1979 became Intel's Chairman and CEO. Together at Intel, Moore and Noyce created new technologies in computer memory, integrated circuits, and the microprocessor and its design. Moore's net worth in 2021 is estimated at $12.6 billion.
Innovation Environment	Dynamic environment with an increasing number of patents issued primarily related to technology in the services sector. Both men contributed to the advance of information technology which was supported by the advances in computer technology and microprocessors.

(*Continued*)

(Continued)

Financing	Both Noyes and Moore were well off financially from their compensation at Shockley Semiconductor. When they started Fairfield Semiconductor, with the support of Arthur Rock a major New York investor in Intel and Chairman of the Board, who convinced **Sherman Fairchild** to start Fairchild Semiconductor. Noyes and Moore were financed by Sherman Fairchild, an American businessperson and investor. Sherman's father was George Winthrop Fairchild, a six-term Republican US Representative from New York. Prior to joining congress, he was a businessperson and investor, best known as the chair from 1915 to 1924 of the Computing-Tabulating-Recording Company which later became IBM. When Sherman's father George died in 1924, Sherman inherited his father's multi-million dollar estate and his father's IBM stock, becoming IBM's largest individual stockholder. Sherman, an American businessperson, and investor, founded over 70 companies, including Fairchild Aviation Corporation, Fairchild Industries, and Fairchild Camera and Instrument. Fairchild made significant contributions to the aviation industry. His **Fairchild Camera & Instrument Corporation, Semiconductor Division** company played a defining role in the development of Silicon Valley. He held over 30 patents for products ranging from the silicon semiconductor to the 8-mm home sound motion-picture camera. Fairchild is also responsible for inventing the first synchronized camera shutter and flash as well as developing new technologies for aerial cameras that were later used on the Apollo Missions.
International Commerce	Intel is an American multinational corporation and technology company headquartered in Santa Clara, California. It is the world's largest semiconductor chip manufacturer by revenue and is the developer of the x86 series of microprocessors, the processors found in most personal computers (PCs). Intel supplies microprocessors for computer system manufacturers such as Acer, Lenovo, HP, and Dell. Intel also manufactures motherboard chipsets, network interface controllers and integrated circuits, flash memory, graphics chips, embedded processors, and other devices related to communications and computing. Intel products are sold globally, and Intel has acquired 34 domestic and international corporations. Intel currently has fab production sites or assembly test sites in China, Malaysia, Israel, Vietnam, Philippines, Costa Rica, and Ireland.
Major success factors	Strong educational backgrounds from excellent universities making them experts in their fields. Located in Silicon Valley a huge innovation center for technology with strong support industries. Connections to very wealthy investors to support their innovations.

In 1975 a new software company was started called **Microsoft** by **Bill Gates (1955–, an American software developer, investor, author, entrepreneur, and philanthropist)** and **Paul G. Allen (1953–2018, an American computer programmer, researcher, investor, business magnate, and philanthropist).** They raised funds by writing the **BASIC** programming language for **Micro Instrumentation and Telemetry Systems (MITS)**. Microsoft became independent from MITS in 1976. In 1980 Microsoft was approached by IBM for an operating system for their forthcoming PC. Microsoft proposed using **86-DOS** developed by **Seattle Computer Products (SCP)** and signed a deal with SCP as the exclusive licensing agent. Microsoft delivered it to IBM as **PC-DOS**. Overnight Microsoft became the leading software company globally and sold **MS-DOS** to all customers other than IBM. Microsoft and Gates sold their first retail version of **Microsoft Windows** in 1985 to offset **Apple's Macintosh**. In 1986 it launched a new operating system, **OS/2**, and in 1998 antitrust litigation began over Microsoft's business practices. The court ruled against Microsoft that it violated the Sherman Antitrust Act.

The year after Microsoft was started, **Steve Jobs (1955–2011, an American industrial designer, investor, media proprietor, and business magnate)** and **Stephen Wozniak (1950–, an American electronics engineer, computer programmer, technology entrepreneur, and philanthropist)** launched **Apple I**. As designed by Wozniak, it had a large memory, a less expensive microprocessor, and a monitor with a screen. In 1977, **Apple II** was released with a keyboard, a color screen, and data stored on external CDs. Programmers were encouraged to develop **applications (apps)** for it, and a spreadsheet program **VisiCalc** made the Apple II a helpful business tool. In 1984 the **Macintosh** computer was mass-produced with a mouse and Graphical User Interface (GUI). It introduced the **desktop publishing industry** with the Apple LaserWriter featuring **laser vector graphics**. New products were introduced beginning in 1997, including **iMac, iTunes, iTunes Store, Apple Store, iPod, iPhone, App Store**, and the **iPad**. In 2001 a new operating system was introduced based on NeXT's NeXTSTEP platform called **macOS**. A modern Unix-based foundation developed by **Mark L. Chambers (1968–, an American hardware technician and technology author)** was also introduced. **Unix** is the established, super-reliable OS that powers most high-performance servers that make up the Internet. Chambers specializes in Macintosh and PC hardware and operating system books under the *For Dummies* brand.

After the war, the computer was used for sophisticated mathematical and statistical calculations, describing these results in graphical figures and charts, and presenting the historical documents of what was done and its importance. As computer technology improved, the speed and complexity of its calculations continued to expand. Meanwhile, the computer's chip size became smaller, enabling it to be embedded in anything. The microprocessor chip's decision-making capability advances using algorithms and artificial intelligence-enabled the computer to learn how to create logical, calculated decisions with improved desired outcomes. Today everyone in the developed and many parts of the developing world relies on the computer for communication, writing, presentations, analysis, and sophisticated calculations.

Case Study #5.2 Significant Disruptive Inventors and Innovations – Computers: Hardware and Software[1–3]

Key Disruptive Inventors	**Bill Gates (1955–, an American software developer, investor, author, entrepreneur, and philanthropist) and Paul G. Allen (1953–2018, an American computer programmer, researcher, investor, business magnate, and philanthropist)** **Steve Jobs (1955–2011, an American industrial designer, investor, and media proprietor, and business magnate) and Stephen Wozniak (1950–, an American electronics engineer, computer programmer, technology entrepreneur, and philanthropist)**
Location	**USA**
Disruptive Invention	They developed smaller and more powerful computer operating systems, attractive computer laptop designs, and ease of use that were less expensive per unit of computing power and storage.
Problem Resolved	Data access, analysis, communication, presentations, and apps to satisfy needs became readily available in one machine.
Solution Impact	New industries and jobs increased labor productivity, and applications expanded continuously with the development and expanded use of the computer.
Economic Impact	Everyone has a computer to improve their quality of life in many ways.
Cultural Impact	Computers and smartphones have become communication, research, analysis, and presentation facilitators.
Inventors Education & Training	Gates's father was a lawyer, and his mother was on the Board of First Interstate Bank, wrote the first program in high school, enrolled in Harvard but left after two years, and started his own company with his parent's support. Allen was a childhood friend of Gates, and both attended Lakeside High School. Allen attained a perfect SAT score of 1600 and went to Washington State University. After two years, he dropped out of college to work as a programmer for Honeywell in Boston near Harvard University, where Gates was enrolled. After that, Gates and Allen started Microsoft. Jobs went to Reed College but dropped out to travel to India and study Zen Buddhism. Wozniak's father was an engineer for Lockheed. Wozniak went to the University

	of Colorado Boulder but was expelled and built his first computer at the University of California, Berkeley. Then he dropped out of school to join Jobs at Hewlett-Packard. In spare time made and sold "blue boxes" for free long-distance calls and launched Apple in 1976.
Innovation Environment	The innovation environment was excellent, with a hot topic for new tech companies and computer technology.
Financing	Gates worked at odd jobs in high school programming to make money, and with four computer friends started Lakeside Programmers Club finding bugs in Computer Center Corporation software. Gates and Allen made traffic counters and designed an algorithm to solve an unsolved problem. Gates joined Allen at Honeywell in 1975. When MITS Altair 8800 computer was launched, they started their own software company Microsoft by selling the BASIC programing language to MITS. Gates's mother introduced Microsoft to IBM's CEO, who needed operating system software for their new personal computer. Gates and Allen dealt with Seattle Computer Products to modify their operating system for Microsoft for $50,000, which they sold to IBM as PC-DOS. They changed PC-DOS to MS-DOS, and with their deal with IBM, they overnight became a major software company. Allen and Gates worked together on writing and configuring the software they developed.
	Jobs' father was Syrian and went to the University of Wisconsin for a Ph.D., and Jobs' adopted father was a Coast Guard mechanic and agreed to pay for his college education. Jobs was fascinated with electronics and befriended engineers, at Homestead High, which had strong ties to Silicon Valley. Jobs met Bill Fernandez and Steve Wozniak. Wozniak built the blue box for free long-distance phone calls, which Jobs sold, showing him that they could beat large companies. Jobs dropped out of school and got a job at Atari as a technician and used his income to go to India for seven months and returned to his Atari job earning $4,650 and paid $350 to Woznick to complete the project. In March 1976, Wozniak completed Apple I, and Apple Computer Company was launched from Job's home. Jobs sold his Volkswagen van to buy a circuit board, Wozniak sold his HP scientific calculator, and 200 Apple I computers were produced. Jobs looked for investors while Wozniak worked on Apple II. Jobs was able to raise about $100,000, and in April 1977, Apple II was released.

(*Continued*)

(Continued)

International Commerce	Microsoft software was the computer industry standard for the operating system for IBM computers used by most major companies worldwide, and Microsoft Windows was launched in 1985. In 1986 they released a new operating system, OS/2, followed by Windows 95. Internationally, Microsoft operates research and development centers in China and India; data centers in Ireland, Singapore, and the Netherlands; and operations and facilities in Ireland and the UK. The company also has offices in India, China, Canada, Australia, Germany, Japan, and the UK. Apple conducts its operations on all continents and has offices, design studios, manufacturing centers, development centers, sales, and marketing offices in the USA, UK, France, Brazil, India, China, Singapore, Australia, Germany, and Sweden.
Major Success Factors	Gates and Allen's friends at the Lakeside Programmers Club were later hired and brought to Microsoft. Gates had strategic industry foresight and ambition, and Allen had exceptional programming, production, and design skills. Jobs had creativity, design, and marketing skills, and Wozniak had excellent computer development, technology design, and programming skills. Each of the four was entrepreneurial in their specializations with complementary dispositions as team members.

Computers, Algorithms, Artificial Intelligence

Mariam-Webster defines a computer as a programmable electronic device that stores, retrieves, and processes data. It processes data according to instructions, and a digital computer stores data in discrete units and performs arithmetical and logical operations at extremely high speed. In computer science, the mathematics of an algorithm is used as a finite sequence of defined instructions to solve problems. It was derived in the 9th century from the mathematician **Muhammad ibn Musa *al-Khwarizmi***, whose Latin name was *Algoritmi*. Algorithms consist of rules that define a sequence of operations, of which all have an end. They were used to solve the decision problem posed by *Entscheidungsproblem* and used as decision trees in computer programing and programming robots.

The birth of artificial intelligence was first explored by Alan Turing's seminal work, "Computing Machinery and Intelligence," published in 1950. **John McCarthy** offers the following definition in this 2004 paper: "It is the science and engineering of making intelligent machines, brilliant computer programs. It is related to the similar task of using computers to understand human intelligence, but AI does not have to confine itself to biologically observable methods." Algorithms have become essential to the way computers logically process data and the programming of robots' functioning. The difference between algorithms and AI is that an algorithm is a set of instructions executed when encountering a trigger. In comparison, AI is a broader group of algorithms that can modify and create new algorithms responding to learned inputs from constantly receiving data. AI can adapt, change, and grow in response to new data and mutate to improve its performance for set goals.

John McCarthy (1927–2011, an American computer scientist and cognitive scientist) was one of the founders of **Artificial Intelligence (AI)**. He developed the **Lisp programming language** family and significantly influenced the design of ALGOL. McCarthy received his advanced education from Princeton University and the California Institute of Technology and spent most of his career at Stanford University. His focus was on mathematical logic for artificial intelligence, and he launched AI as a field of study. In 1959 his paper on "Programs with Common Sense," he used mathematical reasoning to formalize artificial intelligence. McCarthy invented **Lisp** in the late 1950s based on lambda calculus,[ii] and it became the language of choice for AI applications in the 1960s. During the 1980s and 1990s, a significant effort was made to unify new Lisp dialects (mostly successors to Maclisp such as ZetaLisp and New Implementation of Lisp) into a single language **Common Lisp** compatible with the dialects it replaced. In 1994, ANSI published the Common Lisp standard, "ANSI X3.226–1994 Information Technology Programming Language Common Lisp." Today, McCarthy reports the best-known general-purpose Lisp dialects are **Racket, Common Lisp, Scheme**, and **Clojure**.

Will robots displace human workers? Simple robots or machines can function using an algorithm, but as they perform more complex activities, including internal decision-making programs, they rely on AI software. AI software is written in various dialects, like Common Lisp, which is self-determining based on new data resulting in automatic internal re-programming to perform a specific task more efficiently. In *World Development Report 2019*, the World Bank provides historical data that indicates that while robotics replaces workers, technological innovation creates more new industries and jobs typically requiring some retraining of displaced workers.

Atomic Bomb and Nuclear Power

The US atomic bomb and nuclear power development in the Manhattan Project at Los Alamos, New Mexico, was a significant disruptive innovation. A discovery by nuclear physicists in Berlin, Germany, in 1938 made the first atomic bomb possible. Nuclear fission was discovered by **Otto Hahn (1872–1946, a German chemist and pioneer in the fields of radioactivity and radiochemistry), Lise Meitner (1878–1968, an Austrian-Swedish physicist working on radiation and nuclear physics),** and **Fritz Strassman (1902–1980, a German chemist).** When an atom of radioactive material splits into lighter atoms, a sudden, forceful release of energy occurs. The discovery of nuclear fission opened the possibility of nuclear technologies, including weapons. Much of the Manhattan Project work was performed under theoretical physicist **J. Robert Oppenheimer (1904–1967, an American theoretical physicist and physics professor)** and inventor of the atomic bomb. In July 1945, the first nuclear bomb was successfully detonated in a remote desert near Alamogordo, New Mexico. It created an enormous mushroom cloud some 40,000 feet high. To end the war with Japan, one atom bomb and one plutonium bomb were used on August 6 and August 9, 1945.

After the war, nuclear technology developed and harnessed atomic power as a safe and clean way to produce electricity. A nuclear power plant is a thermal power station in which the heat source is a nuclear reactor. In thermal power stations, heat generates steam that drives a turbine connected to a generator that produces electricity. As of 2018, the International Atomic Energy Agency reported 456 nuclear power reactors in operation and 54 additional units under construction in 31 countries. The USA currently has 99 in operation and two other units under construction, France has 58, and China has 46, with 11 more being built.

Nuclear plants are usually considered "baseload" stations since fuel is a small part of the production cost and cannot be easily or quickly activated or deactivated. Their operations, maintenance, and fuel costs are low along with hydropower stations, making them suitable as baseload power suppliers. However, the cost of spent fuel management is high because it remains radioactive material for many years.

Japan has 42 nuclear reactors, but many reactors were stopped after the Fukushima Daiichi nuclear disaster triggered by an earthquake and tsunami on Friday, March 11, 2011, which caused three reactors to meltdown. The Chernobyl disaster was a nuclear accident on Saturday, April 26, 1986, at the No. 4 reactor in the Chernobyl Nuclear Power Plant, near the city of Pripyat in northern Ukrainian. It is considered the worst nuclear disaster in both cost and casualties. It is one of only two nuclear energy accidents rated a seven maximum severity on the International Nuclear Event Scale, the other being the 2011 Fukushima Daiichi nuclear disaster in Japan.

The USA is the largest nuclear power producer, while France has the largest electricity share generated by atomic power. Before the Fukushima Daiichi nuclear disaster, ten nuclear reactors became operational per year but slowed considerably. China has the fastest-growing nuclear power program, with 11 added to the 46 operating. While new reactors are also being built in India, Russia, and South Korea, 100 older, smaller reactors will be closed over 10–15 years. Belgium, Germany, Spain, and Switzerland plan a nuclear power phase-out of operating nuclear power plants.

Jet Aircraft Engines

Jet engine planes were another significant disruptive innovation from WWII. In WWI, aircraft technology had limited use, but it continued to advance and was present in all WWII battles. Propeller-driven aircraft had to fly low and slow when aerial bombing and were easy ground anti-aircraft targets. Jet aircraft's solution was to fly higher and faster. The first jet aircraft was the

German Heinkel He 178 in 1939, followed in 1943 by the **Messerschmitt Me 262**, the first jet fighter aircraft to fly on turbojet power. The Me 262 entered service in 1944 as the fastest conventional aircraft. The turbojet was invented in 1939, independently by **Air Commodore Sir Frank Whittle (1907–1996, a British Royal Air Force air officer, accomplished pilot, and aeronautical engineer)** and later **Hans von Ohain (1911–1998, a German-American physicist and designer of the first operational jet engine)**. The British experimental **Gloster Meteor E.28/39** first flew in 1941, powered by Frank Whittle's turbojet. The Meteor was the first jet as it entered production a few months before the Me 262, which had been in development since WWII. The USA produced the Bell XP-59A using two Whittle engines that General Electric launched in 1942.

Case Study #5.3 Significant Disruptive Inventors and Innovations – Transportation: Jet Engines

Key Disruptive Inventors	**Hans von Ohain (1911–1998, a German-American physicist and designer of the first operational jet engine)** **Frank Whittle (1907–1996, a British Royal Air Force air officer, accomplished pilot, and aeronautical engineer)**
Location	**Germany & British/USA**
Disruptive Invention	In 1937 Ohain and Whittle concurrently developed jet engines for military and commercial aircraft replacing much slower and less stable flights on propeller-driven airplanes. This development launched the rapid growth in commercial jet engine air transport for passengers and freight and accelerated investment and export sales. Jet engines power aircraft by intaking air into a compressor raising the air pressure. A combustion converts ignited air and fuel into a hot gas which emits a powerful jet stream from the engine pushing the airplane forward at high speeds. An afterburner placed before the engine's rear exhaust chamber in which added fuel is burned increases the plane's thrust and speed. It provides a more stable flight for longer distances.
Problem Resolved	Slow and rough travel by propeller planes were easy wartime targets. They were replaced by faster and higher-flying jet planes. Jet passenger planes were faster, smoother, and more comfortable for long-distance flying, reducing distant cities' and countries' costs and time.

(*Continued*)

(Continued)

Solution Impact	Domestic and international travel by airplanes powered by jet engines dominates commercial and military transportation, replacing travel with slower railroad trains, ships, and cars. Jet-powered planes have fewer moving parts than propeller-driven airplanes, can fly at higher altitudes and faster speeds, have increased operation efficiency per weight of the engine, less frequent maintenance, and less expensive fuel costs relative to propeller planes.
Economic Impact	The cost of time became a much more significant factor in people's lives and companies' business operations. International markets became more accessible and serviceable for businesses. The US air force became a dominating global power for securing peace and countering nations threatening democracy in other countries, as occurred in WWII. A 15-hour transatlantic commercial flight between the US and Europe was reduced to about 6 hours on a Boeing 747 with more than 500 passengers and crew in 1969. By 2007 the European Airbus wide-body, double-decker A380–800 could carry more than 850 passengers and crew about 9,756 miles distance at speeds of 560 miles per hour with its four jet turbofan engines. Depending on their configuration, both planes were priced at around \$450 million in 2019. The A380 has flown over 500,000 miles carrying over 190 million passengers. From a US military defense and security perspective, the Lockheed Martin F-22 Raptor is a fifth-generation, single-seat, twin-engine, all-weather stealth tactical fighter aircraft developed for the US Air Force (USAF). As a result of the USAF's Advanced Tactical Fighter (ATF) program, the aircraft was designed primarily as an air superiority fighter and has ground attack, electronic warfare, and signal intelligence capabilities with a cost per plane of \$150+ million. It is planned to be replaced by the superior Lockheed F-35 Joint Strike Fighter (JSF) Lightning II, now in production.
Cultural Impact	Public thought of travel by jet airplane became recognized and considered the norm.
Inventors Education & Training	Ohain earned a Ph.D. in Physics and Aerodynamics at the University of Göttingen, then one of the major centers for aeronautical research. Whittle developed practical engineering skills while helping in his father's workshop. Much of his spare time was spent in the Leamington reference library, reading astronomy, engineering, turbines, and flight theory.
Innovation Environment	Many competing inventions during this period resulted in various patent lawsuits, which adversely impacted the innovation environment.

Financing	Government financing was a primary source of funding entering, throughout and after the war years in Germany, Britain, France, and the US. After the war, private airplane companies established R&D centers to pursue new inventions funded by transportation revenues from passengers, freight shipments, or government military spending.
International Commerce	Commercial and military jet exports became a significant export market beginning in WWII and expanded further after the war.
Major Success Factors	Ohain had a solid educational background in physics and aerodynamics at the University of Göttingen, and his experience was at one of the major centers for aeronautical research. Whittle graduated in 1928 from the Royal Air Force College at 21 and was commissioned as a Pilot Officer. He ranked second in his class in academics, won the Andy Fellowes Memorial Prize for Aeronautical Sciences for his thesis, and was described as an "exceptional to above average" pilot.

Although GE did not invent the mechanical turbosupercharger device, GE engineer **Sanford Moss (1872–1946, an American aviation engineer)** perfected it and made it safe and practical, boosting piston power aircraft. Moss used his patented design to fill the cylinders of an aircraft piston engine with extra air allowing planes to retain their power at high altitudes. Moss designed his turbosupercharger to divert cooling air to the turbine wheel, which helped cool it. The first operational turbojet aircraft, the Me 262, launched in 1944, but mass production did not start until early 1944, too late to impact the war's outcome.

The **Gloster Meteor F.3s.** was the first British jet fighter and the Allies' only jet aircraft to achieve combat operations during WWII. In mid-1944, Britain's Gloster Meteor was used for defense against the V-1 flying bomb and supported ground-attack operations over Europe in the last months of the war. In 1944 Germany introduced the **Arado Ar 234** jet reconnaissance and bomber aircraft, used primarily for surveillance. The **Heinkel He 162 Spatz** single-jet light fighter appeared as 1944 ended. The USSR evaluated its **Bereznyak-Isayev BI-1** in 1942, but Stalin scrapped the project in 1945. The Japanese Navy also developed jet aircraft in 1945, including the **Nakajima J9Y Kikka**, a modified and slightly smaller version of the Me 262 with folding wings. By 1945, the USA had introduced its first jet fighter, the **Lockheed P-80 Shooting Star**, into service, and the UK its second fighter, the **de Havilland Vampire**. The USA entered the **North American B-45 Tornado**, its first jet bomber, into service in 1948. Although capable of carrying nuclear weapons, it was used for reconnaissance over Korea. Britain's **Electric**

Canberra came into service in 1951 as a light bomber designed to fly higher and faster than any interceptor.

The **British Overseas Airways Corporation** (BOAC) operated the first commercial jet service, from London to Johannesburg, in 1952 with the **de Havilland Comet** jetliner. This innovative aircraft traveled faster and higher than the propeller aircraft and was quieter, smoother, and had wings containing hidden jet engines. **William E. Boeing (1881–1956, an American entrepreneur who started Boeing in Seattle)** began buying timberland around Grays Harbor for lumber milling. He built a thriving business shipping lumber to the East Coast via the Panama Canal. In 1916, Boeing went into business with **George C. Westervelt (1879–1956, an American Navy engineer)** and founded Pacific Aero Products Co. The company's first plane was the **Boeing Model 1**, a seaplane. When America entered WWI in 1917, Boeing changed its name to **Boeing Airplane Company** and received orders from the US Navy for 50 planes. In 1934, the US government accused William Boeing of monopolistic practices, and the Air Mail Act forced airplane companies to separate flight operations from development and manufacturing. William Boeing's holding company split into three separate entities, with Boeing focusing on aircraft production. In 1958 the **Boeing 707** began commercial passenger service and dominated civilian airliners. The underslung engines are still evident today in the **Boeing 737** and the **European Airbus A340**. Turbofan jet engine aircraft providing service in the 1950s and 1960s brought greater fuel efficiency and widespread commercial use.

Since WWII, turbofan jet-propelled aircraft travel in the USA and worldwide has expanded dramatically. The commercial jet aircraft transportation industry has become increasingly convenient and dependable and has grown significantly worldwide. The US Department of Transportation reported that in FY2019, the number of annual passengers on all US scheduled airline flights (domestic & international) to and from the USA exceeded 1.1 billion passengers. This expansion reflects the rising load factors and larger aircraft sizes. Nearly 80% of this traffic represented domestic US passenger traffic of 2.8 million average passengers per day for a load factor of 82.7% of available seats. It also reported that the industry creates over 10 million US jobs, generating earnings exceeding $450 billion a year, representing about 5% of GDP.

Pressurized Aircraft Cabins

The rapid expansion of commercial passenger air traffic happened because of the innovation during WWII of pressurized air cabins. To operate at higher altitudes at faster speeds required oxygen and pressurized cabins for fliers to avoid hypoxia, altitude sickness, decompression sickness, and barotrauma. **Charles W. Morris (1907–1994, a US aerospace and automotive engineer)** invented the pressurized airplane cabin. Morris designed the cabin and developed the turbocharged engine for the **B-17** aircraft as an engineer for Boeing Aircraft in Seattle. In 1944, the US military introduced the **B-29**

Superfortress with the cabin's first pressure control system. Pressurization becomes increasingly necessary at altitudes above 10,000 feet above sea level to protect crew and passengers from the risk of several physiological problems caused by the low outside air pressure above that altitude. For private aircraft operating in the USA, crew members must use oxygen masks if the cabin altitude based on air pressure stays above 12,500 ft. for more than 30 minutes or if the cabin altitude reaches 14,000 ft. At altitudes above 15,000 ft., passengers must be provided oxygen masks. The cabin altitude must be regulated and maintained at 8,000 feet or less on commercial aircraft. Pressurization of the cargo hold is also required to prevent damage to pressure-sensitive goods that might leak, expand, burst, or be crushed on re-pressurization during the plane's takeoff and landing.

Space Travel Rockets

The development of rockets for space flight also resulted from WWII with the German invention of the **V2 rocket** used to bomb cities in Britain and Belgium. The V2 rocket was the world's first long-range guided ballistic missile to travel into space. Powered by a liquid-propellant rocket engine, it had a range of about 200 miles and reached an altitude of 65 miles. The German V2 rocket was developed by **Werner von Braun (1912–1977, a German – American aerospace engineer and space architect).** Braun worked as a graduate student at the Technical University of Berlin, assisting Hermann Oberth with liquid-fuel rocket motor tests. **Hermann J. Oberth (1834–1989, an Austro-Hungarian-born German physicist and engineer)** is considered one of the founders of rocketry and astronautics. Similarly significant are **Robert Esnault-Pelterie (1881–1957, a French aircraft designer and spaceflight theorist)**, **Konstantin Tsiolkovsky (1857–1935, a Russian rocket scientist and pioneer of the astronautic theory)**, and **Robert Goddard (1882–1945, an American engineer, physicist, professor, and inventor)**.

Four technologies essential for the success of the **A4** (the precursor of the V2) rocket were: large liquid rocket fuel engines, supersonic aerodynamics, gyroscopic guidance, and rudders for jet control. The Germans never entirely resolved the problem of rocket control for the effective destruction of a specific target, even when using mobile launching trucks. Germany spent $40 billion (2015 dollars) for the V1 and V2 rocket development, and 6,048 were built with 3,225 launched. The V2 also consumed about a third of Germany's fuel alcohol production. The USA and Russia secured the remaining rockets and technology after WWII. The USA shipped three hundred rail-car loads of V2s and parts to the USA and 126 principal designers and scientists, including Werner von Braun and **Walther Dornberger (1895–1980, a German Army artillery officer and mechanical engineer)**. Mathematical equations and design documents, and other German scientific material related to German rocket research were later used by the USA to accelerate its rocket research and success. The Soviets captured enough rocket knowledge and German V2 scientists to launch the **Sputnik satellite** in 1957.

Radio Navigation Systems

During WWII, the airplane was new, its navigation system was not yet developed, and bomber crews were inaccurate. An early navigation system designed by **Robert Dippy (1872–1952, a British radio navigational systems expert)** was the **Gee radio navigation system**. Dippy began work on radar development in mid-1936, but his radio navigational system proposals were not immediately used until 1942 to improve British bombing accuracy. It was successful as a navigation system that brought returning bombers to their home bases, saving many aircraft and crews' lives. Dippy devised Gee as a short-range blind landing system to improve safety during night operations. The range was far better than expected, developing into a long-range, general navigation system. For large, fixed targets like cities attacked at night, Gee offered enough accuracy to be used as an aiming reference without using a bombsight. Although jamming reduced its usefulness as a bombing aid, it remained a navigational aid in Britain throughout and after the war.

Navigation concepts were advanced as **GEE-H,** and in the USA, Dippy assisted in developing **LORAN-A**. LORAN is short for long-range navigation and was a hyperbolic radio navigation system initiated in the USA during WWII. Like the UK's Gee system, it operated at lower frequencies to improve range to 1,500 miles with an accuracy of tens of miles. Its primary use was on ships and aircraft operating in the Pacific during WWII. These systems were used on D-Day to help navigate the massive invasion fleets and airborne forces. In the postwar era, Gee remained a vital part of the British RAF's suite of navigation systems. Several new Gee chains were set up to support military and civil aviation across Europe. The GEE system was replaced in 1970 with the **Global Positioning System (GPS)**, a satellite-based tracking technology used for navigation by road, sea, and air.

GPS was invented by the **US Department of Defense (DOD)** and **Ivan A. Getting (1912–2003, an American physicist and electrical engineer**). Although its application range includes aviation and crime prevention, the technology is associated with highway and address navigation. GPS satellites feature atomic clocks that continuously transmit live time and positional data to GPS receivers on the ground. Of the 24 GPS satellites in orbit, a satellite navigation device must have at least four GPS satellites in unobstructed sight to receive accurate signals.

The history of satellite technology is linked to the military relationship between Russia and the USA. While American engineers were still working on their **Vanguard** project in the mid-1950s, they were surprised by the Soviets successfully launching **Sputnik 1** in 1957, followed quickly by **Sputnik 2**. Both were more advanced and capable than the unfinished American project. **Explorer 1** was the USA's belated but successful satellite launch, followed by

The National Aeronautics and Space Administration's **(NASA)** creation in 1958. Over the next four decades, satellite technology's progress led to GPS's availability for non-military purposes, paving the way for satellite navigation proliferation. GPS is used to track and control crewless aerial vehicles or drones. The first portable navigational device was launched in 2004 by the Netherlands-based TomTom. Today's smartphones have GPS capability built-in, and this technology is now supplemented by GLONASS. Globalnaya Navigazionnaya Sputnikovaya, or Global Navigational Satellite System (GNSS) the Russians' latest contribution. The innovation effectively increases the number of satellites connected to a navigational device, thus improving positional accuracy.

Radar Systems

Heinrich Hertz (1857–1894, a German physicist) first conclusively proved electromagnetic waves in 1886. Hertz demonstrated how solid objects could reflect radio waves, which was the precursor for technological advancements in radar. During the war, the Allies developed the **cavity magnetron**,[iii] allowing more accurate radar systems to be created to detect smaller objects. The cavity magnetron was invented by **John Randal (1905–1984, a British physicist and biophysicist)** and **Harry Boot (1917–1983, a British physicist)** in 1940. A working model was sent to the USA, where Bell Telephone Laboratories created a version that could be mass-produced. The invention of **Radar** (**RA**dio **D**etection **A**nd **R**anging) started with experiments by Heinrich Hertz in the late 19th century that showed that metallic objects reflected radio waves. This possibility was suggested in **James Clerk Maxwell's (1831–1879, a Scottish scientist in mathematical physics)** work on electromagnetism. His most notable achievement was to formulate the classical theory of electromagnetic radiation, bringing together for the first time electricity, magnetism, and light as manifestations of the same phenomenon. Maxwell's equations for electromagnetism have been called the "second great unification in physics" after the first one started by **Isaac Newton**. Not until the early 20th century were systems able to use these principles. **Christian Hülsmeyer (1881–1957, a German inventor, physicist, and entrepreneur)** first used them to build a simple ship detection device to help avoid collisions in fog. Numerous similar systems, which provided directional information to objects over short ranges, have been developed.

The discovery of systems that produced short pulses of radio energy was the key advance that allowed modern radar systems to exist. Timing the pulses on an oscilloscope would determine the range, and the direction of the antenna revealed the targets' angular location. Together the two produced a "fix," locating the destination relative to the antenna. Between 1934–1939, eight nations independently developed systems, including the UK, Germany, the USA, the USSR, Japan, the Netherlands, France, and Italy. All had various land- and sea-based radar and small airborne systems. Radar use widened to include civil aviation, marine navigation, radar guns for police, meteorology, and even medicine. Significant post-war advances are the traveling wave tube to produce enormous quantities of coherent microwaves, signal delay systems that led to phased array radars, and ever-increasing frequencies that allow higher resolutions. Increasing signal processing capability by computers has significantly impacted contemporary commercial radar use.

Microwave Oven

Microwave ovens are a byproduct of WWII radar research and the invention of cavity magnetron. **Percy Spencer (1894–1970, an American physicist and inventor)** invented the microwave oven when he discovered that microwaves from the magnetron stimulate particles that can cook food. Spencer became one of the world's leading experts in radar tube design in 1939. He worked for **Raytheon** and helped guide them to develop and produce combat radar equipment for **MIT's Radiation Laboratory**. Effective radar was the military's second-highest priority project during WWII behind the Manhattan Project. He could cook food by attaching a high-density electromagnetic field generator to an enclosed metal box. Thus, the microwave oven was created, and Raytheon filed a patent in 1945. There were 13.5 million microwave ovens shipped in the USA in 2019 at an average price of $400.

Penicillin Antibiotic

Penicillin was an important discovery in 1869 by **Ernest Duchesne (1874–1912, a French physician)**, who saw that individual molds kill bacteria. Thirty-two years later, **Sir Alexander Fleming (1881–1955, a Scottish bacteriologist, biologist, physician, microbiologist, and pharmacologist)** is best known for his penicillin discovery. His findings include the enzyme lysozyme in 1923 and the world's first applicable antibiotic substance, benzylpenicillin (**Penicillin G**), in 1928. Fleming saw many soldiers dying from sepsis caused by infected wounds during WWI. Antiseptics, used to treat infected wounds, often worsened the injuries as they worked well on the surface, but deep wounds tended to shelter anaerobic bacteria from the antiseptic agent. **Ernst Chain (1886–1979, a German-born British biochemist)** was a chemist and industrialist dealing in chemical products. In 1935, he joined Oxford University and partnered with **Howard Florey (1898–1968, an Australian pharmacologist and pathologist)** to investigate natural antibacterial agents produced by microorganisms. During WWII, research by Howard Florey proved in clinical trials in 1941 the Penicillin drug's effectiveness in curing wounds by stopping infections and allowing their wounds to heal more quickly. Antiseptics were found to remove beneficial agents produced by the human body to protect the patients but not the bacteria. Chain and Florey revisited Fleming's work and discovered penicillin's therapeutic action and chemical composition. They found how to isolate and concentrate the germ-killing agent in penicillin, for which Chain, Florey, and Fleming received the Nobel Prize in 1945.

Andrew J. Moyer (1899–1959, an American microbiologist) developed techniques for the mass production of penicillin, making it useful for people. Penicillin eliminated infection-causing bacteria and helped the wound heal quickly. It likely saved thousands of soldiers' lives by protecting them from infection from diseases and other injuries. The introduction of penicillin in the 1940s began the era of antibiotics and is recognized as one of the most significant advances in therapeutic medicine. A life-saving substance became a widely available medicine still relied on today to cure infections and is the basis for other antibiotics used today.

Synthetic Oil[4–7]

During the war, the Axis powers were in control of most of the world's natural rubber supply, so there was an urgent need for the Allied forces to develop and improve synthetic rubber production. While working for BF Goodrich, **Waldo L. Semon (1898–1999, an American chemist)** invented *Ameripol* (AMERican POLymer) in 1940, which was cheaper to produce and quickly met the Allied need for rubber. In the process, he made over 5000 other synthetic rubber compounds before developing *Ameripol.* Semon is best known for inventing vinyl, the world's second most used plastic. In 1935 he created *Koroseal*, a polymer[iv] made in any consistency. *Koroseal* offers a wide range of commercial wallcoverings and related products for hotels, apartment buildings, office buildings, restaurants, schools, hospitals, and other high-traffic applications. Semon held 116 patents and is known for inventing PVC, widely used in plumbing for transporting water and other fluids.

Germany had a shortage of oil during WWII and needed an alternative and developed a blend of adipic acid ester and polyethylene. The USA also developed a synthetic oil superior to natural oil because it had better start properties in winter and reduced soot deposits. Synthetic oil is a lubricant consisting of chemical compounds that are artificially made. Synthetic greases can be manufactured using chemically modified petroleum components rather than whole crude oil and are synthesized from other raw materials. The base material is still crude oil distilled and altered physically and chemically. The actual synthesis process and composition of additives will vary among producers. However, as soldiers discovered, conventional lubricants have inherent limitations. Distillation cannot remove all impurities detrimental to lubrication, such as waxes that solidify in the cold and prevent engines from starting, as happened to German equipment at the Battle of Stalingrad in the middle of a Russian Winter. Nor can it remove the lighter, unstable molecules that evaporate due to high heat. The extreme conditions of warfare exposed conventional oil limitations, and it quickly became apparent that there was a real need for a better type of lubricant.

Decades before the Battle of Stalingrad, scientists searched for an alternative to petroleum oil. **Charles Friedel (1832–1899, a French chemist)** and his American collaborator, **James M. Crafts (1839–1917, an American chemist)**, first produced synthetic hydrocarbon oils in 1877, marking the first notable step of artificial oil history. But his most important achievement was the discovery with Friedel of one of the most useful synthetic methods in organic chemistry, the Friedel–Crafts reaction. This procedure has brought hundreds of new carbon compounds into existence based on the catalytic action of chloride of aluminum.

In 1913, **Friedrich Bergius (1884–1949, a German, Polish, Argentine chemist)** developed a hydrogenation process for producing synthetic oil from coal dust. Twelve years later, his countrymen, **Franz Fisher (1877–1947, a German chemist)** and **Hans Tropsch (1889–1935, an Austria-Hungary chemist),** developed a process for converting a mixture of carbon monoxide and hydrogen into liquid hydrocarbons.

Meanwhile, in the USA, **Standard Oil Company of Indiana** tried to commercialize synthetic oil in 1929, but they could not generate a demand for the product. A Standard Oil researcher **F.W. Sullivan** published a paper in 1931 that disclosed a process for polymerizing olefins to form liquid products. However, **Lt. Col. Albert J. Amatuzio (1924–2017, an American military jet pilot)** learned that jet engines required synthetic lubricants rather than conventional petroleum-based oil because it is far less tolerant to higher temperatures. Understanding the benefits of synthetic oil in jet engines, he explored the possibility of developing and commercializing a synthetic lubricant for automotive use. If synthetics protected jet turbines so successfully, they would also benefit conventional internal combustion engines since synthetics are cleaner than petroleum-based oil. Amatuzio establishes the company **AMSOIL, Inc.** to become a leader and significant manufacturer of synthetic lubricants. Amatuzio introduced an API-approved fully synthetic motor oil and introduced virtually every successfully marketed synthetic lubricant. He created synthetic transmission fluids, motorcycle oils, gear oils, greases, diesel oils, hydraulic oils, fully synthetic marine oils, and other synthetic motor oil formulations throughout the mid-to-late 1960s. AMSOIL began commercially selling synthetic motor oil in 1968. In 1972, AMSOIL 10W-40 Synthetic Motor Oil became the world's first synthetic motor oil to meet American Petroleum Institute requirements, which prompted the company to adopt the "The First in Synthetics®" tagline. The company introduced several other synthetic lubricants that represented industry firsts throughout the 1970s and early 1980s. AMSOIL distributes products in North America via a network of independent dealers following a direct-marketing business model. Simultaneously, German chemist **Hermann Zorn (1896–1983, a German chemist)** independently discovered the same process. Their discoveries laid the groundwork for the eventual widespread use of synthetic oil. In 1947 Zorn joined a Swiss chemical company and, during his time at several chemical companies, he developed patents for "synthesizing lubricating oils" and contemporary techniques for producing artificial textiles.

Nylon Material and Ropes

The Nylon clothes we wear during freezing weather were also a WWII invention. **DuPont** introduced Nylon as an alternative to the expensive bourgeois silk undergarments. Nylon was more resistant to tearing and later used to make tents, ropes, and other necessary utilities. Nylon is a generic designation for a family of synthetic polymers based on aliphatic or semi-aromatic polyamides. Nylon is a thermoplastic silky material that can be melt-processed into fibers, films, or shapes. It is made of repeating units linked by amide links like the peptide bonds in proteins. Nylon polymers can be mixed with various additives to achieve different property variations. Nylon polymers have found significant commercial applications in fabric and fibers (apparel, flooring, and rubber reinforcement), in shapes (molded parts for cars, electrical equipment, etc.), and films (primarily for food packaging). Nylon was the first commercially successful synthetic thermoplastic polymer. DuPont began its research in 1927, and the first example of Nylon (nylon 6,6) was produced in early 1935 by **Wallace H. Carothers (1924–1937, an American chemist, inventor, and organic chemistry leader at DuPont)**. In response to Carothers' work, **Paul Schlack (1897–1987, a German chemist)** at **IG Farben** developed nylon 6, a different molecule based on caprolactam, in 1938.

Nylon was first used commercially in a nylon-bristled toothbrush in 1938, followed more famously in women's stockings or "nylons," which were shown at the 1939 New York World's Fair and first sold commercially in 1940. During WWII, all nylon production was diverted to the military for parachutes and parachute cord use. Wartime uses of Nylon, and other plastics significantly increased the market for these new materials.

Case Study #5.4 Significant Disruptive Inventors and Innovations – Textiles – Clothing: Nylon and Polyester

Key Disruptive Inventors	**Wallace H. Carothers (1896–1937, an American chemist, inventor, and the leader of organic chemistry at DuPont)**
Location	**USA**
Disruptive Invention	The invention of synthetic fibers such as Nylon and polyester clothing by Carothers was a versatile cloth that became available at a meager price compared with cotton and wool commercially produced by DuPont in 1939.
Problem Resolved	New styles in bright colors and patterns became available to people everywhere. It became the product of the young and constantly changing style and color-sensitive generations and was available at affordable clothing prices to everyone and was easily washable at home.

(*Continued*)

(Continued)

Solution Impact	DuPont began the sale of nylons stockings in 1939, and the socks were first offered in New York in mid-1940, with more than 780,000 being sold on the first day and 64 million in the first year throughout the US 1938 DuPont began to market nylon bristles in toothbrushes. In 1950 by crimping Nylon under heat, the material could become extendable and better fit any leg. In 1959 DuPont created a stretchable fiber called Spandex. The commercialization of polyester fabric began in 1951, Orlon was added by DuPont in the late 1940s, Acrylic fiber in 1941, and Dacron appeared in the 1950s. DuPont had become one of the major producers of synthetic products, plastics, and fibers. Innovation is characteristic of the plastics industry. However, synthetic fibers produced from petroleum such as polyester and Nylon pose a significant risk to the environment because they are non-biodegradable.
Economic Impact	Plastics have a long history during which the only plastics known were composed of natural polymers originally in natural organic fibers (silk, flax, wool, cotton). Synthetic fiber plastics such as Cellulose[2] developed by John W. Hyatt in 1869 in the USA was followed by Rayon's invention by Samuel Courtlands in 1910 in the USA. Subsequently, Leo Baekeland invented Bakelite, a commercially practical thermosetting plastic in the 1900s in the USA, after which Waldo Semon at BF. Goodrich developed synthetic rubber, in 1933 Ralph Wiley developed Saran Wrap, E.W. Fawcett and R.O. Gibson 1938 invented Teflon, and in 1927 Carothers joined DuPont and developed Nylon and polyester clothing.
Cultural Impact	Wool clothing was replaced by cotton, especially in high heat and humidity environments. When synthetic fabrics became available, their low price made them attractive on a vast scale and in every country. Also, because they were less expensive, it was easier to shorten their useful life span as fashions (styles and colors) changed every three years.
Inventors Education & Training	Carothers was born in Iowa, and his father was a vice president of a commercial college. Carothers attended Des Moines high school, became interested in chemistry, went to college at Tarkio College in Missouri, focused on science and chemistry, and received his BA in 1920. He then went to the University of Illinois, earning an MA and Ph.D. in 1924. He taught chemistry at the University of Illinois and Harvard University. Still, research became his main interest, and in 1928 he joined the DuPont Company to lead organic polymer research, but progress was slow.

Innovation Environment	In 1930 at DuPont, Carothers reviewed the chemistry of acetylene polymer and the research of Julius Nieuwland, Belgian American teaching at Notre Dame. Under Carothers's leadership, adding chlorine to the four- or six-stage acetylene polymerization would produce a solid rubber-like material. It was called neoprene, which became produced and commercialized by DuPont in 1931. Later in the 1930s, Carothers and his group discovered synthetic polyester fiber and later synthetic polyamide fiber, and after much experimentation, it became the first commercial nylon fiber polymer. Carothers and his team at DuPont created more than 50 patents between acetylene chemicals and polyamides (synthetic rubber and nylons). A vital change in innovation was a shift to corporate-sponsored research and development. At DuPont, innovation became a tightly managed scientific research-directed activity. Scientists were recruited to pursue activities that the company or its senior management determined to focus on the commercialization of the research results and its impact on its financial performance. This procedure may have partly resulted from the great depression when companies' sales and revenue were depressed because of limited consumer demand. Corporate scientists were told and managed to direct their efforts and focus on product research for market segments that had the greatest need and most significant potential return. This approach contrasted with earlier phases in the Industrial Revolution when more independent scientific research and technological advances were driven more by the impact on society from a particular industry or several industries.
Financing	Financing came from a company's funded innovations either out of their revenues or debt or obtaining competitive grants from government or organizations usually funded by wealthy individuals. The extent to which a corporate bond issuance bank financed the research and commercialization may have facilitated the bond's issuance and resale and managed its servicing. In the 1800s, some of the debt may have been funded by the bank and continued on its books. As financial markets developed and became increasingly regulated, banks or investment banks would participate in the debt to other investors in syndication or, more recently, a securitization. An investment bank might have been facilitated and placed into a mutual fund if innovation and commercialization were financed by issuing equity.

(*Continued*)

(Continued)

International Commerce	The global textile market was valued at $962 billion in 2019 and is estimated to grow 3–5% per year, reflecting the increased demand for apparel, especially in developing countries like China, India, Mexico, and Bangladesh. In US textile imports, cotton accounts for about 35% of the global textile market, while the synthetic textile market share of polyester and Nylon represents about 55% of the total.
Major Success Factors	Synthetic textiles flexibility, comfort, and lower price, whereas cotton retains wetness more readily.

Role of US Government in Financing Innovation

During and after WWII and the Vietnam war, Government funding of research and development was a significant source and sponsorship of important-significantly disruptive innovations. The private sector promoted many government-funded inventions and continued developing and played an essential role in advancing technology. During WWII, the **US Department of Defense (DOD)** funded research by **Fairchild Semiconductor** and **Texas Instruments** to create a device that would make missile targeting more accurate. Today, the resulting product known as **the microchip** is used in every computer, iPhone, and almost any electronic device. In the 1960s, the US DOD funded developing a more reliable communications system to enable time-sharing of computers called **Advanced Research Projects Agency Network (ARPANET)**, a precursor of the **Internet**. The **Internet** is the global system of interconnected private, public, academic, business, and government computer networks of local to global scope, linked by a broad array of electronic, wireless, and optical networking technologies. It uses the **Internet protocol suite (TCP/IP)** to communicate between networks and devices. Inventors **Vint Cerf (1943–, an American Internet pioneer)** and **Bob Kahn (1938–, an American electrical engineer)** played a crucial role in its development.

In the 1970s, The **US Department of Defense** developed the **Global Positioning System (GPS)** to follow the exact location of nuclear missiles and calculate their appropriate flight paths. The **National Science Foundation (NSF)** initiated the **Digital Library Initiative**, a project to index and sort through the growing number of websites. Two Stanford University graduate students, **Larry Page (1973–, an American computer scientist and Internet entrepreneur**) and **Sergey Brin (1973–, a Russian/American computer scientist and Internet entrepreneur),** received support from an NSF Fellowship and wrote the algorithm used to rank web pages by importance. In 1998, Page and Brin founded global search engine **Google Inc**.

Case Study #5.5 Significant Disruptive Inventors and Innovations – Communication and Information: Internet Searching – Google

Key Disruptive Inventors	**Larry Page (1973–, an American computer scientist and Internet entrepreneur)** **Sergey Brin (1973–, a Russian/American computer scientist and Internet entrepreneur)**
Location	**USA, Russian/USA**
Disruptive Invention	Internet information-searching, software prioritization, Page and Brin wrote the algorithm to rank web pages by importance. In 1998, Page and Brin founded the well-known and used global search engine Google Inc. Their idea focused on enhancing the ability to extract meaning from the mass of data accumulating on the Internet.
Problem Resolved	How to effectively prioritize the massive amounts of data continuously accumulates on the Internet regarding its importance or relevance.
Solution Impact	Easier access to knowledge and information about anything anywhere, but there is also a problem of misinformation.
Economic Impact	Reduction in travel reduces pollution, increases remote working, is easier to shop online and hold meetings online.
Cultural Impact	Change in need to meet in person or go to stores and libraries. People are better informed, and goods and services prices are more transparent and more competitive.
Inventors Education & Training	Page holds a Bachelor of Science in computer engineering from the University of Michigan, honors, and a Master of Science in computer science from Stanford University. Brin earned his bachelor's degree at the University of Maryland, College Park, following his father's and grandfather's footsteps by studying mathematics and computer science. After graduation, he enrolled at Stanford University to receive a Ph.D. in computer science.
Innovation Environment	Wartime environments and emergencies often create or highlight beneficial needs for society, such as the internet communication system.
Financing	The Brin family formally applied for their exit visa in September 1978, and both father and mother lost their jobs. For the next eight months, they earned only part-time income. In May 1979, they were granted their official exit visas and allowed to leave Russia. The family moved to Vienna and Paris before Mikhail Brin was hired for a teaching position at the University of Maryland with help from friends. During this time, the Brin family received assistance from the Hebrew Immigrant Aid Society. Larry and Serge met at Stanford. A National Science Foundation

(*Continued*)

(Continued)

	Graduate Fellowship supported Brin. Both worked together on the Stanford Digital Library Project to develop the enabling technologies for a single, integrated, and universal digital library. In 1998, Page and Brin founded the well-known and widely used global search engine **Google Inc.** In 2000, Google began selling advertisements associated with search keywords. The company launched Google News in 2002, Gmail in 2004, Google Maps in 2005, Google Chrome in 2008, and many other products. In 2015, Google became the principal subsidiary of the holding company Alphabet Inc. run by Page and Brin. Both Page and Brin are ranked among the top 20 wealthiest people globally and are actively involved in other technology startups with their estimated wealth above $70 billion each.
International Commerce	Google is becoming a global platform for information and goods and services shipped anywhere. The Internet is a global computer network providing various information and communication facilities, consisting of interconnected networks using standardized communication protocols. It is a worldwide shopping and information platform that supports international commerce.
Major Success Factors	Both men are well-educated, young entrepreneurs committed to effectively prioritizing and cross-referencing the massive amounts of data accumulating continuously on the Internet.

The bar code development used extensively to identify everything today was funded by the **US National Science Foundation (NSF)** for research that developed the **bar code scanners** to read bar codes in the 1970s. The US space agency **NASA** developed an **algae-based supplement** that contains the same nutrients as breast milk **to help recycle oxygen** in the air during space travel. The supplement is now found in all US-produced baby foods today. In the 1970s, **NASA** needed a reliable, **lightweight material for parachute suspension lines** to land objects on Mars. **Goodyear Tire Company** used this super-strong, lightweight material in its tires to make them last much longer than regular tires. In 1996, funding from the **National Science Foundation (NSF)** and the **Central Intelligence Agency (CIA)** for research at the **University of Delaware** developed a sophisticated **touch-screen-based finger tracking and gesture recognition system**. The university introduced the first **touch-screen tablet** in 2001 called the **iGesture Numpad**. In 2005, Apple purchased the technology and modified it to develop the **iPhone screen**.

Between 2006 and 2017, the **US National Institutes of Health (NIH)** invented several life-saving **vaccines for protection from hepatitis A and B, the flu, and the Human papillomavirus infection (HPV),** commonly called warts. All vaccines protect against at least HPV types 16 and 18, which cause the most significant risk of cervical cancer. The HPV vaccines prevent 70% of cervical cancer, 80% of anal cancer, 60% of vaginal cancer, 40% of vulvar cancer, and some mouth cancers.

In the 1980s, **US Defense Advanced Research Projects Agency (DARPA)** launched research projects to improve military **jets' speed and distance**. DARPA's work on **stealth technology** resulted in a prototype of the F-117A that flew successfully in 1977, marking the beginning of the stealth revolution, which has had enormous national security benefits. Today's wind farms use gas turbine engine technology initially developed by DARPA to produce over 8% of US electrical energy through wind power.

Note

All dates, innovator's information, and events have been checked against information in the following sources: *Encyclopedia Britannica, Encyclopedia Americana, Collier's Encyclopedia, Compton's Encyclopedia, Investopedia, and Wikipedia,*

i Moore's Law says that the number of transistors in a dense integrated circuit (IC) doubles about every two years.

ii Lambda calculus (also written as λ-calculus) is a formal system in mathematical logic for expressing computation based on function abstraction and application using variable binding and substitution It was introduced by the mathematician Alonzo Church in the 1930s.

iii The cavity magnetron is a high-power vacuum tube that generates microwaves using the Code Division Multiple Access (CDMA) is a generic term denoting a wireless interface based on code division multiple access technology.

iv A polymer is a chemical compound with molecules bonded together in long, repeating chains. Because of their structure, polymers have unique properties that can be tailored for different uses. Polymers are both man-made and naturally occurring. Rubber, for example, is a natural polymeric material that has been used for thousands of years. It has excellent elastic qualities, the result of a molecular polymer chain created by mother nature. Another natural polymer is shellac, a resin produced by the lac bug in India and Thailand, which is used as a paint primer, sealant, and varnish. The most common natural polymer on Earth is cellulose, an organic compound found in the cell walls of plants. It is used to produce paper products, textiles, and other materials such as cellophane. Man-made or synthetic polymers include materials such as polyethylene, the most common plastic in the world found in items ranging from shopping bags to storage containers, and polystyrene, the material used to make packing peanuts and disposable cups. Some synthetic polymers are pliable (thermoplastics), while others are permanently rigid (thermosets). Still others have rubber-like properties (elastomers) or resemble plant or animal fibers (synthetic fibers). These materials are found in all sorts of products, from swimsuits to cooking pans.

Part II

Global Commerce Following World War II – Globalization Capitalism

6 Importance of Global Commerce for Innovation

Developing global commerce and international trade in goods and services among countries and regions has been essential to human development and improving the quality of life. Both exports and imports are equally important and have significantly contributed to sharing economic growth in all countries over the centuries. International trade has replaced the absence or shortages of goods and services for developed and developing countries. For early immigrants to the Americas, imports of basic necessities were essential for survival. As the colonies crossed the survival threshold, they learned of their comparative advantages and began exporting to pay for imports. International trade has also helped curtail inflation and spread the knowledge of innovations to all countries. The primary method for exchanging goods and services was barter or swapping one suitable good or service for a different good or service. The driving force for that exchange was perceived value and based on what people wanted to keep or needed or sell for what they liked or to satisfy someone else who wanted it. The price or value of what people were exchanging was based on their time making the product (labor's work hours/days or productivity) and the opportunity cost of doing something else with their time and effort. The seller's offer price was compared with the buyer's evaluation of what they considered appropriate for how much effort, thought, and creativity spent producing the product. Also included was any cost incurred for supplies in making the product, marketing, and transporting it.

Historically, a World That Trade Created

International trade promotion has historically been used to support economic growth and supply raw material and agricultural products necessary to fuel that growth. Initially, governments established public companies (like multinational corporations owned by the state) to engage in international sales of home country goods and purchase raw materials or commodities needed for development. Over time, government control or ownership of merchant companies transitioned to private ownership. Public companies like the **British East India** Company transitioned to a public–private partnership type company expanding their international trade involvement. Eventually, sizeable privately-owned family merchant banking companies emerged in the industrial

DOI: 10.4324/9781003024675-8

revolution in Europe and engaged in international trade on behalf of their target market clients, both private and public.

Sea networks linked Asia in ancient times because overland routes were dangerous, challenging, and took many days. The Chinese, Muslims, and Hindus were early prominent trading people. They developed extensive and complex trading routes and built ships appropriate to transport commerce throughout Asia and the Middle East. State concessions and monopolies supported these early traders. The main ports were multinational, with people traveling from many countries as marketers and sales agents for their homeland. Sailors and dock workers from different countries also played a role in moving food, raw materials, finished products, and exchanging knowledge between countries. They were early diasporas from the towns of the producers and shippers who relocated to foreign ports. They spoke the local buyer's and foreign seller's languages. They provided more comfort to importers or buyers than those who did not speak their language or did not understand the quality of their products. The agents understood the seller and buyer's cultures and knew the quality and characteristics of the sellers' merchandise. These trade diaspora merchants preceded colonies and colonial rule and laws. Thus, trade networks grew based on people from the same native place, customs, and language, which helped develop the buyers' trust levels and established traders' reputations.

In the 1850s, European shipping grew stronger with better vessels. European colonial rule became more established as the demand for imports to support city ports, and industrialization grew. Investors and traders from throughout Europe set up overseas trading, distribution, marketing, and sales offices to receive payments in silver and gold. The Chinese used paper currency, silk, tea, and other luxury commodities as "money" for direct exchange or barter. Over time, payment changed to silver, first from Japan, Vietnam, Myanmar, and eventually the USA and Mexico. As trade expanded, it grew from primarily food and clothing necessities such as grains and timber to more discretionary luxury goods. Gradually, there was a spread of information and knowledge of product quality among buyers and sellers of the transaction. The growth of rice spread from eastern Asia to India, then on to Egypt, Morocco, and Spain. The development of cotton crops spread from India to Iraq, Syria, Cyprus, Sicily, Tunisia, Morocco, Spain, and the southern USA. Some species were grown as cereals for human consumption, while some in pastures for animals from Africa and throughout the Mediterranean.

The oceans and seas were considered to belong to everyone until the Portuguese fleet arrived in the late 1500s and started creating forts throughout the trading region between Asia, the Middle East, and Africa. Portuguese controlling power over the seas started to decline in the early 1600s as the age of mercantilism, trade wars, and a British, Dutch, and European-centered world economy was emerging. When these two new European powers arrived in the Indian Ocean and the South China Sea, they witnessed thriving Arab, Indian, and Chinese trade networks. They followed the Portuguese and Spanish to the Americas. The Portuguese in Brazil had started sugar plantations with enslaved Africans and launched the sugar trade with Europe. As the British arrived in

Brazil, they saw the fertile forests and prominent potential enslaved people as an opportunity to initiate coffee production to be exported to Europe, where coffee consumption was expanding rapidly. Coffee growers' land could not be foreclosed on under Brazil's legal system. Since Brazil had no banking infrastructure, the Portuguese arranged financing by borrowing from the British to lend to the plantation owners to grow the coffee with any default exposure covered by the Portuguese. Brazil remains the largest coffee producer globally with 3.6 million metric tons (74% Arabica and 26% Robusta).

Between 1500 and 1750, the Middle East, South, and Southeast Asia offered borderless, open trade between countries. Persian and Chinese entrepreneurs could launch merchant trading and shipping companies and exchange every commodity available. These same entrepreneurs had often won government auctions to collect duties (taxes) on shipping into various ports and gained a valuable advantage over other shippers.[i] As armies grew more prominent with more equipment, the cost of war increased, rulers needed more revenue from trade and agriculture, and tariffs began to spread and rise.

The movement of goods by land was not easy because roads were dirt paths until the city was reached. Consequently, cities' growth and size were limited by transportation, so coastal cities became large and prosperous business centers. Ships needed masts made of larger timbers, so coastal countries with extensive forests near the coast or significant rivers became shipbuilding centers. As a result, most British ships were built in America or Brazil, many Portuguese ships were also made in Brazil, and the Spanish ships were constructed in Ecuador. Winds influenced trading schedules for sailing vessels, controlling the direction and timing of when and how long travel time would take. This influence of wind was particularly true in trade throughout Asia and the Middle East, but wind patterns caused less severe travel constraints in the Atlantic Ocean.

Scottish merchants began developing and building warehouses at major ports to accumulate large stocks of goods, which helped reduce shipping costs. Warehouses reduced the ship's turnaround time because they could be loaded or unloaded quickly near the boat. The Dutch began building larger vessels to carry more cargo and required fewer sailors to manage, which helped reduce shipping costs further. But because these ships were big and slow, they were subject to pirate attacks. The application of the steam engine to power ships and railroads inland greatly removed this wind-sailing restriction, cutting shipping time and costs. It also expanded the number of cities and people participating in trade. Railroads and steamships reduced time and transport costs to ports, resulting in a significant increase in longer-distance global commerce. An important factor that helped reduce ocean-going costs was Britain's successful suppression of piracy in the 18th century, which reduced insurance costs and the need to arm ships with heavy cannons and soldiers crossing the Atlantic.

The need for food in growing cities resulted in shipping beef and lamb from Argentina, Uruguay, and the USA and transporting wheat from Australia, the USA, and India to feed Europe. Japanese mills mixed US, Indian, and Chinese cotton for Europe and the world. The building of the Suez Canal between

1859 and 1869 cut ocean sailing time. The first transatlantic telegraph cable was laid in 1858 and became functional in 1865, significantly improving the Americas and Europe's trade and information flow. China pulled out of the large shipbuilding business and shipping, leaving them both to the European countries. The Chinese departure resulted in a new pattern of world trade. European trade merchants benefited from the Portuguese, who had charted the seas and skies and created navigational instruments such as the quadrant to determine latitude to enrich themselves in Africa and the East Asian markets. International trade was necessary for food and survival and influenced the size of cities. If cities grew too fast, food prices would rise, raising wage demands and pushing up product prices, increasing dependence on imports.

A second significant factor in promoting international trade and survival of the new migrants to North America was the emergence and expansion of warehouses along the USA and Canadian East Coast. Independent Scottish traders built and managed the warehouses, and over the next 75 years, directly helped retain the US export competitiveness. The emergence of warehouses meant that goods could be sent to ports ahead of the ship's arrival, cutting the time and sailor boarding costs in port before ships could load and leave. Also, ship owners would hire merchants as sailors and provide free passage for their services in exchange for cargo space onboard ships. Exports helped the new settlers from Europe get out of debt and paid for traveling to the USA. It also paid for the housing and clothing items that could only be imported from Europe. US exports were grain from New York and Pennsylvania, rice, naval stores,[ii] and cotton were sent from North and South Carolina, and tobacco was grown and processed from Virginia and Maryland. Sugar shipped from American investments in Jamaica and Brazil became a primary export.

As shipping costs fell, Europeans demanded an increasing number of American exports. In exchange, Europe shipped luxury goods to America, and there was always some space for immigrants wanting to go to the Americas. During the 300 years leading up to the 1800s, about 1.6 million Europeans came to the Americas, and 8 million people came from Africa to work in the southern cotton and tobacco plantations. About 4 million Chinese came to California during this same period to clear land for farming and build the railroad. The Chinese immigrated as farmers and planted sugar, tobacco, and coffee for exports globally. In the latter part of the 19th century, 12 million Europeans moved *en masse* to the Americas from the turmoil in Europe. Global commerce expanded dramatically after the Suez Canal opened in 1869 and cut travel time from Marseilles, France to Shanghai, China from more than 100 days to under 40 days, resulting in European trade with Asia expanding.

Steam Engine Locomotives Expand Global Commerce

The development of the steam engine locomotive led to the global expansion of railroads that cut land-based freight costs by over 90% and further boosted international trade growth everywhere except in India. In 1910, India had the fourth-largest rail network, but it did not spur international trade because it was primarily inland and to more impoverished cities, where rail shipment was expensive. Furthermore, railroad building had no spillover impact to train skilled people who could transfer their knowledge of steelmaking, engineering, or coal mining to other people in India. However, as people became more affluent in any country, they began to drink, smoke, and eat exotic plants. These items included coffee, tea, cocoa, tobacco, and sugar. These products became the most valuable agricultural goods in international trade between producers in America, Asia, Africa, and consumers in Europe, the Middle East, and Asia. Opium became widely traded in the 19th century and served as an engine of growth, especially for Britain and China. The British forced China in the Treaty of Nanjing to open its markets to trade and import opium exported from India. India's opium export earnings help it import textiles, railroads, and other industrial products from Britain. India also exported rice, cotton, and indigo dye to Britain. Much of Britain's financial investments in America's growth were earned from export profits of sales to China and India, illustrating the importance of free international trade and capital mobility for investments and the associated direct and indirect benefits for economic growth.

Cocoa became Mexico's major agricultural export to Europe. Coffee produced in Yemen was exported through the Middle East and then to Britain and Europe in the late 18th century after it was separated from its sediment, and honey and milk were added. By the late 19th century, the USA became a major coffee importer overnight to wake up in the morning with their elixir to start the workday, as coffee became known as the business drink. In the USA, food was exported to Haiti's large sugar plantation of enslaved workers, who became workers on coffee plantations, and coffee was shipped to the North-Eastern states. When the workers revolted in the 1790s, coffee production was shifted to Brazil by the Portuguese merchants, and Brazilian plantations began to ship coffee to the USA in 1809. Several years later, the Portuguese also developed sugar plantations in Brazil for shipment to the USA for their coffee. An estimated 10 million Africans were shipped across the Atlantic Ocean to work on sugar and coffee plantations in exchange for US and European imports of their labor in Haiti. Haiti's French rulers and merchants did not invest their profits from sugar and coffee in Haiti but sent them back to France to be invested.

The leaves of the coca tree found in Bolivia and Peru, chewed initially by Native Americans working in silver mines under harsh conditions, began to be sold to the Spanish for export. German chemists converted the coca leaf into an anesthetic called cocaine and used it for medical purposes. Cocaine growers in Colombia and Mexico became major exporters of the drug in the 1970s, shipping it to the USA, Britain, and Europe, although it was an illegal substance.

In the mid-1800s, gold was found in California and later in Australia, Alaska, and South Africa, which also discovered diamonds. The discoveries enriched the world and increased the global money supply, stimulating economic growth via international trade. Guano, bird droppings found on islands off Chile's coast became a valuable fertilizer import for farmers in England and the USA to increase crop yields. Similarly, the discovery of enormous amounts of oil near the surface of desert lands in Saudi Arabia by the so-called "seven sisters" comprising the seven major oil companies were exported to the USA and Europe. In WWII, oil demand was driven to support the global mobility of ships, tanks, airplanes, and military vehicles. In the meantime, the availability of oil enhanced transportation innovation of the internal combustion engine, which contributed to the increased demand for oil. Likewise, Europe's growing wealth endorsed increasing its hunger for beef imports from Argentina. The demand for rubber was driven by the increased need to produce tires for bicycles and later cars in the USA and Europe. This demand resulted in a sharp increase in the production and export from Brazilian rubber trees. Rubber tree seeds were transplanted in plantations in British tropical colonies, and Indian and Chinese labor was used to increase output to meet the growing demand.

Turpentine was initially discovered as a solvent for rubber in 1764 by **Francois Fresnau (1703–1770, a French botanist and scientist)**. In 1820, **Charles Macintosh (1766–1843, a Scottish chemist)** rediscovered this solvent for rubber and invented "a waterproof fabric" by painting liquified rubber on two sides of cotton fabric, creating a raincoat and rubber boots. **Giovanni Fabbroni (1752–1822, an Italian naturalist, economist, agronomist, and chemist)** discovered the rubber solvent naphtha in 1779. In 1839, **Charles Goodyear (1800–1849, an American chemist and manufacturing engineer)** re-developed and patented the vulcanization of rubber. Goodyear discovered that applying heat to natural rubber to remove the sulfur made it waterproof and winter-proof without losing its elasticity. The growth in rubber demand from the USA, Germany, Japan, and Russia eventually exceeded supply sparking innovation by Dupont chemists, leading to synthetic rubber to meet growing US and world demand.

In 1735, **Charles de la Condamine (1701–1744, a French explorer, geographer, and mathematician)** had learned about a process from local Mesoamerican tribes while working in the Amazon rainforests of Peru. The process could harden rubber into a seamless form such as a tube or tire. The bicycle's development stimulated **John B. Dunlop (1840–1921, a Scottish inventor and veterinary surgeon)** to re-invent the pneumatic (inflatable) rubber tire with a much less expensive process than initially developed. The original inventor of the vulcanized rubber pneumatic tire was **Robert W. Thomson (1822–1873, a Scottish inventor)**, and he also invented the first pneumatic tire and the fountain pen. **William Harvey du Cros (1846–1918, a Dublin-born financier)** founded the pneumatic tire industry by supporting John B. Dunlop's innovations and mass-producing his tires. While the bicycle spurred the pneumatic tire, the automobile's invention significantly expanded the demand for pneumatic rubber innertubes for tires. During WWI and WWII, the increasing demand for rubber gave rise to synthetic rubber for tires, replacing the labor-intensive effort of cultivating wild rubber trees in Brazil and British Malaya. Brazil's rubber exports were overtaken by the growing export demand for coffee, sugar, and soybean products.

Case Study #6.1 Significant Disruptive Inventors and Innovations – Transportation: Pneumatic Tires

Key Disruptive Inventors	**John B. Dunlop (1840–1921, a Scottish inventor and veterinary surgeon)** **William H. du Cros (1846–1918, a Scottish financier and founder of the pneumatic tire industry supporting John B. Dunlop and mass-producing Dunlop's tires**
Location	**Both in Scotland**
Disruptive Invention	Dunlop re-invented pneumatic tires for his child's tricycle, unaware of the prior patent of the original inventor of the vulcanized rubber pneumatic tire by Robert W. Thomson, a Scottish inventor. Du Cros supported Dunlop's research and development and started mass-producing Dunlop's tires.
Problem Resolved	Solid rubber tires were hard, rough riding, heavy, and did not roll as far as pneumatic tires, which used less material than solid rubber or metal tires and were less costly. The process could use natural or synthetic rubber, and the latter was less expensive and easier to obtain.
Solution Impact	It supported a much more comfortable ride for bicycles and auto tires and was less expensive than the solid rubber tire.
Economic Impact	Dunlop became a major multinational producer of tiers for bicycles, autos, trucks, and airplanes, supporting the development of related industries, particularly the auto industry, trucking, and multinational aircraft industries.
Cultural Impact	People became much more mobile and willing to explore and commute more significant distances from urban suburbs into cities
Inventors Education & Training	Dunlop studied to be a veterinary surgeon at the Dick Vet, University of Edinburgh. Du Cros was educated at The King's Hospital in Dublin, an independent co-educational day and boarding school.
Innovation Environment	The environment was a very innovative period, and the need for tires was great and growing.
Financing	Dunlop supported his research and experimentations as a veterinary surgeon. Du Cros made himself Ireland's boxing champion and fencing champion for his health and started and led his team to win the Irish Rugby championship. In his late twenties, du Cros had formed his six sons into a successful racing cyclist team. Unfortunately, his sons lost to a rider using pneumatic tires. Du Cros saw a commercial opportunity to produce pneumatic tires. As a well-known Irish businessperson, he partnered with his friends J. M. Gillies and William Bowden. He persuaded Dunlop to promote the new company that du Cros successfully floated its shares, keeping ownership under his control. In

(*Continued*)

(Continued)

	1896, du Cros sold the company to investors for 3 million pounds. The same year, the company was relisted as the Dunlop Pneumatic Tyre Company on the stock market. It produced its first car tire in 1900 after Michelin, a French multinational tire manufacturing company, started in 1889.
International Commerce	Dunlop tires were first exported and then produced globally following the worldwide sale and production of bicycles, cars, and trucks.
Major Success Factors	Dunlop was a veterinary surgeon familiar with flexible tubes or blood vessels and could transfer sheet rubber into a pipe or tire, eventually becoming a manufactured seamless tire.

US gold production and exports rose sharply between 1848 and 1860 from northern California. The westward movement of east coast immigrants searching for new opportunities led **John Sutter (1803–1880, a Swiss immigrant of Mexican and American citizenship and the first northern California land developer)** to leave his family and explore the USA. He arrived in California, which was then controlled by Mexico. The local governor gave Sutter 50,000 acres to develop and bring European immigrants to his New Helvetia colony. Sutter built a fort to protect against Native Americans and used the fertile land to grow wheat, peas, corn, beans, and grapes for wine. Sutter also introduced shipping on the Sacramento River and built a lumber mill to supply wood for housing and other buildings. On the Sacramento River, gold was found in 1847 by one of Sutter's employees, **James Marshall**, and nine days later, California passed from Mexico to the USA. As the word of the discovery of gold spread, immigrants began pouring into California, with the Chinese becoming the primary international nationality.

The gold discovery caused substantial growth between 1848 and 1860, and imports from Europe and other countries increased as gold revenues flowed abroad in payment. California's world trade increased threefold between 1850 and 1870 and resulted in the emergence of the shipping industry to support the growing international commerce of California. Chile and Peru exported wheat to California, and El Salvador, Costa Rica, and Guatemala began exporting coffee along with Brazil. South America, Hawaii, and Asia, particularly China and Japan, opened their markets to US goods and began to expand trade through the west coast ports of San Diego, Los Angeles, and San Francisco. During this transition and opening of the California economy, Hawaii exported sugar and pineapples to California. Production on the US west coast and in the Hawaiian Islands, particularly Maui, continued to expand over 25 years. In 1898, the USA annexed Hawaii as a US territory that removed all barriers to trade between the two countries and began US tourism to the tropical islands.

The Spanish brought cattle to Argentina and abandoned them when they left the country. The grass-fed cattle expanded rapidly on the open pastureland, and

Argentina developed a significant meat exporting industry with the USA and Europe. Europe's demand for beef grew with its urbanization and the steamship development, which could transport more cattle faster across the Atlantic Ocean, and as freight costs declined, volume grew. Beef bouillon became available to feed the more impoverished people in Europe. As refrigeration emerged, enormous amounts of dressed, chilled, or frozen beef became known to European consumers. Cattle farming became big business in Argentina, and cattle ranchers began to fence off the pastureland to control quality and increase output. Gradually the work of 4–5 gauchos became replaced by a man with a herding dog. Italian and Spanish immigrants were brought to farms to prepare the ground for growing feed.

In the Midwest around Chicago, farmland was sold to new immigrants in 160-acre units[iii] of highly productive flatlands that receive good rains in summer, lots of sun, and snow for water in the winter. The problem was finding labor to work the farm, which supplied the opportunity and incentive for machinery innovations to help the farmer. This need was the incentive for **Cyrus McCormick (1809–1884, an American inventor and businessperson who founded the McCormick Harvesting Machine Company)** to invent the mechanical reaper, which he brought to Chicago for sale to farmers. The cut crop had to be brought to the thresher, and **John Appleby (1840–1917, an American inventor)** invented the automated tying machine attached to the thresher-binder. The new apparatus (cut, gathered, bound, and hauled the grain) enabled two men to produce low-cost food to send to the east coast states. The binding twine[iv] was imported from Mexico, made from cactus, and cut by hand.

During its first 100 years, the USA imported technology primarily from Britain and Europe via immigrants and travel. By 1900, the USA began exporting technology improvements in agricultural farming machinery to these countries and China. Shanghai, Tianjin, and Qingdao imported equipment for mechanized textile mills for which longer-fibered cotton was imported from India and the USA. The Chinese also began to replace short-strand Chinese-grown cotton with the longer-strand US cotton seeds. This replacement increased US cotton production by about 30% per acre and helped reduce the cost of textiles exported to the USA and Europe from Britain.

At first, Spain's discovery of the Americas resulted in gold and silver exports. The revenue was used to purchase more European exports, including tobacco, coffee, cocoa, and sugar, expanding trade. Eventually, the USA began producing sweet corn exported throughout the world. Potatoes were shipped from the Andes in Peru to become the world's fourth-largest food crop. These crops required little labor, yielded more calories per acre than rice and wheat, and supplied many vitamins,[v] and they could be stored for extended periods in dry climates. They were first exported to China and then later to Europe and Ireland. Since both were quickly grown with little cost and maintenance, they became a popular crop among the poor. It was an inexpensive food for armies and low-paid industrial factory workers in the British textile industries. As British wages and living standards improved, potatoes' demand moved to Eastern Europe, particularly eastern Germany and Poland. After the French revolution in Europe and Russia, potatoes became an essential food source and were used by many armies.

West Africa, an exporter of enslaved people, needed an alternative when slavery ended as a significant export. An option was to use enslaved Africans to grow products for export out of Africa. In this way, Ghana became a substantial exporter of several agricultural products, including cocoa, palm oil, rubber, and gold. In some cases, European immigrants developed colonies and set up companies in Africa in the Congo and southern Africa, where locals were not well treated. In addition, it was challenging work clearing jungle growth for planting cocoa and other crops.

Rubber grew naturally in Brazil's Amazon rain forests. The randomness of trees made it inefficient to tap it profitably, and the leading consuming countries of the USA and Europe could not grow rubber trees. Britain and the Dutch grew rubber trees in Malaya and Indonesia for export. **Harvey Firestone (1868–1938, an American businessperson and founder of the Firestone Tire and Rubber Company)** was one of the first global producers of automobile tires. He tried to employ local Liberian managers to get locals to work the plantations and was condemned by the League of Nations in 1930, but rubber exports continued to grow. The American **Henry Ford (1863–1974, an American industrialist, business magnate, and founder of the Ford Motor Company)** purchased several million acres in Brazil to develop a rubber tree plantation for exports to the USA. It quickly failed because caterpillar pests moved from tree to tree to destroy the farm as the trees had been planted too close together. Germany came to the rescue by developing synthetic rubber, fearing the loss of imports if it went to war with Britain. The German artificial rubber process was shared with DuPont and Standard Oil of New Jersey to help after the war in producing improved airplane fuel.

The Japanese tried to seize Malaya and Indonesia to take over the rubber plantations from the British and Dutch. There was a growing need for natural rubber because synthetic rubber could not be used for heavy trucks or airplane tires, which required the strength of natural rubber. Improved artificial rubber production based on oil-based synthetics grew to supply about two-thirds of market demand in the 1970s. However, since the volatility in oil prices impacts synthetic rubber's price, natural rubber still accounts for about half of the total consumed rubber.

America's Development by Immigrants

The colonization of America opened the opportunity to a land rich in resources, and its greatness resulted from industrious and creative immigrants from many countries. Unfortunately, the native American was not appreciated and was moved to isolated, unproductive areas. The financial need to launch a new business was small and most often funded with family money. This funding changed with the steam engine's development and its application to power the railroads' growth. For this, significant capital was needed, and the investment return took years to be realized. The English and Dutch recognized a need for a corporation with substantial investment capital to have a long and permanent life. In addition, many unrelated partners would be needed. Such significant capital needs set the stage for corporate monopolies or oligopolies, which carried extensive inventories stored in warehouses close to major ports for exporting. Once exported, the partners might pay dividends as the company grows. The spread of the global transportation revolution reduced shipping costs from the First Industrial Revolution. It also led to the Suez Canal construction and opening in 1869 to accommodate trade expansion to East Africa and Asia. Later, a similar development occurred with the Panama Canal construction in 1914, shortening the Western USA's shipping route to Europe via the Pacific Ocean, further accelerating global commerce.

Setting Time Zones

England was the first to develop railroads and set train times based on Greenwich time rather than any specific time zone. Globally the world was divided into 24 time zones. The European powers imposed a standard time on the rest of the world, making global travel more accessible, especially for air travel when it became popular. Time standards were adopted in 1847 according to so many hours ahead or behind **Greenwich Mean Time (GMT)**. GMT is the mean solar time at the Royal Observatory in Greenwich, London, measured from midnight.

In the USA, railroad companies joined together to establish national time zones in 1883. This standardization of time allows callers to synchronize a meeting or calling time worldwide. Time became a vital measure in deciding when workers should work in a factory as the factory machinery could not run unless they were all at their position. The development of railroads and train travel scheduling was also dependent on time, and later it was also crucial for sea and airplane travel. More recently, it is essential to schedule and determine car travel time for work, meetings, trips, and today to schedule Zoom video conferencing sessions.

International Trade Standards and Currency

Expanding global commerce and capital flows required laws and standards for goods and services, exchange rates, and banking and financial markets. Quality controls were put in place to protect consumers and control agricultural diseases. Products also were monitored to ensure tariffs on certain products were enforced and collected. A considerable amount of documentation was required on imports to provide that the products were what the buyer ordered and in acceptable condition and on exports to protect hostile countries from receiving confidential trade secrets. Regarding pricing and payment settlement in international trade, the exchange of gold and silver was accepted during the 1800s, and currencies' gold backing determined their exchange rates with foreign currencies. In the mid-1900s, the US dollar became the standard for global trade and capital flows and a key international reserve currency for governments following the Bretton-Woods Agreement in 1944. This development built a fixed exchange rate system where the IMF was established to ensure the system works. Fixed exchange rates were considered the best means of promoting international commerce. International trade is more straightforward when a single widely accepted currency like the US dollar is used for pricing and payments. The agreement's collapse led to exchange rate volatility and the birth of floating currencies. Market arbitrage innovation dealt with exchange rate fluctuations based on changing economic conditions to reduce risk by developing currency hedging instruments such as forwards, futures, swaps, and options. While these instruments increase the cost of doing business globally, they resolve the currency volatility problem for importers and exporters. The major commercial banks provided these hedging instruments innovations that also served as currency exchanges for individuals, companies, and governments. There was also a regionalization of currency blocs into trading areas. Former colonies initially became part of currency trading zones for international settlement in British pounds, French francs, and later US dollars. The Euro replaced individual member European country currencies with a basket of the major countries' currencies to determine the Euro's value against the US dollar. The Euro fluctuated within a narrow margin around this base rate, depending on the USA's differing economic performance versus Europe. This system is still in effect today, and the Euro is the second most important currency unit used in international trade after the US dollar.

Creating an international grain market around 1900 helped determine price differentials between various agricultural products. Railroad storage elevators homogenized wheat and other agricultural products produced by different farmers. Agreements on weights, measures, and instruments helped standardize agricultural and industrial measurement for traded goods globally. Arbitrage between other markets for the same commodity eventually resulted in a single global price for goods, excluding shipping costs. The price differential between different commodities would cause farmers to adjust what they would grow to the extent they could, based on price expectations, weather trends, and expected return. Farmers could eventually purchase hedges against price volatility by agreeing to sell their product forward for future delivery if they expected the current price to move against them by falling. In 1898, the **Chicago Mercantile Exchange** became the primary market for all commodity trading, pricing, and eventually hedging in the USA. In London, coffeehouses were financiers' original transaction meeting place to conduct mercantile exchange, stock, and bond market activities. An insurance and reinsurance syndicating market like **Lloyds of London**[vi] had long been established in 1688 to protect against losing ships, ship's cargo, and warehouse products.

By the 17th century, silver pesos became the most widely circulating currency globally. Pure and consistent content set the world's standard for coins and provided the means for Europe to pay for imports from Asia of spices and silks. Brazil discovered gold which brought 300,000 Portuguese, and it supplied the world's gold demand. Silver became no longer used as the standard currency for international trade as the standard shifted to gold because of its higher value. Gold revenue was used to import enslaved people from Africa to work on the Brazilian coffee and rubber plantations and pay for clothing and spices imported from the countries around the Indian Ocean. Significant gold discoveries in California, Australia, and Brazil sparked an unprecedented boom in world trade growth between 1848 and 1873. Gold discovery in South Africa and Alaska resulted in gold appearing more reliable metal to base a monetary system. International banking and commerce growth made it clear that a single stable monetary system or standard was necessary to expand global trade. Accelerated trade was aided by lower transportation costs between Europe and Asia because of the opening of the Suez Canal in 1869. Europe could pay with goods that it had previously paid for with silver. Western European and US capitalists began investing in Mexican railroads, mines, ranches, and factories after 1880, stimulating economic growth. Meanwhile, since Brazil defaulted on its foreign debt, it was not favored by foreign investment and continued to rely on its gold exports to purchase imports.

Rothschild Family Founders of International Finance

The **Rothschilds** in Frankfurt developed a new business method, which became the groundwork for expanding world markets during the last 200 years. Frankfurt became the center for international merchant banks. **Mayer Amschel Rothschild (1744–1812 was a German Jewish banker and the Rothschild banking dynasty founder)**. He was also referred to as a "founding father of international finance." He earned his income by changing money, and the Rothschilds made their money by moving funds and goods across international borders, which helped speed economic transactions. It also created substantial amounts of investment capital and consolidated nation-states. The Rothschild family spread across Europe, and the brothers pooled their money in consortia and used carrier pigeons and fast ships to disseminate information quickly. They financed wars for rich monarchs with whom they worked closely, and they gained knowledge on financial and commercial activities and profited from it. The Rothschilds pushed limited liability laws that gave birth to corporations that issued stocks to build capital. They invested in gold, silver, copper, and mercury mines in Mexico, the USA, Spain, South Africa, and Australia. They brought together the consortia of international bankers to remove the barriers to capital flows. They became underwriters of loans and bonds for anonymous third parties and stood behind their issued loans. They preferred enormous, low interest, and safe loans, and the family is still a principal player in international finance today.

Case Study #6.2 Significant Disruptive Inventors and Innovations – International Finance and Banking

Key Disruptive Inventors	**Mayer Amschel Rothschild (1744–1812, a German Jewish banker and the Rothschild banking dynasty founder and a founding father of international finance**
Location	**Germany**
Disruptive Invention	International finance and banking supporting world trade and investment.
Problem Resolved	The difficulty of financing trade between different countries easily at reasonable costs.
Solution Impact	It became easier to purchase products from various parts of the world.
Economic Impact	International trade and finance grew, supporting domestic growth in GDP and the transmission of innovations and knowledge, and enhanced connectivity across borders.
Cultural Impact	The world became exposed to new foods and products from different countries, which helped change the way people lived, the type of food they consumed, their clothing, and how other cultures lived.
Inventors Education & Training	One of eight children of Amschel Moses & Schönche Rothschild and Amschel's father had a business in goods trading and currency exchange and supplier of coins to the Prince of Hesse. He secured an apprenticeship with Jacob Wolf Oppenheimer, at the banking firm of Simon Wolf Oppenheimer in Hanover, in 1757. Samuel Oppenheimer's grandson taught Rothschild about foreign trade and currency exchange and then returned to his brothers' business in Frankfurt in 1763.
Innovation Environment	The environment was beginning a very innovative period. The Rothschilds introduced the financing instruments and practices to support growth, and creative finance's helped support Britain and Europe's economic growth. Rothschild family banking businesses pioneered international high finance during the industrialization of Europe. They supported railway systems worldwide and complex government financing for projects such as the Suez Canal.
Financing	Mayer became a rare coin dealer and represented Crown Prince Wilhelm of Hesse in this regard, who had also worked with Mayer's father. Rothschild's coin business grew to include several wealthy royal clients. He expanded his banking activities for Crown Prince Wilhelm. The company expanded rapidly following the French Revolution when Rothschild managed payments from Britain to recruit Hessian mercenaries. In 1798, son Nathan Mayer Rothschild was sent to England to further the family interests in textile importing with £20,000 capital to establish the first foreign branch. Nathan became a naturalized citizen and established a bank in the City of

	London in 1804. Mayer provided partnership agreements with his three oldest sons sending Jacob to Paris in 1811 to coordinate the family's operation throughout Europe. This enabled the Rothschilds to profit from financing Wellington's armies in Portugal, which meant purchasing massive quantities of gold on behalf of the British government. Nathan's sons furthered the family fortune across Europe. Eldest son Amschel Mayer took over the Frankfurt bank, and Salomon moved to Vienna. Nathan turned the London branch into one of Europe's most powerful banking institutions, Calmann (Carl) set up a unit in Naples, and Jacob ("James") opened de Rothschild Frères, which grew to become a significant force of finance in Paris. The Rothschild family possessed an enormous private fortune in the world during the 1800s. During the 19th century, the family purchased much of Mayfair, London, and accumulated numerous large estates through Europe and Britain.
International Commerce	World commerce began expanding as countries started to explore other continents and the Rothschilds became a significant source of financing this expansion.
Major Success Factors	Management control was kept within the family, which was large and spread throughout the world. The family developed strong economic and political connections through Europe and Britain. Another essential part of Mayer Rothschild's strategy for success was to keep control of their banks in family hands, allowing them to maintain complete secrecy about the size of their fortunes.

Grain Markets, Transportation, and Consumer Tastes

Consumer tastes vary for different grains, and it is difficult to substitute one for the other, which generates international trade. Wheat is an Atlantic world staple, and rice is a Pacific and Indian world staple. As shipping costs fell for wheat that came through the Panama Canal to New York to be shipped to Europe, lower wheat prices helped it compete with rice to become an acceptable staple throughout Europe. Later it was sent through the Suez Canal to Asia and China. The use of grain elevators that mix various farmers' grain into one category by season and the development of the railroads and preloading boxcars with warehoused grain from storage elevators helped lower transportation and wheat price to compete with rice. As grains were mixed and became listed by season spring, summer, or winter crop, this made it possible to develop a futures and options market at the **Chicago Board of Trade**, allowing farmers to hedge wheat price fluctuations. Wheat, therefore, became a commodity. Rice stores and ships better than wheat, and significant rice consumers strongly prefer to grow the rice or where it is grown. But when shipped to Europe, price became the primary consumer driver for what they purchased. India was a major grower and exporter of grain. Consumers in India were indifferent between wheat and rice and bought based on price, which impacted how much wheat or rice was exported. As a result, a global wheat market developed.

In the 19th century, the USA ran a significant trade deficit importing everything needed to start and develop a new nation until it became more self-supporting and independent. It could finance its imports because of substantial capital investment inflows from Europe. As large US companies emerged after the great depression, the USA was transformed into a creditor nation. US financiers like **J. P. Morgan (1837–1913, an American financier and entrepreneurial banker)** used their excess liquidity for mergers and acquisitions (M&A) and built some of the world's largest corporations. Morgan dominated corporate finance on Wall Street as CEO of the banking firm **J.P. Morgan and Co.** Morgan was a driving force behind the US wave of industrial consolidation during the late 19th and early 20th centuries. Other prominent entrepreneurial and wealthy US families include **William A. Rockefeller (1851–1929, an American businessperson and financier)**. Rockefeller was a co-founder of Standard Oil with his elder brother **John D. Rockefeller**, and he helped build the **National City Bank of New York**, which became **Citigroup**. Rockefeller was part owner of **Anaconda Copper Company**, the fourth-largest company globally in the 1920s. He also worked with **E.H. Harriman (1848–1909, an American railroad executive and rebuilder of bankrupt railroads).** In addition, Rockefeller worked with several European investors like **Meyer Guggenheim & Family (1828–1905, a Swiss-born-American entrepreneur)**. Guggenheim made his fortune through mining and smelting in the USA, Mexico, the Caribbean, and later other parts of South America. These entrepreneurial investors were trying to gain control of natural resources and their transportation. **E. H. Harriman** invested in building rail and ship networks throughout the Americas. **William Rockefeller** focused on building a petroleum and copper empire and, for a time, worked with Harriman to ensure he had transportation facilities to move his end products to markets in the USA and other countries. The **Guggenheims** invested in Mexico's refining industry, focusing on silver, lead, and copper. They became significant producers of these products for export to the USA and globally. The American financiers **James Speyer** of **Speyer and Company** and **Jacob Schiff (1847–1920, a German-born Jewish American banker at Kuhn Loeb, businessperson, and philanthropist)** used European capital sent to the USA to buy a controlling interest in Mexico's major railroads. **James Speyer (1861–1941, an American banker)** in New York City and his brother **Edgar Speyer (1862–1932, an American-born financier and philanthropist)** were international financiers. They headed a company known as **Speyer and Company** in the USA and **Lazard Speyer Elissen** in Britain. They established an American commercial bank in Mexico and made US dollar loans to the Mexican government, for which they floated a bond in France. Speyer and others later issued a $500 million bond in the USA and Europe to fund the **Mexican National Railroads** system. The Mexican government collaborated with the international financiers to get the money they needed to build their economy. They used trusted financial intermediaries like **Rothschild's, Baring's**, and **J.P Morgan** to show that Mexican investment risk was acceptable. They sold portions of the investments to other investors via financial syndicates. The final part of the transaction is reassurance by a neutral third party like the International Monetary Fund or The World Bank for loans and a private credit-rating agency like Moody's or Standard and Poor to set bond's risk ratings. As US investment banks placed money in companies' and governments' financial instruments globally, this export of funds helped stimulate the development of the global economy and increased international commerce. It resulted in debt service payments back to the US investors to repeat the process.

As the USA became the dominant world economy, confidence in the US dollar value for transactions and international reserves grew. This global confidence was reflected in the growth of the **Eurodollar market in London** after WWII. The Eurodollar market is one of the most significant financial post-WWII innovations. Eurodollars are dollar deposits from governments, corporations, or individuals held by banks primarily in London that any qualified entity can borrow. US banks became large borrowers of these funds overnight because of their low-interest rates and certainty of being available in large amounts to cover loans to their many clients. It was also reflected with the accumulation of **petrodollars** or dollar payments to the **Organization of Petroleum Exporting Countries (OPEC)** for oil imports and the flow of the funds from OPEC and other countries into US dollars at the sign of any financial, economic, or military crises. Gradually the Eurodollar market expanded to become the **Eurocurrency market** to accommodate the need for dollars and other currencies by multinational banks and corporations to fund international trade and investments.

Impact of Trade on Industrialization

Raw material exporting countries depended on trade to support economic growth. The early factory housed production was found in the sugar mills of Latin America, where sugar cane is crushed, boiled, and made ready for its transatlantic journey and where the laborers were imported from Africa. International trade also was a significant part of the textile industries in Britain, and several factors helped boost trade expansion as the British navy opened markets worldwide. British dominance of India's leading textile exporting region gave Britain access to the textile markets of the Ottoman Empire, Persia, Southeast Asia, and parts of Africa. Industrialization eventually gave British producers a comparative advantage in replacing India's producers, and cotton was a necessary import that Britain could not grow at home.

For industries impacted by industrialization, raw material had to be imported and the finished product exported. This process is also valid for the workers during industrialization. They would not eat without food imports or access other desired products without importing them from other countries. Consequently, industrialization, stimulated by innovations, was accompanied and supported by an expansion in international trade. Also, shortages of certain raw materials needed in larger quantities than available domestically had to be imported to support industrialization. With global trade, the supply of raw materials increased, lowering the price and reducing the cost of producing final goods. As total demand surged, aggregate supply and demand increased and led to global growth. Therefore, industrialization expanded employment and development in the industrializing country, further boosting raw materials imports.

As technologies supporting industrialization in one country become known and available in other countries, beneficial employment and economic growth effects are passed on to other countries via international trade, capital flows, and movement of human capital. Sometimes specific politicians or governments may limit the spread of knowledge of the new technological processes with policies that can preserve monopoly control of the latest innovation. In such cases, reverse engineering the latest technology product by scientists of other countries can reveal new innovations that provide even better technologies that may not violate patent rights. Thus, society benefits from lower costs or innovative ideas gained from foreign trade even with a trade deficit.

Protectionist policies by these governments inhibit trade and knowledge transfer. Considerable damage to society occurs if no innovations for improved industrialization are implemented because of trade protectionism fears. Specialization in a county's production with a comparative advantage does not guarantee that all countries gain equally. Still, it does ensure that all nations or societies are better off with international trade. Participating in international trade and investment or globalization opens the door to increased technological alternatives and provides consumers with better choices and lower prices than available without international trade.

Logic Behind the Importance of International Commerce and Innovation

What is the basis for comparative costs and comparative advantage supporting international trade? A country's ability to produce goods and services is a function of its available natural resources, workforce, capital, innovation, and entrepreneurship. Technological change impacts how these factors are used most efficiently and are driven by understanding and knowledge of the different production areas. Countries are endowed with varying production factors to educate labor, create awareness, invest in technology and physical capital, and support entrepreneurship with sophisticated financial markets. The result is increased productivity, economic growth, and development. This development has explained the differences in the country's relative factor prices and productivity. From a demand-side perspective, there are significant differences in per capita incomes and wealth between developed, developing, and emerging market economies. This difference is reflected in higher-income countries' stronger demand for higher quality and more sophisticated products than lower-income countries. Therefore, higher-income countries' manufacturers and producers will first produce goods for the domestic market. Then, as they satiate the domestic need, they will explore exporting to the international markets with a similar demand structure and appropriate per-capita incomes, cultures and tastes, and geographic proximity. Different varieties of the same product are exchanged between similarly developed countries because of taste and reputational differences such as automobiles, wines, clothing, etc. Technology is rising fast, costs are falling, and modern designs are constantly innovating. They are creating competition among nations to gain a larger share of the global market. Some countries have achieved their goals using the latest technologies and innovations to reach demand beyond their borders.

The openness of the worldwide market assists governments in increasing per capita income through exports. A prerequisite to compete globally is to improve the local economy's competitiveness to help increase production and create more jobs. Innovations lower costs, which will enable producers to sell their products globally and attract foreign investors. Exports assistance can be used as an opportunity for developing economies to expand their production capacity, boosting economic growth, reducing unemployment, and promoting employment opportunities. However, tariffs or subsidies will misallocate scarce resources from what is truly a competitive advantage.

International trade and capital flows represent an educational and learning opportunity of what people worldwide are learning and doing with their knowledge. The first physical exposure to innovative ideas and innovations often comes from international trade in goods and services. Worldwide trade and capital flows are a barometer of countries' competitiveness and innovations. The comparative advantage principle supports the importance of international trade and specialization based on the differences between countries' relative costs of producing comparable products. Comparative cost differences are linked to the country's production function and its production factors and innovations, representing the supply-side argument supporting the value of international trade to a country and its people. A demand-side perspective also emphasizes consumer preferences in different countries for various goods. Early economic theories justify the benefits of specialization. Each country has a comparative cost advantage in a product, and both countries gain by specializing and trading, increasing both products' output. Even if one country is more efficient in producing both products, specialization will increase total output. This gain occurs when each country focuses on developing the product with the most significant comparative advantage or least comparative disadvantage.

Comparative advantage can also be explained with opportunity cost, which is the cost to a country resulting from not producing another product or service. A country's production of an additional unit of any product can be measured by the value or opportunity cost of the number of units of the product that is not produced when all factors of production are fully utilized. If there are unemployed factor resources, then the opportunity cost of using them is zero because they were not being used. The country would be below its production possibility frontier. If there are differences in comparative costs between countries, there are opportunities for domestic production and international trade specialization. The terms of trade or ratio of a country's exports relative to the country's imports determine how much of one product exported is traded for units of another product imported. Thus, only production specialization and international trade will allow a country to obtain more of what it wants and physically produce with its production factors without sacrificing any domestic demand for the product it makes domestically. When there are differences between countries' comparative costs for products, both countries gain from specialization and international trade. This possibility enables countries to reach a larger output more quickly than provided by their average economic growth rate.

Consequently, both countries get a better price than the domestic price for products each country sells in international trade, incentivizing trade with other countries. The amounts exchanged and gained are determined by the countries' size of the differences in their terms of trade. Certain higher technology products that incur high startup fixed costs have increasing returns to scale or decreasing average costs as output expands, such as differentiated products by reputation or style. Like other developed countries, there are many income groups in the USA, and each has different income-expenditure levels and tastes. Lower-income levels are more cost-sensitive, whereas higher income levels are usually more quality or innovative, state-of-the-art focused in their demand. The developed country will scale its product varieties to satisfy the needs of these distinct categories of consumers. They extend this practice in exporting products to perceived similar markets in foreign countries. Eventually, exports become customized specifically to satisfy local consumers' demands, regardless of income. Gradually foreign markets may imitate the exporting country's higher technology imported products and produce them for the local market. Lower production costs and new product varieties may also generate exports to be sold back to the originating country. Alternatively, the originating developed country manufacturer may establish a production facility overseas and modify its product to satisfy local demand. Either way, technology is eventually transferred to the importing country.

Once initiated, the international trade cycle may move the competitive advantage to developing countries to sell domestically, replacing imports, and exporting products to pay for additional imports. Thus, the competitive advantage originating from innovations in the USA, Europe, and Japan are transferred through international specialization and trade to countries that can adopt the technology and improve their competitiveness like South Korea, Taiwan, Hong Kong, and China have done. These developing country markets continue to gain a relative competitive advantage and extend the trade cycle by exporting technology imitations at lower costs to the developed countries that initiated this dynamic process. As these emerging markets become more advanced, their productivity and per capita incomes grow, and they import higher quality products from developed countries. Thus, exporting and capital flows transfer knowledge to other countries via multinational corporations exporting or investing overseas. Over time, this helps stimulate R&D investment in innovative technology in developed countries, perpetuating the international trade and investment cycle to promote trade and investment in less expensive raw materials and labor in emerging market economies. This technology transfer learning cycle model may take 20–40 years to be completed and stimulate per capita GDP growth globally, depending on the technology's degree of sophistication.

In a recent study by Ana Maria Santacreu and Jesse LaBelle, "Technology Transfer and Regional Trade Agreements (RTA)," St. Louis Fed, when RTAs include protection of Intellectual Property Rights (IPR), there is a significant increase in technology transfer. This pattern contrasts with RTAs that do not have IPRs that experience less technology transfer from developed countries. IPRs also increase the local incentive for investment in innovation when IPRs are enforced.[vii] With the growing importance of global supply chains in an increasingly connected world and because patents can only be protected within the borders of each patent office, innovators have an incentive to obtain patents in many countries where they do business. Since 1980, US companies' growth in international patenting has outpaced their domestic patenting growth. International patenting by US inventors has shifted toward Asia, particularly Japan, China, India, Hong Kong, Singapore, Malaysia, and Thailand.[viii]

The economist **Raymond Vernon (1966) (1913–1999, an American economist)** formulated the Product life-cycle theory of US exports, first published in 1966. He identified a three-stage international trade model to transfer technological products from high-wage advanced countries. The first stage of innovation and production is in the innovating country, and most attention is focused on the home market economy. Proximity, familiarity with regulations, consumer demands, and low transportation costs drive market considerations. Product modifications and adjustments will be made for the home market by the original company or new companies with their imitations and improvements within the confines of patent protections for the originating company. Since the originating company has a competitive advantage, they control the new product's price and pass on innovation costs of any improvements or refinements.

In the second maturing product stage, foreign demand grows, and the new product becomes exported to satisfy growing overseas orders. In some cases, certain countries may have import tariffs or non-tariff barriers on certain products. This situation may result in locating a production facility behind the tariff wall, where demand supports this investment. It will also reduce transportation and servicing costs and, perhaps, lower labor costs. Eventually, increasing competition from other companies may erode the originating firm's freedom to control the product's price.

In time, a third stage occurs as the product becomes standardized or commoditized. This situation will lead a company's production to the lowest-cost locations in developing countries. Output from these low-wage countries will be exported to the larger markets in the high-wage developed countries. At this point, price competition is the primary factor driving market share.

This dynamic international trade and investment model explains the rapid increase in worldwide commerce that has exceeded the rise in real GDP and contributed significantly to the growth in global output. There has been an increasing degree of international economic integration globally. The size of international trade in goods and services and global investment has increased many countries' GDP. This evolution originated in industrialized countries' manufacturing sectors and has spread to these countries' communications and transportation sectors via supply chains. The slowing growth in advanced countries' manufacturing sectors has contributed to the slowing in GDP growth in developed industrialized nations. Manufacturers have shifted to developing countries with lower labor costs and less restrictive environmental regulations.

Higher technology manufacturing is less sensitive to labor costs. The advance of the Fourth Industrial Revolution with the increasingly integrated use of digital analytics, microprocessors chips, robotics, artificial intelligence, and more efficient coordination could reverse this trend. In addition, growing evidence from the COVID-19 pandemic supports a re-shoring increase of overseas production facilities because of restrictions on access to labor and the disruption caused to global supply chains of critical products for domestic manufacturing applications.

In the 1900s, the business paradigm changed as private specialized marketing and sales companies emerged, such as **Woolworths, Sears & Roebuck, J.C. Penny's**, etc., advertised via newspapers, flyers, catalogs, and sold many products produced by many companies. Manufacturing companies outsourced their sales and distribution to retail stores throughout the country, with a location in every city with over 50,000 people. Individual stores sold products from local and national manufacturing companies, specializing in products like shoes, baby clothes, jewelry, books, etc. As more products became readily available and sold by national marketing and retail sales stores across the country, prices became determined by supply and demand market forces. Larger urban centers would have multiple retail stores conveniently throughout the standard metropolitan area. These stores eventually became part of shopping centers or a common enclosed, more comfortable shopping center called "a mall." Malls often included restaurants to help attract more shoppers and keep them shopping longer. This model eventually expanded throughout developed countries and gradually into developing countries.

Thus, there developed companies producing a specific line of goods and stores like Sears specialization in retail and commercial products' marketing and sales. Out of this emerged the establishment of regional warehouses to hold inventories of products, serving as distribution centers for the surrounding retail stores. Initially, railroads transported products to the distribution warehouses for inventory as shelf space was limited and costly in retail stores. Then the trucking industry emerged to accelerate and deliver smaller amounts of multiple products based on current demand from large centralized warehouses to the urban retail stores for final sales. This logistics system was vital because it could quickly adapt to consumer demand changes in an overall retail store system and reduced inventories. It could also introduce new products with seasons, styles, tastes, and reduced delivery time to the consumer market. This more efficient logistic process significantly reduced the time gap between equalizing production supply and consumer demand.

With advances in computers and communications such as telephones, the telegraph, fax, internet, the smart cell phone, and GPS, a more efficient logistics system and industry was invented. The procedure improved the communications between the producers, the marketing and distribution companies, and the delivery and transportation distribution system of trains, trucks, and planes. Since this product distribution network had a standard communications system connecting all moving parts, it significantly improved the efficiency and marketing responsiveness of producers, distributors, marketers, and retail consumer shopping stores. It also allowed companies to manage inventory better, reducing costs. The next step was the emergence of electronic shopping with massive online stores such as **Dell Computers**, which customized assembly and sold all computers and related electronic goods from global electronic equipment producers. Dell would purchase various computers and parts from different global manufacturers, assemble a personalized computer under its brand name for consumers, and customize computer systems for large companies. One further innovation in the process was to connect each retail outlet directly to the production factory so that changes in consumer demand as to style, color, functionality, or whatever could be relayed throughout the system and accelerate the responsiveness to changes in consumer tastes.

A leading example of this accelerated responsiveness to consumer tastes changes was Zara, the retail clothing store launched by **Amancio Ortega (1936–, a wealthy Spanish businessperson and innovator)**. He is the founder and former chairman of Inditex fashion group, best known for its chain of Zara clothing stores. He opened the first Zara store in 1975 in central Spain and today is worldwide with 2,213 stores across 93 markets and 39 online markets. The first store featured low-priced lookalike products of popular, higher-end clothing fashions. Ortega opened additional stores throughout Spain and expanded globally in the following years. During the 1980s, Ortega changed the design, manufacturing, and distribution process to reduce lead times and react to new trends more quickly, called "instant fashions." The improvements included using information technologies and using groups of designers instead of individuals. In addition, he used **Radio Frequency Information Data (RFID) chips** located in the security tags removed from clothing when purchased to be reused. The chip allows the company to take inventory by detecting RFID tags' radio signals quickly. When an item is sold, the stockroom is immediately notified to be replaced in the correct size and color.

The most recent service innovation has been the emergence of **Amazon,** which is an online retailer and marketer for all products and recently began including groceries. The company has also built a rapid delivery network like FedEx. Amazon is a multinational technology company founded by **Jeffery P. Bezos (1964-an an American internet entrepreneur, industrialist, media proprietor, and investor).** His great-grandfather John Jørgensen immigrated to the USA from Denmark in the late 19th century. In 1993, Bezos decided to establish an online bookstore, and with $300,000 from his parents, he founded Amazon in 1994 from his garage in Seattle. In 2021 Amazon will use warehouses to accelerate delivery to all USA, Europe, and other countries. Amazon created its delivery services of planes and trucks in the USA and provided a one-day delivery for its *Prime* service. In 2020–2021, Bezos became the world's wealthiest person according to the Forbes Real-Time Billionaires ranking with over $200 billion in net worth. National discount chain stores like Walmart and Target have combined large physical stores for shopping and online sales and shipping or pick-up in response. They have also begun providing groceries as Amazon did with its purchase of Whole Foods. These discount marketing stores selling all products have also expanded internationally, following the example set by US fast-food restaurants like McDonald's, KFC, Wendy's, and Starbucks.

Case Study #6.3 Significant Disruptive Inventors and Innovations – Internet Retail Sales and Delivery[1,2]

Key Disruptive Inventors	**Jeffery P. Bezos (1964–, an American internet entrepreneur, industrialist, media proprietor, and investor)** **Amancio Ortega (1936–, a Spanish "fast fashion" entrepreneur)**
Location	**America, Spain**
Disruptive Invention	The creation of Amazon's internet online web shopping for everything marketing model. Founder of Inditex fashion group and Zara clothing and accessories.
Problem Resolved	Save people time from going to the store and interacting with other people during the COVID-19 pandemic. It also makes price comparison more transparent and easier – lowering overall prices. The latest fashions that women want are provided almost immediately at reasonable prices.

Solution Impact	Reduces COVID-19 risks and provides more time for other higher-value activities. Over 6000 Inditex stores globally sell the Zara brand to customers worldwide.
Economic Impact	It contains inflationary pressures, and easier consumer spending may contribute to more substantial real GDP growth and reduced energy usage for a better environment. Inditex employs more than 92,000 people providing the latest affordable fashions. The price of Zara's contemporary styles was attractive, making them more available to women everywhere.
Cultural Impact	Reduction in time socializing in stores encourages every home to have internet and a device to access the internet. This access will be beneficial for the increased amount of education delivered online. Zara's 6,500 stores in 88 countries provide the latest changing fashions that women want for themselves at reasonable prices. Consumers are attracted by the fashionable products produced to meet their immediate demand, and they purchase products because of relatively low prices and limited supply.
Inventors Education & Training	Bezos attended grammar and high school in Houston and Miami and then his graduate studies at Princeton University, receiving a Bachelor of Engineering Science Degree in Electrical Engineering and Computer Science (BSE) from the Department of Computer Science after changing his Physics major. He graduated in 1986 *summa cum laude* from Princeton University. He worked on Wall Street in various financial positions building a network for international trade, product manager at Bankers Trust, and D.E. Shaw & Co. working on mathematical modeling for the hedge fund. Ortega was the youngest of four children whose father worked for the railroad in the town of Tolosa. He left school at 14, worked for a local shirtmaker Gala, and learned to make clothes by hand. His first business was Confecciones Goa producing bathrobes. He opened his first Zara store in 1975 with his wife Rosalia Mera and made clothes rapidly, replicating popular fashions to sell in his stores. Zara used a vertically integrated supply chain, in which the company has tight control over most of the design production and distribution system to its chain of retail outlets. The proximity of production units

(*Continued*)

(Continued)

	helps Zara provide timely and flexible production to supply the ever-changing demands of consumers more efficiently than its competitors. Zara does not outsource its production to Asian developing countries, unlike its competitors. In 2021 Zara Online was launched, increasing the ease of purchasing products. In the 1980s, Ortega introduced technology improvements, including using information technologies and using groups of designers instead of individuals. Importantly, Zara is built on solid brand values is now an industry capable of offering trendy products at affordable prices, and the company wants to be close to young people. Products are made in limited editions, so Zara stores must sell products quickly at full price without returns, boosting profits. Zara's highly responsive, vertically integrated supply chain enables the export of garments 24 hours, 365 days of the year, shipping new products to stores twice a week. After designing products, they take around 10–15 days to reach the stores. All clothing items are processed through the distribution center in Spain, where new clothes are inspected, sorted, tagged, and loaded into trucks. In most cases, clothing items are delivered to stores within 48 hours. This vertical integration allows Zara to retain control over areas like dyeing and processing and have the on-demand fabric-processing capacity to provide the correct fabrics for new styles according to customer preferences. It also eliminates the need for warehouses and helps reduce the impact of demand fluctuations.
Innovation Environment	Bezos left his job at D.E. Shaw and drove from New York to Seattle developing his business plan for Amazon as an online bookstore out of his garage on July 5, 1994, and 3 years later did an IPO, taking the company public. Ortega found the environment very responsive to Zara, achieving a faster response to rapidly changing fashions.
Financing	Bezos received an estimated $300,000, which he invested in Amazon's startup, and by the end of 1998, he had expanded Amazon's products to consumer goods. The $54 million raised from the IPO was used to finance the acquisition of smaller competitors. In 2000, Bezos borrowed $2 billion from banks to pay

operational costs and, in late 2002, laid off 14% of his workers to cut costs. In 2003 the financial picture improved, and Amazon registered $400 million in profits. Amazon Kindle was launched in 2007. In 2013 Amazon Web Services received a $600 million contract from the CIA. In 2018 he sold stock to launch Blue Origin, and Amazon earned $2 billion in profits and gave his US workers a salary increase to a minimum of $15 per hour. Bezos also sent his senior vice president Agarwal to India with a $5.5 billion budget to localize operations and link them to Amazon's supply chain routes. In January 2020, Amazon India announced an investment of $1 billion and committed to digitally enabling 10 million small companies, driving e-commerce exports worth $10 billion, and creating one million additional jobs from 2020 to 2025. Amazon added 300,000 direct and indirect employment and added 250,000 new salespeople. It currently exports $3 billion and has recruited one million jobs in India. More than 2.5 million small companies work with Amazon, including sellers, artisans, weavers, delivery, logistics services, etc. In late 2020, Amazon scored a victory when it won an injunction from an arbitrator in Singapore to temporarily halt a significant deal between two major Indian retailers Future Retail and Reliance Industries, which could have severely slowed Amazon's growth in India.

Ortega financing was generated by starting several small family-supported businesses. Because his business strategy supported a more rapid response to consumer desires, his company captured market share rapidly. Shorter lead times (and more fashionable clothes), lower quantities (through scarce supply), Zara produces more styles faster than competitors, and customer-co-creation. One of the secrets to Zara's success includes using Radio Frequency Identification Technology (RFID) in its stores. The brand utilizes cutting-edge systems to track garments' location instantly and makes those most in-demand rapidly available to customers.

(*Continued*)

(Continued)

	Additionally, it helps to reduce inventory costs, provides greater flexibility to launch new designs, and allows fulfillment of online orders with stock from stores nearest to the delivery location, thereby reducing delivery costs. Tapping into the growth in demand pulled Ortega's business strategy to success and outcompeted traditional fashion leaders. Zara empowers its sales associates and store managers to be at the forefront of customer research. They intently listen and note down customer comments, ideas for cuts, fabrics, or a new line, and keenly observe new styles that its customers are wearing that have the potential to be converted into unique Zara styles.
International Commerce	Amazon sells globally and only provides delivery service to 65 countries but only one day service in the USA. Zara and Inditex source materials produce current fashion clothes. And sell globally through local stores in major cities and Online technology at very competitive prices.
Major Success Factors	Bezos says the four factors to success ranked by importance are: • Customer obsession, • Eagerness to invent, • Long-term thinking, • Operational excellence. Ortega has remained faithful to its core values that define all his stores: beauty, clarity, functionality, and sustainability. The secret to Zara's success has mainly been driven by its ability to keep up with rapidly changing fashion trends and showcase them in its collections with minimal delay. Using chips to track inventory sales, Zara understands the customers' needs and responds to their needs very quickly.

Ever-Changing Machine Age Enters the Fourth Industrial Revolution

Specialization and focusing on what a company and its employees can do best has also resulted in a separation of companies into one of the following categories: production of a specific group of products or services; distribution and logistics companies focused on getting goods to warehouses; internet marketing and sales companies that make consumers aware of goods like Amazon which is now the second-largest retail store with $386 billion in net sales in 2020. And physical stores where people can examine goods in-person and purchase products like Walmart, the largest retailer at $520 billion in net sales in 2020. Also, there are a group of specialized companies that sell a specific product category like grocery stores (Walmart, Kroger, Ahold Delhaize, Publix, ALDI), drug/pharmacies (Walgreens, CVS, Walmart, Rite-Aid), home improvements (Home Depot, Lowes, Menards, Ace Hardware), electronics (Amazon, Best Buy, Apple, Walmart), apparel (TJX, Nike, Gap, Nordstrom), and business supply stores (Staples, Walmart, Office Max). According to the Deloitte, *Global Powers of Retailing 2020*, 23rd *Annual Report*, almost two-thirds of the top 250 retailers have foreign operations. Over half of the leading retailers are in the fast-moving discount consumer goods product sector, including clothes, cleaning supplies, toiletries, furniture, kitchen appliances, electronics, school, office supplies, and recently added groceries. Today, their focus for growth, except Amazon, which is only online, has been opening new warehouses domestically and overseas, developing their e-commerce business, and opening online ordering pick-up locations. Many boutique retail stores in shopping malls have remote factories for production, marketing, sales, and distribution facilities. They are also expanding overseas in developed and developing countries with an emergence of a middle class. This increased specialization by task or function has resulted in additional sub-specializations in target market sales such as business-to-business, business-to-consumer, and the global supply chain.

Notes

All dates, innovators' information, and events have been checked against information in the following sources: *Encyclopedia Britannica, Encyclopedia Americana, Collier's Encyclopedia, Compton's Encyclopedia, Investopedia, and Wikipedia.*

i Pomeranz, Kenneth and Steven Topik, *The World That Trade Created,* M.E. Sharpe, 2013 3rd edition, Chapter 1.

ii The term naval stores originally applied to the resin-based components used in building and maintaining wooden sailing ships, a category which includes cordage, mask, turpentine, rosin, pitch, and tar.

iii One hundred and sixty acres and larger farms were very large by European standards.

iv The leaves of *Agave fourcroydes* cactus yield a fiber called henequen, which is suitable for rope and twine but not of as high a quality as sisal. It is the major plantation fiber agave of eastern Mexico, being grown extensively in Yucatán, Veracruz, and Tamaulipas.

v A medium sized potato *with its skin provides*: Calories: 161, Fat: 0.2 grams, Protein: 4.3 grams, Carbs: 36.6 grams, Fiber: 3.8 grams, Vitamin C: 28% of the Required Daily Intake (RDI), Vitamin B6: 27% of the RDI, Potassium: 26% of the RDI, Manganese: 19% of the RDI, Magnesium: 12% of the RDI, Phosphorus: 12% of the RDI, Niacin: 12% of the RDI, Folate: 12% of the RDI and many antioxidants. It may improve blood-sugar levels, digestive health, and it is naturally gluten free.

vi A partially-mutualized marketplace within which multiple financial backers, grouped in syndicates, come together to pool, and spread risk.

vii https://research.stlouisfed.org/publications/economic-synopses/2021/09/20/technology-transfer-and-regional-trade-agreements (Accessed 12/30/2021).

viii https://research.stlouisfed.org/publications/economic-synopses/2021/12/03/the-rise-of-asia-as-a-destination-for-u-s-Patenting#:~:text=Third%2C%20this%20shift%20toward%20Asia%20has%20focused%20on,%28the%201st%20largest%29%20within%20a%20couple%20of%20years. (Accessed 12/30/2021).

7 Financing Innovations

Financing and investment in innovations are critical to the research, discovery, and success of a country's productivity growth, economic development, and global competitiveness. During the First and beginning of the Second Industrial Revolutions, the primary funding innovation source was self-funded bootstrapping from a person's savings or loans from family and friends. Family and friends' trust in the innovator and understanding the innovation was essential. Investors wanted to share emotionally and financially in the person's success. Family funding is still used today, but change began after the First Industrial Revolution as corporations became the primary source of innovations.

Corporations employed scientists offering attractive salaries and benefits, provided them with a laboratory, required materials, and copyrighted their inventions in their name. Corporations cover the copyright expenses, finances the innovation launching and production of the product or service, pays marketing and advertising expenses, and benefit from the innovation's financial success. This ownership change occurred as innovations became more significant in their sophistication, impact, and reward. A second change was the funds required increased as technical sophistication rose, and additional financial support was needed to achieve the most efficient production scale. Third, new forms of financial innovation begin to be invented in the financial markets for generating the required funding. A more comprehensive range of non-traditional financial investors in innovations emerged, such as institutional investors, retirement and pension funds, family offices, and foreign public sector wealth funds. Also, non-bank corporations began providing lower-cost financial services and allocated a specific portion of their exposure to startups and innovations as a new investment asset class. In addition, modern technologies like Internet crowdfunding enabled middle-income investors to participate in innovations. In addition, there has been increased global investment in startups and new innovations, reflecting the expansion in the number of worldwide millionaires and billionaires. Fourth, there are many inventions and innovations each year in more developed and developing countries resulting in greater competition.

The technological lifespan of new inventions has been shortened as new innovations replace the previous technological advance more rapidly. This shorter technological life cycle increases the financial risk of investing in an innovation that

DOI: 10.4324/9781003024675-9

might quickly become obsolete and requires higher immediate returns. But missing that once-in-a-life-time investment opportunity could be emotionally devastating. Fifth, it is increasingly challenging to control innovation opportunities as alternatives become reverse-engineered, with marketing improvements easily added to appeal to consumers. Sixth, universities and corporations' R&D departments and corporate-sponsored R&D laboratories have emerged and attracted, retained, and provided research support and security for innovators. Their activities and objectives are altering the motivations behind the financing of innovations. They have become the primary source of innovations, impacting market competition. The innovation process has become more structured by industry, and corporations now manage innovations to maximize their business performance from a market control, and profitability perspective. First, going from invention to innovation is increasingly controlled by the universities and corporations to suit their organizational strategy. So, innovations are subject to being managed on a cost-benefit basis to determine their financial significance more rapidly or be discontinued. Second, if the invention or innovation is successful, the company, university, or research lab manages the patent application and innovation process and related marketing costs. The inventor(s) name is usually on the patent to recognize their discovery, but the university or corporation retains the financial benefits. Third, there is often a gap or wedge between independent private innovators and employed innovators by a university or corporate R&D departments. The wedge is between a desire for financial return, research and development costs, the timing and risk results tolerance, and degree of independent personality. Fourth, the innovator may behave differently in selecting from the previous options depending on the alignment of their values, expectations, and self-confidence.[i] Fifth, the dependence on stock markets to provide an exit strategy for investors who funded the innovation is not always available to manage supporting capital flow to finance new innovations. Patent law reduces the risk facing existing innovations and investors, which implies a better rate of return over a more extended time. However, this protected, artificial environment may inhibit new innovations as the financing threshold rises. The following four innovation financing case studies illustrate various methods of financing successful startups. A first case is a group of wealthy Scottish investors providing funding for Scottish immigrant farmers to the USA using the farm as collateral for the loan.

Financing Case 7.1 The Scottish Immigrant Agricultural Financing by Scotland's Alliance Trust

Scotland's people were creative innovators, building business networks, and intelligent investors in Britain even before the First Industrial Revolution. According to Charles W. Munn. *Alliance Trust: A Short History 1888–2008*, Scots were known to travel widely and proved that they could assimilate to local conditions wherever they visited. They also had a reputation for demanding work, honesty, thrift, and taking calculated risks. They were attracted to America as they saw opportunities, and several investment companies in Edinburgh and Dundee began exploring the Midwest and Western agricultural and mineral opportunities. Dundee grew to be the primary center for the whaling industry in Britain. A shipbuilding industry had developed, so it had business connections in many of the world's major ports. During the US Civil War, the evenhanded businesspeople in Dundee sold sandbags and tents to both sides of the military and linen to plantation owners in the South. With investment returns low in Scotland, they explored America for better returns.

Several leading Dundee businesspeople met in October 1873 and decided that they wanted to lend money to farmers in Oregon and Washington. Neither area had many people, but the land was fertile, hills wooded, gold discovered, and the rivers had salmon, and they needed capital. A company was established in 1873 to make mortgage loans only on land close to centers of population and transport links, with a loan size equal to one-third "based on the land's agricultural value, excluding any mineral value." The lending strategy was to have a network of agents trusted to make accurate judgments about a property's value to set the loan amount. The Dundee Mortgage and Trust Investment Company was formed and registered to operate anywhere in the USA and Canada. Australia and New Zealand with an authorized capital of £500,000 as only £300.000 was called. By 1879 the shareholders were receiving an annual dividend of 10%. By 1876, returns were good enough to encourage expanding the business to other US areas.

The success of savings banks in California. which were not allowed in Oregon and Washington, resulted in The Oregon and Washington Mortgage Saving Bank being incorporated in Scotland in 1876. The business model was to invest funds in first mortgages secured by real estate. By 1879 deposits only equaled £11,600 from 150 depositors, and the bank had mortgages of £19.400 on 80 farms. The annual net profit was £670, of which £150 was held in reserve, and the dividend to shareholders was 6%. The Dundee Land Investment Company was established in 1878 with an authorized capital of £100,000 as only £15,000 was called, and £75.000 borrowed, and its policy was highly speculative and ambitious. Land for quick sale or rental was acquired in Indiana, Illinois, and Iowa and selected Texas, Kansas, and Nebraska areas through its local 14 agencies. It was hoped that Scottish settlers would purchase the land, secured by crops either in the ground or above the ground. This expenditure would help to reduce weather risk. Another way to minimize weather and other supply or price risks emerged in a commodity hedging instrument. Banks and other financial markets were also used to hedge against foreign exchange risk. Thus, if the farmers thought the crop price would rise, they might sell the product forward when they believe it would be higher. This hedging instruments cost was less expensive than investing in storage facilities to hold the product until the price moved to a higher level. Dundee Land also bought a three-quarter interest in 162,000 acres of timber and grazing land in Tennessee and Kentucky for $37.000. Then they also bought 250,000 acres in New Mexico and 200,000 acres of Mississippi bayou in Arkansas at between 50 and 75 cents per acre. These large land tracks brought fraud, squatters, policing costs, and little or no revenue. The Board of Dundee Land hired a Scot with an agricultural background to oversee the agents and inspect the purchased land. Despite the USA's recession in the mid-1880s, the Dundee Land Company had success with land in Texas's panhandle and the 800,000-acre Matador ranch, transferred from a Texan to Dundee ownership sold in 1951 for a handsome profit. In 1880 returning from Australia, the Oregon and Washington Savings Bank Chairperson set up the Hawaiian Investment and Agency Company with 218 shareholders, of whom 170 were in Scotland and 17 in Hawaii. The return on land investments was less than in Texas, so a new, more conservative company, the Western and Hawaiian Investment Company, was created and eventually became the Second Alliance Trust in 1923. In 1884 the new company returned 16% on its capital, but its share price was below par.

In the early 1880s, it was a boom period for the range cattle industry. Texas Land and Cattle Co., the Matador Land and Cattle Co., and the Hansford Land and Cattle Co. were established by Dundee businesspeople who joined together to become Alliance Trust. Alliance retained shares in the mineral interests through the company Toreador Royalty. A former Indian Scout and Texas Ranger, Charles Goodnight became one of the great Texas cattle owners, and his ranch was part of the Dundee mortgage portfolio. In 1888, due to US legislation, to enable them to continue in the USA, they needed to operate the same business in Scotland. The Dundee Mortgage and Trust and the Dundee Investment Company merged to create the Alliance Trust with an authorized capital of £950,000, of which £220.000 was paid up, £700,000 was in debentures, and £160,000 in preference stock. The new Alliance Trust began diversifying its investment portfolio to include railroads. As deal size grew for large development projects, more deals were funded through syndications, which helped diversify risk. The 1893 financial panic in the USA hurt agricultural prices, and the cost of land fell. As farmers defaulted, Alliance Trust took over the management of the farms and cotton plantations. By the time the US economy recovered before WWI, Alliance had added $12 million in 3,500 mortgages on the security of US land covering 2 million acres and US railway bond holdings reached £1,000,000, and by 1915 the Alliance Trust dividend was raised to 19%. In the 1920s, Alliance Trust began to invest more in US securities and bonds and less into US mortgages, and the dividend was raised to 25% in 1926. Under US law, it is possible to separate land surface ownership from minerals ownership, which Alliance Trust did whenever surface land was sold.

Alliance sold the Chavez Grant in New Mexico to the US Government, and it became part of the Los Alamos atomic development in 1941. In Texas, Oklahoma, and Louisiana Alliance made leases for oil, gas, and coal with prospecting companies, many of which went into total production, paying a standard royalty of one-eighth of receipts (12.5%). In the 1950s and 1960s, Alliance Trust switched out of fixed interest securities into equities when they rose remarkably. US investments remain a significant share of Alliance Trust's operations today.

Source: Adapted from Alliance Trust: A Short History 1888–2008 by Professor Charles W. Munn, OBE, FCIBS, University of Dundee and used by permission of Alliance Trust PLC.

In Britain's agriculture sector, the farm's size was initially small, un-fenced, and most plowing, planting, and harvesting were done by hand, with the output primarily feeding the family. The development of the animal-drawn plow enabled the farmers to provide for their families and sell or trade a small part of the harvest with others. However, the end of feudal landowners and the emergence of farmer land ownership, the growth in the size of farms, and the larger farm's fencing enclosure also helped expand productivity and output. The introduction or expansion in animal fertilizer further helped to raise crop yield. By investing in these developments, the farmer could accumulate surplus funds to sustain the family in harsh weather or infestations and expand the farm's output. On the demand side, urban centers' growth created an increasing need for food, putting pressure on farmers to change traditional farming methods.

Farmers did not immediately accept the invention of agricultural machinery because of its cost, and it was untried. Gradually, it became possible for farmers to invest in new machinery and grow their farms' size to expand productivity and output, lowering the cost per production unit. Lower food prices increased the demand, enabling farmers to grow their businesses and invest in additional mechanization from more significant revenues. The production of agricultural machinery required iron and eventually steel and became manufactured in factories in larger quantities lowering costs and giving rise to more jobs, increased incomes, and the demand for healthier meals. Farmers' focus shifted to considering the number of acres appropriate for their new machinery and the amount of time between growing seasons to prepare the soil for the next planting, fertilizing, and harvesting. Financing Case 1 provides insights into how these innovations were funded.

Financing Case 7.2 The Cyrus McCormick Financing Story

Cyrus McCormick and his family financed from farm income and friends the construction of the reaper. It took nine years for the farmers' culture to change before the first reaper was sold. After that, all reapers were built in the family farm blacksmith shop to control costs. In 1843 Cyrus finally sold 29 reapers and 50 reapers the following year for $100 each. Then McCormick licensed someone in Brockport, NY, and Cincinnati, OH, to make and sell reapers in specific areas, and by 1846, about 190 reapers were sold. In 1847 McCormick moved production to Chicago, which was closer to the prairies and incredible lakes. With limited financing available, McCormick had to find a business partner. Cyrus partnered with an earlier licensee Mr. Gray and began building a larger factory to produce his reaper and made 500 for the 1848 harvest season. Gray sold to William Ogden, a Chicago developer and investor W.E. Jones, a total of 1,550 reapers for the 1850 harvest.

After that, Cyrus ran his business without partners and recruited family members to join him in Chicago to run the McCormick Harvesting Machine Company. He created a manufacturing system equipped with the best possible tools and a marketing, sales, and distribution system run by family members. In 1848, he raised his reaper's price to $120 and provided a written guarantee, with the farmer paying $30 at purchase and the rest in six months at the end of the harvest season. The sale was conditional on the machine cutting 1.5 acres an hour with a full refund if the device failed. The following year, the price was raised to $125, with the farmer paying $35 cash plus freight from Chicago and the balance due December 1, and 6% interest on the loan balance from July 1. Cyrus set up 19 agents and warehouses at specific high crop production customer locations to improve sales and increase access to reapers to ease delivery and provide better service and repairs.

McCormick became a millionaire after relocating to Chicago, and during the Panic of 1857, the McCormick family invested heavily in Chicago real estate. In 1858 he married Nancy Fowler, a good business partner and advisor to Cyrus. The Chicago fire in 1871 destroyed their factory. They rebuilt a more contemporary and extensive factory at the original location with a capacity of up to 15,000 machines per year. McCormick's engineers improved the self-raking reaper, self-binder machine, mowers, etc., and only one person needed to operate his advanced reaper. In 1902 the McCormick Harvesting Machine Company became part of the International Harvester Company.

Angel Startup Financing

Wealthy individual investors looking for opportunities continue to play a significant role in financing innovations, as illustrated in Financing Cases 2 and 3. The process has become more formalized by the startup's development, survival, and expected persistence. Today, many countries' startups are financed by "Angels" and "Accelerators" that offer support services and funding opportunities for launching a new business. Companies that use Angel investors or business Accelerators are typically early-stage startups and beginners that have moved to the "concept" stage. Angel investors are often wealthy individuals that provide a reliable financial support source to allow innovators to take the initiative to step toward proof of concept and production. The term "Angel investor" refers to people who choose to invest in startup businesses and often are experienced entrepreneurs who can recognize a promising idea based on their own experience in a particular industry. When they contribute a certain amount of money to a new company, the Angel investors will gain an ownership interest in the startup. If the startup is successful, the Angel investor may share an agreed percentage in its profits.

Financing Case 7.3 James Watt Financing the Steam Engine and the Birth of the Factory

James Watt's steam engine development is an excellent example of the early financing manufacturing of products in a factory. In 1754, Watt's mother and brother died, and his father suffered a financial loss from a shipwreck. At age 18, Watt took a position as an instrument maker apprentice and then took a job at the University of Glasgow as a "Mathematical Instrument Maker" in the physics department. He partnered with a Chemistry Professor, Joseph Black, and made nautical instruments. In the early 1760s, Watt met Professor John Robinson, who introduced James to the Newcomen steam engine as the university was studying why large machines used so much steam to operate. His solution was that since steam was elastic, it would rush into a vacuum cylinder and be condensed without cooling the cylinder. He incorporated a separate condenser chamber into which moisture would move by the piston's force. During the following couple of years, Watt improved the Newcomen steam engine by eliminating atmospheric pressure. In Watt's engine, the piston's downstroke was caused by a vacuum in the cylinder below the piston by evacuating steam from the cylinder into the condenser chamber. Watt also improved the seal around the piston by using grease and lowered the condenser steam temperature to enhance the piston chamber's vacuum. He located the steam chamber alongside but below the level of the piston cylinder. The steam chamber was attached to a pump with a piston operated by a thin rod connected to the main pumping beam, making the engine's operation automatic. The effect was to reduce the amount of heat used to drive the cylinder's pumping force, which reduced the amount of coal needed to about 70% of the Newcomen's engine. This change reduced the operating cost and pollution of the Watt engine.

Watt's next challenge was to produce a full-scale model engine and commercialize his invention to meet the industry's needs. Watt had received financial support from his friend at the University, Professor Joseph Black, who had provided Watt a significant loan. In 1769, Watt obtained a 14-year patent for his engine and gave John Roebuck two-thirds ownership of the patent to pay off Watt's loan from Professor Black. Black had earlier introduced Watt to John Roebuck, a part-owner of Canon Iron Works and a coal mine owner with a water flooding problem.

In 1768, Watt became close friends with **Matthew Boulton (1728–1809, a British manufacturer and business partner of Scottish engineer James Watt)**, a wealthy and successful Birmingham manufacturer. Boulton's wealth came after he married a wealthy heir Mary Robinson who died in 1753 childless. Watt had previously visited Boulton's Soho machinery factory, which was one of the largest factories, and Boulton wanted to manufacture Watt's steam engine. However, Roebuck, who owned two-thirds of Watt's steam engine patent, only offered a license to sell the machines in a limited Midland area. Boulton declined the offer because the area was too small to cover building the production facilities. Instead, Roebuck agreed to finance Watt to construct a full-size engine over his mineshaft. Unfortunately, Roebuck's men did not have the skills to complete the job, and Roebuck began to run out of money and eventually became bankrupt in 1773 when credit availability collapsed. Boulton was a significant creditor of Roebuck, and in settlement of the latter's debt, he took Roebuck's share of Watt's steam engine patent in 1773, and Watt's partnership with Roebuck ended.

Meanwhile, Watt had taken a surveying job to sustain himself and his family. In 1774, at age 38, Watt quit his survey job, left Scotland, and moved to Birmingham (where Boulton resided), the second-largest metropolitan area in England. Watt's steam engine's 1769 patent was to expire. In 1783, Boulton and Watt applied to Parliament for an extension, and in 1775 it was extended 25 years and covered Scotland and England. Bolton's collateral became his two-thirds share of Watt's steam Engine Patent. Thus, the Boulton and Watt partnership to build steam engines began and was the main driver of the First Industrial

Revolution. Watt was the inventor, and Boulton provided the commercialization, substantial capital, management expertise, business initiative, and ability to influence Watt. Boulton made Watt's inventions a commercial success and excelled at marketing and negotiating deals with customers.

Watt developed creative improvements to the steam engine between 1774 and 1787 and with Boulton's skillful ironworkers' help they produced high-quality products. Watt's prototype was disassembled and moved to Soho, where Boulton's machinists reassembled and modified the steam engine making several simplifications that improved its efficiency. Watt knew the seal between the piston and the cylinder needed to be improved to become an even more efficient energy producer. Watt arranged a meeting with John Wilkinson, who had developed a new water-powered, precision drilling mill that could bore a smooth, uniform barrel hole for the cannons he produced. In 1775, after receiving Wilkinson's new iron cylinder and piston, Watt and Boulton quickly rebuilt an improved, more efficient operating steam engine that used less than half the Newcomen engine's fuel. Wilkinson installed five-Watt steam engines in his foundries to power blowers for blast furnaces and pumped water out of his coal mine. Other foundries followed the Wilkinson example and purchased Watt engines. One of the Watt engines had a 50-inch diameter piston for pumping water out of a mine to give an idea of the machines' size. Wilkinson also used Watt–Boulton steam engines to power a tilt hammer for pumping in Paris's waterworks and powering a 70-foot steel barge.

To expand the Watt–Boulton steam engine's market and uses, Watt pursued additional patented inventions such as rotating motion, which was the type of action used by most machines in cotton and textile factories. Wilkinson continued to be responsible for boring the cylinder holes for the pistons for Watt's engine for the next 20 years. Boulton and Watt also developed a creative sales agreement for their steam engine. They would deliver and install the engine free of charge, and the buyer would pay only an annual rent amount equal to one-third of the cost of the fuel saved by replacing the Newcomen engine with the Watt engine. In 1781 Boulton saw new markets in corn, malt, and cotton mills and urged Watt to invent a steam engine's rotary motion. Watt developed his so-called sun-and-planet gear to replace the steam engine's original reciprocating action, using a shaft that produced two revolutions for each steam engine cycle. The sun and planet gear converted reciprocating motion to rotary motion by fixing a cogwheel at the end of the rod connected to the steam engine's main beam. With the main beam's movement, the cogwheel (planet) revolved around and turned the second cogwheel (the sun), a second rotating cog or gear fixed to the drive shaft generating a rotary motion. When both sun and planet have the same number of teeth, the drive shaft completes two revolutions for each double stroke of the main beam. The planet gear is fixed to the connecting rod and thus does not rotate around its axis. The following year Watt patented the double-acting steam engine, in which the piston was pushed and pulled by injecting steam above and below the piston.

Over time the startup funding process has become more structured into steps or stages of successful performance allocations than in the 1800s when there were far fewer new inventions than today. Also, the funder is segmented by industry specializations. Starting a company today, an Angel investor might invest as much as $10,000 to $50,000 to help with research, development, and proof-of concept-costs, and they may become a partner in the venture. If the invention proves successful and the business takes off, Angel investors expect their initial funding to return and a certain profit percentage. Often, Angel investors know well and have been actively involved in the business in which they invest. Therefore, Angle investors are connected to a network of other investors and are familiar with relevant industry specialists, engineers, accountants, lawyers, and marketers who can help startups develop a successful business and marketing strategy to drive profitability.

Consequently, startup inventors should make sure that they are compatible with the Angel investor's personality. If inventors want to benefit from an additional, genuine interest in their business, Angel investors are worth considering. Angel investors will only invest in companies they believe can generate a high Return on Investment (ROI). Once they contribute funds to an idea, they will support it through its entire journey and do all they can to help the venture succeed through its launch stages. An Angel investor can serve as a credible option for new innovations that do not yet qualify for a business loan if they are willing to give up part of their control and ownership of the new company. Investor confidence in the invention will determine the number of financing stages or rounds necessary before its product or service becomes an innovation with its own growing income stream. The greater the investor uncertainty of the invention's impact, the more the financing rounds of smaller amounts. Each funding round may be smaller until the investors become convinced that the idea is reasonable and doable. If it is believed to be a potential "unicorn," this significantly impacts innovation and commercialization. Unicorns often turn quickly to the IPO option to fund themselves and, if successful, can raise billions almost overnight.

Financing Case 7.4 The Guglielmo Marconi Financing Experience

A different early financing model is Guglielmo Marconi, born in Italy to a wealthy Italian business family whose mother was Scotch-Irish and taught Marconi to speak and write English. Marconi was privately educated in Bologna and studied college-level physics under several well-known professors. He was interested in science and knowledgeable of Maxwell, Hertz, Lodge, and Righi's works in electromagnetic waves. Righi was a neighbor of the Marconis and familiarized Guglielmo with Hertzian electromagnetic waves, which Marconi reproduced. Then, using Lodge's coherer device, he began experiments in generating and receiving wireless signals at home. Marconi continued to expand the signal's distance by using antennas and location reflectors to obtain a directional beam that could travel over hills and beyond sight. When the Italian government showed little interest, Marconi went to England and found the British postal system interested and filled for a patent in 1896 in London. He returned to Italy to demonstrate to the Navy land to ships at sea communications. His British patent was approved, and he applied for an Italian patent and established the Wireless Telegraph & Signal Company (later, he changed Wireless to Marconi).

Marconi returned to England to perform a transmission test for Lloyds over 18 miles, and the newspaper Daily Express obtained news using Marconi's system. In 1898 Marconi began to commercialize and market his wireless communication system. There were reports on events like yacht racing to help Queen Victoria who received radio messages about the Prince of Wales's health from the royal yacht at sea. SOS help signals sent from a sinking lightship sent lifeboats to rescue the ship's crew, and news of the event increased Marconi's wireless system sales. Marconi continued expanding the distance of wireless signals reaching 75 miles in 1899. He began having permanent transmission/receiving stations built in several locations. In New York the same year, Marconi communication equipment broadcast Admiral Dewey's victory in the Spanish-American War. Newspapers began using Marconi's equipment to broadcast America's Cup yacht races with the US defeat of England.

Marconi formed his American Marconi Company and launched his Marconi Internal Marine Communications Company for installing land-to-ship communication systems. He applied for another US and British patent for a tunable type of continuous-wave transmitter and receiver machines that could communicate at distinctly different frequencies to overcome the interference between several transmitters and receivers.

Marconi continued to expand the distances over which wireless communication signals could be transmitted using new patented inventions for sending and receiving. He also built his companies' businesses by commercializing his innovative technology, including microwave and beam technology.

Since the 1800s, many funding innovations have been developed as incomes have risen for the upper 10% of the population. More people have been educated about the value of innovations for economic growth and competitiveness, and they have witnessed the value of a unicorn's startup. As workers' income rises, they are more willing and able to invest more in startups. Often funding happens in a specific area started by launching a perceived unicorn company, as illustrated in Financing Case 4. Other startups in the same field as the unicorns often benefit by attracting funds from investors that could not afford or missed the opportunity to invest in the unicorn. They may also see unicorn-related startups as possible M&A targets if it takes off on their growth path to success. This action is a type of funding herd-effect that often gains momentum, attracting funders that do not want to miss being a part of something that is thought of as the product or idea of the future or potential launch of a whole new industry.

Professional Crowdfunding Fundraisers[1,2]

During the First and Second Industrial Revolutions, it was not easy to find financial backers unless the inventor was a member of the wealthy class with good connections. This challenge began to change during the Third Industrial Revolution with the innovation of the Internet. Other funding sources and opportunities have developed more recently. For example, with the emergence of the Internet, "**Crowdfunding**" is a more contemporary way of raising smaller amounts of investment funds for startups from many smaller investors and an occasional prominent investor in addition to family and friends. These smaller investors are willing to risk smaller amounts of money for possible significant returns on startups that usually have a couple of years of operating and performance data.

There are two types of Crowdfunding donation-based and investment-driven. Initially, funders would donate to support a common goal in return for various rewards. Investment-based is where businesses need capital and sell ownership positions online in the form of equity or debt shares and have a potential for financial return. Crowdfunding is increasingly an online business model of smaller, specialized, local funding shops that bring together a broader investor audience of doctors, business executives, professors, and retired professionals. Crowdfunding has had a more positive experience with Kickstarter's launch as a way new tech and non-tech companies can raise seed funding and validate their new products or services. **Kickstarter** was launched in 2009 by **Perry Chen**

(1976–, an American artist with the idea), Yancey Strickler (1978–, an American author and music critic), and Charles Adler (an American product builder and entrepreneur) with global investors. Kickstarter fees are if your project is successfully funded, the following fees will be collected from your funding total: Kickstarter's 5% fee and payment processing fees (between 3% and 5%). If funding is not successful, there are no fees. Many more crowdfunding copycats help raise funding for new and continuing startups.

For example, *Kickstarter.com, Crowdfunder.com, Somolend.com, Seedinvest.com*, and a continually growing number offer online platforms for operating startups looking for second-stage and higher funding. Crowdfunding accelerates Angel investing and allows startup management to pitch to a sizeable Internet audience via regular Zoom video conference briefings and quarterly performance update reports. The audience can track and ask questions about the young company's performance and plans. The amounts raised during the pre-arranged funding window may vary between a couple of hundred dollars to $50,000 or even larger sums in anticipation of sharing the benefits of the startup company's initial public stock offering (IPO) or acquisition by another major company in the same industry. Crowdfunders usually charge 5% if the target amount is raised.

Crowdfunding is about raising money and building relationships with a larger group of potential customers who would benefit from the product/service and demand for it. As the innovation barriers are eased, additional small to mid-size tech companies will participate due to more affordable engineering and Crowdfunding. This process is an excellent opportunity for small businesses to raise additional funds from investors who have already invested in them. Crowdfunding is popular among startups because it can raise funds at a lower cost and more efficiently than traditional methods of raising capital. It allows startups, who are legally responsible for funds raised, to raise funds in a much shorter time, which means they can potentially raise much more money for their startup, which supports their success. Thus, Crowdfunding provides advantages over other strategies like venture capital and Angel investing, which require the new venture's entrepreneur to raise funds.

Commercial and Industrial Banks[3–7]

Commercial banks are among the smallest funding sources for startups because of their higher risks of success and loan repayment concerns. However, there are specialized commercial banks that will fund innovators through various stages of growth. **Silicon Valley Bank** is one of the best-known sources of innovation startup financings with offices in significant innovation centers. Its home office is in Santa Clara, California, the USA's most important innovation hub. Silicon Valley Bank has helped fund more than 30,000 startups throughout the USA. Specialized smaller business banks offer personalized loans or short-term equipment loans or leases to second and later-stage startups requiring financing. Bank loans are usually short-term loans for up to a couple of years unless they have government small-business-supported lending programs.

The limited amount of bank financing for new venture financing may well be the absence of an identifiable source of consistent revenue to cover the debt-servicing costs and loan repayment. When developing an innovation pitchbook for your investor audience, keep this concern in mind if you pitch to a bank. Even if you decide not to pitch to a bank for funding, you may want it to provide its business services for the company you are starting.

Private Equity Venture Capital Financing[1,2,7–9]

The next level of funding for new companies as they qualify for additional funding rounds or growth stages consists of specialized investment or private equity new venture companies. There are two significant data providers on **Venture Capital (VC)** funding by all startup and later development stages and industry sectors for the US and global markets provided by *Preqin* and *Pitchbook*. They identify more than 35 thousand VC investors participating in over 400 thousand deals with 90 thousand VC-backed companies and close to 20 thousand VC funds. Private equity and venture capital are primarily used in the USA, Europe, Israel, and Australia.

Venture capital is a form of equity financing relevant for young companies with innovation and growth potential but untested business models and no history. The development of the venture capital industry is considered a vital framework to stimulate innovative entrepreneurship. US venture capital financing for startups or young companies with innovation and growth potential employing less than 20 people has increased since 2000. VC financing is now a significant source of entrepreneurial funding in the USA and continues to expand globally. Since 2010 VC investments have been increasingly concentrated in the Information and Communication Technologies (ITC) sector, followed by the life sciences sector. VC seeks to generate significant returns, primarily in industries with low capital requirements on small initial investments, such as ICT and life sciences. In sectors with higher capital requirements such as real estate, infrastructure, mining, and raw material processing attract smaller VC funding. At the same time, private equity and venture capital investments are usually held for seven to ten years for payout. However, there is an active secondary market in which portfolios of startup assets can be sold a couple of years after launch to free up capital for more attractive opportunities or changing market trends. Leading secondary investment firms with current dedicated secondary capital above $5 billion include Lexington Partners. AlpInvest Partners, Ardian (formerly AXA Private Equity), Capital Dynamics, Coller Capital, and HarbourVest Partners. Additionally, major investment banking firms, including Credit Suisse, Goldman Sachs, JPMorgan Chase, and Morgan Stanley, have active secondary investment programs.

The Riverside Company is a global private equity firm focused on investing in growing businesses valued at up to $400 million. Since its founding in 1988, *Riverside* has made more than 850 investments. The firm's international private equity and structured capital portfolios include more than

140 companies. *Riverside* seeks to foster long-term growth through fundamental operating improvements and add-on acquisitions. *Riverside* often partners with sellers seeking to remain involved in the company and aligning interests to drive growth. *Riverside* strives to add value for all of its stakeholders by using an operating-intensive approach, expertise in various industries, and systems and strategies designed to make companies bigger and better. *Riverside* seeks to grow companies organically via new products, expanding markets, enhancing operations, and improving processes. It also carefully considers strategic add-ons that can accelerate growth.

The preceding examples of funding sources for innovators operate on the production or supply side of launching and developing new companies by innovators. Every commercial bank helps innovators by providing credit to support consumer demand for their purchases, including innovators' new product(s) or service(s). This type of bank consumer financing is indirect or broad support. It offers electronic payment services, cash management services, credit cards, credit instruments, home equity, and other loan types to consumers to buy the product they would like to own or use. It is like having an in-house bank to provide credit to your product or service buyers. Because this funding carries less risk associated with the financing, the number and types of finance available are more numerous and readily available.

Commercial banks' lending is directly influenced by economic conditions, inflationary pressures, and a specific bank's financial condition and strategy. These factors are under the influence of the country's regulatory and economic policies of the Central Bank. 2021–2022 is an excellent opportunity to launch a business as interest rates are low with liquidity readily available. As the COVID-19 pandemic has slowed during the first half of 2022, economic activity is recovering, and M&A activities are expanding. One exception has been the COVID-driven healthcare technology investment which in 2020 rose 50% to a new high exceeding $50 billion, bringing the total outstanding healthcare investment from all sources to $10 trillion. More robust investment sectors include early detection diagnostics like lateral flow tests, early intervention therapies, and precision medicine for different illnesses. For example, investment in nanomedicine alone has increased annual average growth by 50% over the past five years.

After a startup company passes through all the primary financial support sources, its next opportunity is to be acquired by a larger company, remain a private company, or go public with an **Initial Public Offering (IPO)**. More extensive, established companies usually have their in-house Research & Development (R&D) departments to research and initiate further innovations, products, or services. They also monitor the launch of new startups that might compete with their existing products or have a new product or service they would like to own and add to their complementary business line. In this case, they would try to acquire the startup company based on their perceived future value of the acquired company's new product(s) or service(s). The acquired company becomes part of the existing firm, which may or may not retain the startup's innovator(s) to help manage the company's future growth.

The second option is the **IPO** and offering shares in the new company on a public stock market to raise capital for growth while retaining its ownership. If the startup company has performed well, the IPO can be gratifying without surrendering direct management control from a financial and ownership perspective. However, it does become subject to market approval regarding its performance, and its stock price may vary accordingly. Suppose the IPO is not an option a startup wants because of the accompanying follow-up and regular government reporting requirements and costs. In this case, it can seek the advice of a Venture Capital company or an Investment Bank's professional advice to remain independent (private) or support the startup through an M&A process.

Another alternative is to sell itself to a **Special Purpose Acquisition Company (SPAC)**. A SPAC is a shell corporation listed on a stock exchange to acquire a private company, making it public without a lengthy and costly initial public offering. According to the US Securities and Exchange Commission, "A SPAC is explicitly created to pool funds to finance a merger or acquisition opportunity within a set timeframe." The opportunity usually has yet to be identified. Selling to a SPAC can be an attractive option for the owners of a smaller company, often a private equity fund. First, it can add up to 20% to the sale price compared to a typical private equity deal. Being acquired by a SPAC can also offer business owners a faster IPO process under the guidance of an experienced partner, with less worry about the swings in broader market sentiment. SPACs raised a record $82 billion in 2020, and nearly $90 billion in SPAC funding was raised in the first half of 2021.

The Expansion of Corporate Innovations[2,8,9]

In Britain, the USA, and Europe, beginning with the First Industrial Revolution, the golden age of innovation was launched, which continues today. Entrepreneurs collaborated with wealthy industrialists who understood the industry's needs and sought educated people in the field, well experienced and creative. Inventors began working in university and corporate research laboratories funded by the parent business entity, wealthy individuals and families, or other successful inventors. The inventors required good personal and professional references and needed to understand the complexities of the challenge. For example, James Watt improved Thomas Newcomen's first steam engine's efficiency with the invention of an improved and more efficient atmospheric steam engine. It brought about an unknown energy source to power machinery in factories anywhere and birthed the large factory corporation. As corporations grew, they quickly realized they would have to innovate to keep up with continually changing customer needs to remain competitive domestically and internationally to survive.

As corporations realized the link between long-term and sustainable profits and innovations, they began to create internal Research and Development (R&D) and Laboratory Research operations and recruit proven scientists to develop the next innovation. These researchers had the certainty of employment with a respectable income plus benefits. If they (usually working in teams with other scientists) were successful in their research, the patent would be in their names(s) with a small bonus. However, the company would own all rights to the invention and bear the innovation and commercialization costs. This arrangement provided guaranteed income and benefits, employment security, and recognition for the inventor. Still, the company covered all the innovation costs and received all the benefits, including revenues, as they owned the patent and invention. Corporations removed the inventor's uncertainty, and today, over three-quarters or more of patents are designated to inventors working for companies. Unlike those very disruptive events driving the First and Second Industrial Revolutions, there is an increase in many more minor impact-continuous innovations.

The emergence of corporate innovation has not replaced independent innovators, but it has become the largest funding source of R&D and innovations. Even if a non-corporate inventor(s) launches an attempt to commercialize its product or service, it may be bought by a large company that the new startup could disrupt. Consequently, large companies, particularly technology oligopolists in their industry, protect their existing product line and reputation and control innovation competition from outside by individual innovators. Granted, the corporate acquirer rewards the real unicorn very well with an attractive salary and desirable research facilities.

Government Funding[7,10–12]

Spending by government agencies on research and development (R&D) is best represented by **America's Defense Advanced Research Projects Agency (DARPA)**, which other developed nations are now trying to duplicate. DARPA contracts out its work like financing Moderna to explore messenger RNA to make vaccines, resulting in their COVID-19 vaccine seven years later. DARPA's other successes include the computer, Internet, GPS, drones, stealth technology, etc. In addition, another growing source of funds supporting research and innovations comes from governments in providing scientific grants. **Government Grants** from various departments are for several years and focus on specific scientific research projects with objectives. These grants and loans, in some cases, fall under general government grant and loan guidelines that may contain specific rules and regulations regarding patent ownership which require careful review before committing to the grant. For example, US Government grants (www.usgrants.org/) are non-repayable financial awards and incentives from federal agencies, public for-profit, and not-for-profit organizations. They are given to individuals, businesses, and professional organizations to stimulate/grow the economy and create job opportunities. Substantial grants are often funded through a university or company research department (medical, agriculture, technology, physics, chemistry, mathematics, etc.) and require monthly or quarterly reporting of progress and expenditures. Table 7.1 summarizes the various startup and small business funding sources by the funds needed and the innovation business stage.

Table 7.1 Sources of Funding for Inventions and Innovations

Family & Friends	*Special Investor Funds*	*Major Financial Centers*	*Corporations*	*Government Grants & Loans*	*Not-for-Profit Foundations*	*Foreign Investors*
Relatives	Angel Investors Accelerators	Banks Large & Medium-Sized	Private Public	Federal & State	Universities	Banks
Crowdfunding	Incubators	Investment Banks	R&D	All Agencies & Departments	Foundations	Funds Investors
Personal Loan	Venture Capital Loan	Mutual Funds	New Product Development	www.grants.gov	Wealthy Families	Diaspora
410k Roll Over Business	Microloans	HELOC	R&D Research Labs	Government Research Labs	Top 100 Nonprofit Organizations	Remittances Wealthy Families
Startups	Small Business Credit Cards	SBA loan				Abroad
Reward-Based Crowdfunding	Venture Capital Companies	Personal Loan for Business				Foreign Corporations
Kickstarter	*FundingPost*	Equipment Financing				
Equity-Based Crowdfunding:	IPO companies	Purchase an Existing Business				
Donation-based						
Investment-based						

Source: Authors

Banking and Finance Infrastructure in the Global Economy[3]

The evolution and development of the world's financial systems was an exceptionally long process beginning with humanity's creation and the emergence of consumers' and producers' needs. Initially, farmers and craft families negotiated transactions to buy and sell goods and services to meet their needs. Since not all countries have the same resources or are not at the same economic development stage, international trade has many advantages. There are several benefits to businesses that participate in international trade. A domestic business's value is access to a larger market and a diversification of its market risk since, typically, not all countries are in the same business cycle phase. Foreign buyers' economies may have more robust demand and purchasing power for the seller's products or services than the home country. Since inventions and innovations are built on earlier innovations, international commerce provides the most significant exposure for new creations. Increasingly, small domestic and especially foreign startups in the USA and Europe need only a computer, website, and access to the Internet to start a business selling to friends internationally.

International trade became more complex as more countries were formed, and trade between countries grew. During the First and Second Industrial Revolutions, buyers and sellers in different countries searched for a common medium of exchange they could trust and rely on to make it easier to price and exchange their goods and services globally. Gold and silver coins were nice but cumbersome to carry and subject to fraud and robbery. Furthermore, a few countries' gold production has historically been controlled, raising concerns regarding their supply reliability. Global gold output has averaged a 1% annual growth rate significantly below most countries' full-employment or natural growth rates. There is concern about whether the total gold output growth is sufficient to support full-employment growth rates or maintain a fixed exchange rate between countries' currencies. Therefore, tying a country's currency to gold becomes a severe constraint on growth and employment.

There are two parts to establishing a global vehicle of exchange. First, a currency must be acceptable to facilitate transaction needs within a country. Secondly, it should be a stable medium of exchange to finance trade between nations. Two countries' currencies may change in value at different rates over time, creating a risk of losing the importance of purchasing power by one of the countries' currencies in each transaction. The problem becomes even more complicated when transactions do not occur immediately but happen over time. There are now 200 different countries, and most have separate currencies. If they used single or common currency, they would require a standard monetary and economic policy management system. Not all countries are at the same stage of development or the same phase of the business cycle. Some countries, usually former colonies of an advanced country, continue to use the developed colonizing country's currency if that developed country is still its principal trading partner. The International Monetary Fund (IMF), *Annual*

Report on Exchange Arrangements and Exchange Restrictions, identifies countries' primary common currency. They are the US dollar area consisting of 38 countries and the Euro currency area with 25 participating countries. According to the Bank for International Settlements (BIS), over 80% of global trade is conducted on a US dollar currency and value basis. This development has dramatically benefited the expansion of international trade and capital flows. Volatile currency risk becomes part of the cost of international business, and there exist hedging instruments to protect against a potential exchange rate change for most international transactions. Coordination among countries on economic policies through international organizations such as the IMF helps stabilize currencies and reduce currency risks, enhancing international commerce and the movement of capital.

The increasing interlinkages of an ever-more-open global economy stimulate further global business expansion. The US dollar provides four critical functions to ease this growth: a medium exchange, unit of account, store of value, and standard for deferred payments. Society and countries learned from experience that supporting a stable and reliable currency requires a sound financial system. And this requires a Central Bank to manage the money supply, interest rates and facilitate the government's borrowing and debt service payments. It also is expected to ensure the soundness of a prudential banking system, payment system, and financial infrastructure that supports real GDP growth to achieve full employment levels. Avoiding financial crises enables increased economic stability, a steady full employment growth rate, and a continuous innovation environment.

Future Evolution of Financial Markets

As the world economy grows, the need to finance transactions using modern technologies and processes to ease efficient financial settlement is rapidly changing. This evolution will affect and change the current roles of money, currency, banking, central banking, and the existence of the multiple specialized types of product-specific and risk-specific financial markets. To better understand this change, let us first explore the world's structural financial emergence.

Tipping Point: Cultural Change Toward a More Creative Europe

In Europe, the First and Second Industrial Revolutions induced growing populations, burgeoning cities, and increasing demand for food, goods, and services. This demand was met by both old and new methods of production. The shift toward larger farms and animal herds and commercial crops such as wool and grains, capital investment in machinery, and servile labor's freeing completed the manorial system's decline in agriculture. Aided by the steam engine's invention, manufacturing boomed, especially for products used in armies and fleets' outfitting – cloth, armor, weapons, and ships. New mining and metalworking technology made the profitable exploitation of large-scale capital investment in the rich iron, copper, gold, and silver deposits in central Germany, Hungary, and Austria.

One measure of Europe's economic development is the spectacular growth in the population of specific cities. For example, Antwerp doubled its population in the second half of the 15th century and doubled it again by 1560. Under Habsburg's patronage, Antwerp became the primary European entrepôt for English cloth, an international banking network hub, and the principal Western market for German copper and silver, Portuguese spices, and Italian alum.[ii] By 1500 the Antwerp Bourse (stock and commodity exchange) was the central money market for much of Europe. Other cities profited from their circumstances. Lisbon became the Portuguese maritime empire's home port. Seville was the Spaniards' gateway to the New American World. London served initially as the capital of the Tudors and became the center for Britain's textile industry and banking activity. Lyon was favored by the French kings as a market center and capital of the silk industry. Augsburg served as Germany's principal north-south trade route and was the Fugger Family merchant banker's headquarters.

During the Renaissance period of the 15th and 16th centuries, cities appeared as markets for a culture where beliefs stressed human beings' potential value and goodness, emphasized everyday human needs, sought rational ways of solving human problems, and launched an educational and creative environment. The tipping point for the launch of the Renaissance was the impact of the Black Plague, one of the most destructive pandemics in human history, killing people throughout Asia and Europe as it spread along trade routes and through trading ports.

New mechanical and mathematical discoveries of **Copernicus, Harvey, Kepler, Galileo, and Newton** transformed traditional science. Translations of ancient Greek scientific works increased interest and knowledge in physics, astronomy, medicine, botany, and other disciplines. Renaissance philosophers formulated the rules of the deductive and inductive methods by which scientists worked. The Renaissance made its most significant contribution to modern science in mathematics, particularly arithmetic and geometry.

One of the most critical technological advances was the emergence of printed books. They documented progress in many fields resulting in the spread of knowledge and the cross-fertilization of ideas with new perspectives. With movable metal type, printing about the mid-15th century in Germany was invented by **Johannes Gutenberg (1398–1468, a German goldsmith, inventor, printer, and publisher).** Gutenberg drew from block printing on wood and papermaking by the Arabs from China and the Flemish oil painting technique to create a new printers' ink. **Johann Fust (1400–1466, a German painter, goldsmith, lawyer, and financial backer of Johannes Gutenberg)** and **Peter Schöffer (1425–1503, a German printer and manuscript copyist)** developed casting metal type and locked it into a wooden press. The development of printing amounted to a communications innovation that transformed human learning and enlightenment. At this entrepreneurial development stage, people learned from others across civilizations and how to apply new tools for analyzing data.

Development of Currency

Goldsmiths (jewelers) in England had been craftsmen, bullion merchants, money changers, and money lenders since the 16th century. They learned to be financial intermediaries from the scriveners (record keepers who could read and write) who were the first to record deposits for relending them. The Gold Standard in England became official in 1816, and guidelines were set up to issue standard banknotes representing a certain amount of gold. Merchants preferred to store their gold with London's goldsmiths because they had private, secure vaults. In exchange for each precious metal deposit, the goldsmiths issued receipts certifying the quantity and purity of the metal they held in trust. These receipts could not be assigned, so only the original depositor could collect the stored goods. The goldsmith's function of relending on behalf of a depositor was the basis of modern banking. Promissory notes were issued for money deposited, which by custom and law was a loan to the goldsmith and allowed them to make advances to other customers. This practice was a form of fractional reserve banking. Promissory notes developed into assignable instruments, circulating as a safe and convenient form of money backed by the goldsmith's promise to pay. Hence, goldsmiths could make loans in gold, promissory notes, or checking accounts.

The growth of urban centers and the emergence of industrialization stimulated finance and banking development. As companies' size, cost of machinery, and industrial factories grew, banking began to replace the self-financed more miniature craftsman family firms. Some of the Goldsmiths became the forerunners of great English banks as banks began issuing paper "banknotes," which circulated the same way government-issued currency circulates today. In the US, this practice continued through the 19th century, and at one time, there were more than 5,000 distinct types of banknotes issued by local US commercial banks. Only the notes issued by the largest, most creditworthy banks were widely accepted.

Since banks issued notes far more than the gold and silver they kept on deposit, sudden loss of public confidence in a bank could result in bankruptcy or "run on the bank" by depositors. Thus, in 1694, The Bank of England was granted sole rights to issue banknotes in England. In the US, the Federal Reserve Bank was granted similar rights after its establishment in 1913, and until 1933, government-authorized currencies were partially backed by gold or silver. The Great Depression in the 1930s was the first stage of failure of the Gold Standard. The price of gold was devalued when the US gold standard backing its currency was revised. In 1944 the Bretton-Woods agreement revived the gold standard with the US dollar exchanged for gold at $35 per ounce. The system was modified in 1971 when the USA realized that the dollar no longer required gold backing with the US government-backed confidence. The US dollar was recognized as the keystone of the international monetary system. The US Federal Reserve assumed the role of providing financial support to enhance the growth of the global economy. After that, global economies grew more rapidly, nearer their natural full-employment capacity. They were no longer constrained by insufficient gold production controlled by a few producing countries.

Emergence of Modern Banking Promotes Trade

With international trade expanding between countries, attention focused on developing a payment medium to finance international transactions smoothly and efficiently. Banking as we know it is traceable to medieval and early Renaissance Italy, to the prosperous cities in the north such as Florence, Venice, and Genoa. International banking spread from northern Italy throughout the Holy Roman Empire and northern Europe in the 15th and 16th centuries. The original banks were "merchant banks" that Italian grain merchants developed in the Middle Ages. Merchants and bankers grew in stature based on cereal crops' trade. Many displaced Jews fleeing Spanish persecution also were attracted to finance and commerce. They brought ancient practices from the Middle East and Asian silk routes and applied them to finance grain production and trading.

Development of International Trade Finance[10–12]

Gradually the British goldsmiths began to lend money on behalf of the depositor. A foreign draft is a bill of exchange drawn in one country and made payable in another country. It is a written order used in international trade that binds one party to pay a fixed sum of money to another party on demand or at a predetermined date and bypasses purchasing foreign currency and facing exchange rate risks. The bill of exchange takes the form of a bank draft, and the issuing Bank guarantees a fixed amount in whatever terms are agreed to by both parties after showing enough funds in the issuing Bank's account. The discounting of interest to the depositors against what could be earned by employing their money in the banks' trade soon developed. It was selling an "interest" to them in a specific transaction. This practice overcame the usury objection against charging an interest rate on the loan. It was also used as an ancient method of long-distance financing for the transport of goods. At trade fairs, money changers contributed to banking's growth by issuing documents redeemable at other fairs in exchange for hard or convertible currency. These documents could be cashed at a future fair or a fair in a different country and would often be discounted or the face value reduced by an amount comparable to the current interest rate. These documents evolved into bills of exchange, which could be redeemed at any office of the issuing banker and made it possible to transfer large sums of money without carrying large sums of gold.

Christians were forbidden to charge and accept interest on loans by the sin of usury, defined as lending at interest (Islam makes similar condemnations of usury). Non-Christian Jewish newcomers initiated a way to lend to farmers against crops in the field, a high-risk loan at what would have been considered usurious rates by the church. In this way, they could secure the grain-sale rights against the eventual harvest, and they then began to advance payment against the future delivery of grain. They made their profit from the current discount against the future price. This two-handed trade was time-consuming, and soon, a class of merchants was trading grain debt instead of grain. The Jewish trader performed both financings (credit) and underwriting (insurance) functions. Financing took the form of a crop loan at the beginning of the growing season, which allowed a farmer to cultivate (through seeding, growing, weeding, and harvesting) their annual crop. Underwriting a crop or commodity with insurance guaranteed the crop's delivery to its buyer, typically a merchant wholesaler. Also, traders performed the merchant function by planning to supply the crop buyer through alternative sources-grain stores or alternate markets, for instance, in case of crop failure. They could also keep the farmer (or other commodity producers) in business during a drought or other crop failure by issuing crop (or commodity) insurance against losing their crop.

Merchant banking progressed from financing trade on one's behalf to settling transactions for others and then holding deposits for the settlement of notes written by the people who were still brokering the actual grain. These deposited funds were intended to settle grain trades but were often used for the merchant bank's transactions. And so, the merchant's Bank in the large grain markets became centers for holding money against a bill of exchange or check.

By the end of the 16th century and during the 17th century, the traditional banking functions of accepting deposits, moneylending, money-changing, and transferring funds were combined with bank debt issuance that served as a substitute for gold or silver coins. New banking practices promoted commercial and industrial growth by providing a safe and convenient means of payment and a money supply more responsive to commercial needs and by "discounting" business debt. By the end of the 17th century, banking was also essential for war finance for European states' funding requirements. Increased war funding by banks led to government regulations and the first "Central Banks." New banking techniques and practices in Amsterdam and London helped spread the concepts and ideas elsewhere in Europe. The first Bank to begin the permanent issue of banknotes was the Bank of England in 1695. Initially hand-written and issued on deposit or as a loan, they promised to pay the bearer the note's value on demand. By 1745, standardized printed notes ranging from £20 to £1,000 were circulated. Fully printed currency for total flexibility in payment to anyone that did not require the payee's name and the cashier's signature first appeared in 1855.

In the 18th century, banks offered more services, including clearing facilities, security investments, checks, and overdraft protection. Checks were invented in the 1600s in England, and banks settled payments by direct courier to the issuing bank checks. Around 1770, banks began meeting in a central location, and by the 1800s, a dedicated space was established, known as a bankers' clearinghouse. The London clearinghouse used a method where each bank paid cash to the clearinghouse and then was paid cash by an inspector at the end of each day. The Royal Bank of Scotland created the first overdraft facility among banks in 1728.

The First Industrial Revolution and growth in international trade increased the number of banks, especially in London. At the same time, new types of financial activities broadened banking scope beyond its origins. The merchant-banking families dealt in everything from underwriting bonds to originating foreign loans. These new merchant banks facilitated trade growth, profiting from England's emerging dominance in seaborne shipping. Two immigrant families, **Rothschild** and **Baring,** established merchant banking firms in London in the late 18th century and dominated world banking in the next century. These banking and trade activities also provided funding for innovations in industry, business, education, and the arts. However, the emerging banking systems often suffered from fraud, mismanagement, and speculation causing financial crises. Crises necessitated increased government involvement and the emergence of bank regulations and **Central Banks** to enforce them.

Early Emergence of Merchant Bank's Financial Innovations

The credit providers and purchasers of debt were the merchant bankers involved in global commerce. Large family entrepreneurial empires and fortunes were created. **Cosimo de Medici and the Medici Family of Florence (1389–1464; until 1737)** were global entrepreneurial lenders, manufacturers, investors, importers, and exporters. **Jacob Fugger and Fugger Family of Augsburg (1459–1526; until 1640)** was an entrepreneurial urban merchant and financier of credit for debt and interest from many bourgeoisie local merchants and their families. They were also global entrepreneurs and traders and mobilized international merchant banking, money transfers, letters-of-credit businesses, insurance, and venture capital. These families also created corporations for mining, communications services, and cartels to promote monopolies like mining copper. Not all merchant bankers were successful. **John Law (1671–1729, a Scottish economist)** distinguished money, a means of exchange, from national wealth depended on trade. He participated in banking, gambling, the tulip price bubble crash, and the collapse of the Mississippi Company of France.

In contrast, **Richard Arkwright (1769–1843, a British inventor and a leading entrepreneur)** marketed and sold surplus UK and US goods through

Canton's port to a Chinese trader, **Wu Bingjian** or **Howqua (1769–1843, a Chinese entrepreneur).** Howqua was the most senior of the *hong* merchants in the Thirteen Factories and the Canton Chong leader. As a "hong" merchant, he was one of the few authorized by the Chinese government to trade silk and porcelain with Europeans in Canton (now Guangzhou) in the early 19th century. He became the richest man in the world.

Notes

All dates, innovators' information, and events have been checked against the information in the following sources: *Encyclopedia Britannica, Encyclopedia Americana, Collier's Encyclopedia, Compton's Encyclopedia, Investopedia, and Wikipedia.*

i Bergman, Dirk, and Ulrich Hege, "The Financing of Innovation: Learning and Stopping," Rand Journal of Economics, 2005.

ii Alum is a colorless astringent compound that is a hydrated double sulfate of aluminum and potassium, used in solution medicinally and in dyeing and tanning.

Part III

Global Innovation Expands World Interdependence – Entrepreneurial Capitalism

8 Value of Standards, Measurement, and Manufacturing

As the world emerged from the First Industrial Revolution, a transition occurred, moving production from the craftsperson's skills working out of their home to large factory mass production. In some cases, skills were passed on from the parents. The arrival of the factory focused on larger-scale production, and the larger workforce became more categorized and specialized by specific skills. Factory workers increasingly specialized their skills or functions depending on preference, experience, and training. Companies trained workers in new skills required to produce goods and integrate innovative technologies into the production process.

Specialization required focusing on worker objectives and how long the worker had to complete a function or activity before the product went to the next person. If one person or a group with a particular specialization could not do their job within a specific period, the whole production line would stop. Factory maintenance and holidays required an inventory of goods to give the factories' salesforce immediate access to products if sales rose unexpectedly. As machines became more advanced and controlled the production process, engineers designed, developed, and maintained the machinery with periodic updates in response to changes in demand and technology updates. Various manager levels were required to keep everyone on the production line executing their function to produce and assemble correctly on time. Senior-level management required knowledge about the industry, technology, economy, and changing customer needs to maintain market share and anticipate future demand and disruption risks for longer-term planning and stable growth.

Consequently, the timing and coordination of specific tasks had to be done to keep everyone full-employed and maintain factory efficiency and productivity. Since machinery is tireless and represents a considerable investment, there could easily be two or three shifts of 8–10 hours with a break for lunch and two short rest or coffee/tea breaks. Working schedules of three eight-hour shifts daily became common in the high-capital intensive industries like steel production, car production, electronics, and home appliance output.

While the engineer showed each specialized worker what work skills they needed to keep the production process working in unison, this function was eventually replaced by a production manager and the human resource

DOI: 10.4324/9781003024675-11

department (HR). The production manager assumed responsibilities to ensure all workers were in their positions and functioning as required to achieve the desired output. HR ensured that new hires had the desired skills and upskilled existing workers to meet changes in production needs. The next concern of the production manager became the quality of the product produced and reducing waste. Too many mistakes could drive up costs and not satisfy the sales force's demand, adversely impacting profits and reputation. Therefore, the importance of quality and production speed became increasingly crucial. More significance was assigned to the standardization of parts and substitutability of the components between the various models. Improved measurement devices to ensure standards of quality, size, or strength were required to maximize the effectiveness of these standardized and interchangeable parts along with the correct tools to install them appropriately and efficiently.

The increased demand for transporting goods grew during the First and Second Industrial Revolutions, resulting in more advanced road transportation and railroad development modes. Eventually, the same standardization would also apply to meet the rails' weight and speed bearing strength of the passenger or freight trains. And so that the train was not delayed by constant rail or wheel repairs. During the Civil War, the US government recognized the military and economic advantages of having a standardized railroad track gauge that measured 4 feet, 8½ inches. This track width was the same size as England when early railroad trains were developed. Subsequently, this gauge was mandated for the US Transcontinental Railroad in 1864, and by 1886 it became the standard width for all future train tracks. This decision involved the Federal Railroad Administration, the US Department of Transportation agency, the Association of American Railroads, and the US Department of Defense's Defense Standardization Program Office. By standardizing the railroad gauge, US cities experienced tremendous growth in the 20th century, bringing increased prosperity.

The continued growth in cities' size and infrastructure complexity indicated that a unique set of national standards would be necessary to ensure city dwellers' safety. Common standards became even more evident when a fire broke out in 1904 in Baltimore. The fire quickly spread to engulf an 80-block area. As firefighters came from New York, Philadelphia, and Washington, DC, they realized that their fire hoses could not connect to Baltimore's fire hydrants. Consequently, the fire burned for more than 30 hours and destroyed 2,500 buildings. A US survey of fire hose couplings found over 600 coupling types. A national standard was created one year later and established the US National Fire Protection Agency International and the National Safety Council. Building standards were also necessary, especially as buildings became skyscrapers and, in some locations, faced earthquakes, hurricanes, tornadoes, and tsunamis.

Interchangeable Parts

Gun making was considered a skilled craft in the 18th century, and firearms, including pistols and muskets, were all constructed by hand. Every gun was one-of-a-kind, and a broken weapon could not be easily repaired. During the First and Second Industrial Revolutions, machines replaced the manufacturing work previously done by men, and factories replaced artisans' workshops. The groundwork for this change introduced interchangeable parts in the firearms industry.

In the mid-18th century, **Honoré LeBlanc (1768–1861, a French gunsmith)** pioneered using interchangeable or pre-manufactured parts. He suggested that the gun parts be made from standardized patterns and easily replaced if broken. In 1785, LeBlanc demonstrated the value of the large-scale interchangeability of complex mechanical parts by disassembling musket locks, mixing the elements, and assembling them again. Le Blanc was inspired by French artillerists' work of **Jean-Baptiste Vaquette de Gribeauval (1715–1789, a French artillery officer engineer)** on interchangeability in artillery. Blanc's work and other French military officers led first by General Gribeauval and **Major Louis de Tousard (1749–1817, a French artillerist)** were taken to the new American Military. They were the basis for the later development of interchangeable manufacture by US military contractors. He wrote two influential books about a school for officers that became the blueprint for West Point and a manual for artillery officers.

Lieutenant General Gribeauval was a French artillery officer who revolutionized the French cannon – creating a new production system that allowed lighter, more uniform guns without sacrificing range. The Gribeauval system, replacing the de Vallière process, was essential to French military victories during the Napoleonic wars. In addition, Gribeauval is credited as the earliest known advocate for the interchangeability of gun parts and interchangeable manufacturing development.

Jean-Florent de Vallière (1667–1759, a French artillery officer) in 1726, became Director-General of the Artillery Battalions and Schools and reorganized and standardized the King's artillery. He standardized the French artillery pieces by limiting Canons produced for 24, 12, 8, and 4-pound cannonball weights. He improved the method used for founding cannons, replacing the technique developed by **Jean-Jacques Keller (1635–1700, a Swiss gunfounder)**. The de Vallière system used core drilling of bronze developed by **Jean Maritz (1680–1743, a Swiss inventor).** Maritz invented a vertical and horizontal drilling machine that provided higher precision of the canon bore shape and surface and higher shooting efficiency. The arrival of the Gribeauval system involved the standardization of cannons and shells. LeBlanc applied these concepts to muskets and used gauges and filing jigs to bring duplicate parts to interchangeability. Previously the parts' uniformity was achieved via cut-and-try methods, using jigs, gauges, and master models to guide hand filing.

LeBlanc was not alone in understanding the interchangeable part system. **Samuel Bentham (1757–1831, a British naval engineer)** pioneered uniform features in producing wooden pulleys for sailing ships. LeBlanc's idea did not catch on primarily because competing gunsmiths quickly realized the negative effect on their craft and livelihood. When LeBlanc tried to interest other European artisans, they were unreceptive due to skepticism about the system viability and fear that their employment and status might be threatened. LeBlanc turned to Thomas Jefferson, who was the US Ambassador to France. In 1789, Thomas Jefferson visited LeBlanc's workshop and was impressed by his methods and realized that such a system would free the USA from dependence on European sources for military equipment. Jefferson tried to persuade LeBlanc to move to the USA but was unsuccessful, so Jefferson wrote to the US Secretary of War with the idea and worked to fund its development. President George Washington approved the idea, and in 1798 a contract was issued to Eli Whitney for 10,000 muskets to be built with interchangeable parts.

In 1797, Congress voted to prepare the nation for war with France and allocated funds for new weapons. By 1801, Whitney failed to produce any promised weapons and was called to Washington to justify using Treasury funds. Whitney demonstrated assembling muskets by choosing from a supply of parts he brought and received renewed federal support. Although the last 10,000 muskets ordered came eight years late, they were judged to be of superior quality, and Whitney was asked to produce 15,000 more muskets within the next four years. Interchangeable parts became standardized in the USA when Whitney used unskilled workers to quickly assemble many weapons at a lower cost, making gun repair with replacement parts more acceptable.

Today interchangeable parts are taken for granted. If an M12 bolt is produced in the USA and an M12 nut imported from China, they fit together. World trade in manufactured goods requires worldwide standards for bolts, nuts, and screws, and today most of the world has adopted a common metric screw standard. The idea and benefit of interchangeability were realized before Honoré LeBlanc.[i] However, these were either loose tolerances, elementary parts, or expensive samples. For example, in Venice's Arsenal, wooden pieces for ships like benches were pre-cut so that they could be assembled with only minor adjustments. In 1720, **Christopher Polhem (1661–1751, a Swedish scientist, inventor, and industrialist)** developed interchangeable clock parts, but it did not spread beyond his workshops. In 1785, LeBlanc demonstrated the first large-scale interchangeability of complex mechanical components. Gribeauval continued this standardization, and by 1780, wooden pieces for canon carriages became interchangeable. Gribeauval also pushed for standards in the manufacture of the cannons themselves. "Go gauges/no go" to ensure that a cannonball fits in the barrel has been used since medieval times. In addition to the "Go/no go Gauge," Griebeauval added a second "no-go gauge" to check if the ball was too small. Only balls that passed through the go but not the "no-go gauge" were within acceptable tolerance limits. Later, additional requirements prevented egg-shaped balls from passing through a series of gauges. Musket locks have a much more complex design. A small piece inside the tumbler lock is necessary to fire the gun and has a complex shape and tight tolerances. The first to prove interchangeability for musket locks was **Guillaume Deschamps** in 1723, but his locks were too expensive.

The French Army tried to lower costs and increase quality by putting pressure on French gunsmiths. The gunsmiths supplied weapons to the American Revolution soldiers for profit and were less fussy. The French Army's attempt to force gunsmiths to sell their products to them was unsuccessful, and the Army was in danger of running out of weapons. Out of this problem, the idea was born to introduce interchangeable parts and replace the annoyingly stubborn craftsmen with more docile unskilled labor paid a lower wage. The French Army's purpose had nothing to do with ease of assembly or the possibility of in-field repairs under combat.

LeBlanc also developed many tools and gauges to ensure accuracy and hardened the parts slowly to avoid warping. The French government provided him with a workshop to produce interchangeable parts. He disassembled 50 locks, picked 25 locks at random, and assembled them again. The workshop was destroyed during the French Revolution. Le Blanc set up a second workshop and produced large quantities of interchangeable gun locks at a low cost before dying in 1801. The opponents of LeBlanc stopped the production of interchangeable parts, and France lost the knowledge of interchangeable parts.

Mass Production

UK mass production of interchangeable parts was first achieved in 1803 by **Marc I. Brunel (1769–1849, a French-born British engineer).** Brunel collaborated with **Henry Maudslay (1771–1831, a British machine tool innovator and die maker)** and **Simon Goodrich 1773–1847, a British engineer to the British Navy Board).** All three collaborated with **Brigadier-General Sir Samuel Bentham (1757–1831, a British mechanical engineer and naval architect),** the Inspector General of Naval Works Portsmouth Block Mills. The British Navy required 100,000 pulley blocks manufactured a year during the Napoleonic Wars. Bentham had already achieved remarkable efficiency at the docks by introducing power-driven machinery and reorganizing the dockyard system. Marc Brunel and Maudslay, a founding father of machine tool technology, developed the first industrially practical screw-cutting lathe in 1800 with standardized screw thread sizes. They also collaborated on designing block-making machinery. By 1805, the dockyard had been fully updated with the new purpose-built machinery. It took 45 machines to perform 22 processes on the blocks, to produce three sizes. The machines were made of metal, improving their accuracy and durability, and used markings on the blocks to ensure alignment. An advantage of this new method was increased labor productivity due to reduced labor-intensive managing the machinery. Labor productivity was increased since ten men could do what previously took more than a hundred. By 1808, the annual output reached 130,000 blocks, and some of the equipment was still in operation as late as the mid-1800s.

Eli Terry (1772–1852, an American inventor and clockmaker) used interchangeable wooden parts in clocks made with a milling machine as early as 1800. All clock pieces were interchangeable, and each part was labeled and interchanged as needed. The first mass production using interchangeable parts in the USA was the 1806 Porter Contract, producing 4000 clocks in three years. Terry crafted 4,000 wooden gear tall case movements when the expected annual average was about a dozen. Unlike Eli Whitney, Terry manufactured his products without government funding. Terry anticipated the potential of clocks becoming a household object. He produced clock wheels and plates a few dozen simultaneously using a milling machine. Jigs and templates were used to make uniform pinions to assemble all parts using a production line, making clocks affordable for the average US citizen.

Case Study #8.1 Significant Disruptive Inventors and Innovations – Mass Production and Interchangeable Parts: Clocks

Key Disruptive Inventors	**Eli Terry Sr. (1772–1852, an American inventor and clockmaker)**
Location	**USA**
Disruptive Invention	Mass-produced with interchangeable parts clocks at lower prices for everyone.
Problem Resolved	Clocks were produced by artisans one at a time and were expensive.
Solution Impact	Clocks became affordable for the average citizen, and factories set fixed working hours.
Economic Impact	Factory workers had access to inexpensive clocks to get to work on time.
Cultural Impact	Humans could switch from sunrise to sunset to track time using inexpensive clocks.
Inventors Education & Training	Terry served as an apprentice under Daniel Burnap, the forerunner of manufacturing. He opened his first clock shop at home in 1793, using wooden components for his clock mechanism. He received the first US patent for an equation clock granted by the US Patent Office. An equation clock is a mechanical clock that includes a tool that simulates the equation of time so that the user can read or calculate solar time, as would be shown by a sundial.
Innovation Environment	Favorable and active with the US Patent Office granting patents, Terry was awarded five patents by 1825 and was later granted more patents for advances in clock-making. Terry's former partners Seth Thomas and Silas Hoadley began making similar clocks on their own, as did other clockmakers who copied Terry's techniques and clock models.

Financing	Terry was self-financed by his clock-making and repair shop, and in 1804 Terry signed the Porter contract to produce 4,000 wooden clocks. Terry used low-cost apprentices to make rough-cut wooden wheel parts for journeymen to shape precisely into clockworks. He substituted waterwheel-powered machines to run saws and lathes to produce rough parts and replace apprentices. Terry created jigs and fixtures to make many interchangeable critical clock parts accurately and inexpensively, enabling Terry to sell many lower-priced shelf clocks. He produced 3,000 clocks compared to six to ten produced by a skilled craftsman per year. He sold his clock factory to his team member Chauncey Jerome who later owned the world's largest clock factory. Terry also produced tower clocks and the mass production of standardized wooden clocks, which enabled him to accumulate a modest fortune.
International Commerce	Most of Terry's wooden clocks were sold in the USA.
Major Success Factors	His major success was introducing mass production to clock-making in the USA, which emphasized producing large quantities of accurate interchangeable parts for the clocks keeping their price affordable.

As the third president of the USA, Thomas Jefferson successfully promoted interchangeability, and two armories were built, one in Springfield, Massachusetts, and one in Harpers Ferry, West Virginia. Harpers Ferry produced the first interchangeable locks. Gunmaker, inventor, and proponent of interchangeability **John H. Hall (1781–1841, an American inventor of the M1819 Hall breech-loading rifle and a mass production innovator)** was sent to Harpers Ferry to set up a workshop. Hall realized that interchangeability was about precision, and if conventional gun lock parts had an accuracy of ±0.2 mm, he needed ±0.02 mm for interchangeability. Hall achieved this interchangeability using 63 gauges to verify the tolerances of the components of a lock. He also invented new measurement techniques, developed more robust and more stable machines to reduce vibration, and improved the latest milling technology. By 1824 all the parts for his gun locks were interchangeable.

The crucial step toward interchangeability in metal parts was initially undertaken by **Simeon North (1765–1852, an American gun manufacturer).** In 1816 North created one of the first accurate milling machines in the USA to do metal shaping previously done using a file. Before 1832 both Simeon North and John Hall were able to mass-produce complex machines with moving parts like guns, using a system of rough-forged features. Followed by a milling machine that adjusted the components to near-correct size and then "filed to gage by hand with the aid of filing jigs."[ii]

The next step was interchangeability across various workshops, which was achieved in 1834 so that parts, wherever produced by North and Hall factories, were interchangeable. In 1849, the Springfield Armory earned interchangeability. After the war, hundreds of machinists and technicians working for the armories eventually moved to other industries and brought knowledge of interchangeable parts. Many new complex products benefited from the armories' experience, such as bicycles, sewing machines, adding machines, typewriters, and eventually automobiles. Sewing machine maker **Isaac M. Singer (1811–1875, an American inventor and businessperson)** and most auto parts producers achieved interchangeability mid-1850s.

Case Study #8.2 Significant Disruptive Inventors and Innovations – Mass Production and Interchangeable Parts: Sewing Machine

Key Disruptive Inventors	**Isaac M. Singer (1811–1875, an American inventor and businessperson)**
Location	**USA**
Disruptive Invention	He made significant improvements in the design of the sewing machine and developed an electric sewing machine for households. He was the founder of the first American multi-national business with the Singer Sewing Machine Company.
Problem Resolved	Walter Hunt and Elias Howe had patented sewing machines before Singer, but they were not readily usable.
Solution Impact	Most families could own singer sewing machines to produce and repair family clothing and other household textiles.
Economic Impact	The industrialization of garment and textile manufacturing and sewing became a global industry, creating new jobs.
Cultural Impact	Many homemakers and young women learned how to sew, make, and repair clothes at home, and some of them became particularly good and started their work at home sewing craft business.
Inventors Education & Training	Singer was one of eight children born to German immigrants and left home at 12 to join a traveling stage act.
Innovation Environment	The innovation environment was improving rapidly, and patent protection was well established.
Financing	In 1839 Singer obtained his first patent for a machine to drill into rock and sold it for $2,000, which he spent forming a traveling acting troupe for five years. He then developed and patented a machine for carving wood and metal in 1849 and went to New York to build a working prototype for which he received an advance

from A.B. Taylor & Co. After an explosion destroyed his prototype, he met G.B. Zeiber, who became Singer's financier and partner and moved to Boston to market his new wood carving machine prototype to printers, but there was little interest. Singer was asked to repair Lerow & Blodgett sewing machines. He received a patent to make several improving modifications to the device.

In 1856 Singer and several other manufacturers met in New York. Rather than fight each other about patents, the lawyer Orlando Potter set up the first "Patent Pool," enabling the production of complicated machines without legal battles over patent rights. Sewing machine manufacturers Singer, Grover & Baker, Wheeler & Wilson, and Elias Howe agreed to form the Sewing Machine Combination and not contest each other's patents. In 1856 the I. M. Singer Company produced 2,564 sewing machines, 13,000 in 1860, and continued to expand production after building a New Jersey plant, and by 1876 sales had reached 262,300. Singer invested in mass production based on interchangeable parts, cut his price in half while increasing his profit margin by 500%, and targeted the home market. At the same time, his competitors focused on the industrial market. Singer was also helped by his partner Edward C. Clark, who developed installment purchasing plans and a new trade-up program by accepting trade-ins, which caused sales to increase sharply. The Singer sewing machine was user-friendly and could sew 900 stitches per minute, far more than the accomplished tailor. As Singer cut his home use machine price to $10, he continued to dominate and grow his household market's significant share in the early 1880s. In 1885, Singer produced the first "vibrating shuttle" sewing machine, significantly improving the transverse shuttle design. He expanded into the European market and built two massive sewing machine factories next to railroad stations for easy and fast distribution. One is to make machines for home use and one for industrial use. 3,500 workers produced an average of 8,000 sewing machines per week, and as demand grew, he added more production floors and built his power station. Bombs severely damaged the factory, workers, machines, and surrounding areas during WWI. After the war, Singer rebuilt his factories and expanded production. His company offered tens of thousands of sewing classes for women and eventually teenagers' courses on making their attractive, stylish

(*Continued*)

(Continued)

	dresses. Home Education Classes for young women began to include sewing instruction and exercises. In 1863 the I.M. Singer Company was dissolved, but The Singer Manufacturing Company continued production with Singer on the Board, and he held 40% of the shares. In 1889 Singer demonstrated the first electric sewing machine and began mass-producing domestic electric machines. Poor pay and worker relations, including union disruptions and major factory accidents resulting in significant loss of worker lives, finally resulted in the Equal Pay Act in 1970 to raise compensation for some women workers. In the 1960s, the Japanese introduced improved production efficiency and aluminum body machines and products below the cast-iron sewing machines and eventually outselling Singer sewing machines. The textile and garment markets moved to the lowest-cost labor countries in Bangladesh with deplorable working conditions and many accidental deaths from fires and factory building collapses.
International Commerce	In 1885 Singer built a large plant in Glasgow and began to market his machines overseas. His sewing machine sales and offices expanded throughout developed countries to finish clothing and produce textile products at low costs. As a result, developing countries' clothing output became traded globally, and sewing machines became owned worldwide by most families.
Major Success Factors	Singer's improvements in the industrial sewing machine met the tailoring and leather companies' demands for a heavier and more powerful machine. Singer focused on mass production and interchangeable parts in his sewing machines to reduce prices below competitors. He also used creative time payment plans for his customers and offered training classes for homemakers. Teenage sewing classes became part of required Home Education classes in grammar and high schools.

Development of Standards and Measurements

Standards to reduce costs, improve efficiency, and support mass production are required. The shift from craftsperson design and custom-made products to industrialization and factory manufacturing to satisfy a growing population's demands required standardization and precise measurement. In addition, increasingly accurate measurement for design, production, servicing, and repair of manufactured products required establishing industry standards and sizes supported by global agreement and acceptance. These needs and the interchangeability of parts called for agreed-upon standards and measurements for all industries by their respective engineers and scientists. In some cases, the standards needed to be enforced by law/regulation to avoid segmentation in each industry and boost competition.

As the steam engine and the railroad emerged, the need for more accurate measures and standards grew. The British **Winchester Standards** emerged for a yard being 3 feet in length, a foot of 12 inches, with each inch equal to 3 barleycorns of about one-third of an inch each. Units of capacity and weight also became specified in the Winchester Standards. By the 17th century, the statute had set the measure of an acre (4,840 square yards), a rod (16.5 feet), and a furlong (660 feet). It took 8 furlongs to make a mile equal to 1760 yards. Several weight measures included the troy ounce for gold and silver metals and the avoirdupois pound for other goods sold by weight. **The Weight and Measures Acts of 1824 and 1878** established the **British Imperial System**, moving toward more precise measures. For example, a gallon was defined as equal to 10 pounds of distilled water at 62°F with the barometer reading at 30 inches, or 277.42 cubic inches. In the USA, the gallon was measured as 231 cubic inches at about the same time. In the UK, **The Weights and Measures Act of 1855** made the avoirdupois pound the primary unit of mass, **The Weights and Measures Act of 1985** defined imperial base units in terms of their metric equivalent, and the UK completed its transition to the metric system in 1995,

National Institute of Standards and Technology (NIST)

The National Institute of Standards and Technology (NIST) was established in 1901 by US Congress as a physical sciences laboratory and a non-regulatory agency of the US Department of Commerce. Its mission is to promote US innovation and industrial competitiveness by advancing measurement science, standards, and technology to enhance economic security and improve the quality of life. Today, NIST's activities are organized into laboratory programs that include nanoscale science and technology, engineering, information technology, neutron research, material measurement, and physical measurement. NIST's measurement standards laboratory, known as the National Metrological Institute (NMI), employs about 2,900 scientists, engineers, technicians, and support and administrative personnel. NIST also hosts 1,800 guest researchers and engineers from US companies and foreign countries and partners with 1,400 manufacturing specialists and staff at 350 affiliated centers worldwide. The **"Handbook 44"** published by NIST provides the specifications, tolerances, and other technical requirements for weighing and measuring devices. Congress made the metric system in commerce a legally protected activity through the **Metric Act of 1866**. In May 1875, 17 out of 20 countries signed the Metric Convention or the **Meter Treaty**. This Treaty also established the **International Bureau**

of Weights and Measures under the control of an international committee elected by the **General Conference on Weights and Measures**.

NIST is headquartered in Maryland with a Colorado facility, and its activities are organized into laboratory programs and extramural programs. In 2010, NIST was realigned by reducing the number of **NIST laboratory units** from ten to six consisting of Communications Technology Laboratory (CTL), Engineering Laboratory (EL), Information Technology Laboratory (ITL), Center for Neutron Research (NCNR), Material Measurement Laboratory (MML), and Physical Measurement Laboratory (PML). NIST also supports the **Manufacturing Extension Partnership (MEP)**, a nationwide network of centers helping small and mid-sized manufacturers create and retain jobs, improve efficiencies, minimize waste through process improvements, and increase market penetration with innovative growth strategies. The **Technology Innovation Program (TIP)** is a grant program where NIST and industry partners cost-share the early-stage development of innovative but high-risk technologies. The Baldrige Performance Excellence Program administers the **Malcolm Baldrige National Quality Award**, the highest performance and business excellence award.

NIST's Colorado laboratories are best known for NIST-F1, which houses an atomic clock that serves as the nation's official time source. From measuring cesium's natural resonance frequency, which defines the second, NIST broadcasts time signals via longwave radio station WWVB and shortwave radio stations WWV and WWVH from Colorado and Hawaii. NIST also runs a neutron science user facility, the **Center for Neutron Research (NCNR)**, which provides scientists access to various neutron scattering instruments. They use NCNR to research materials science, fuel cells, biotechnology, etc. Established in 1961, the **SURF III Synchrotron Ultraviolet Radiation Facility** serves as the US national standard for source-based radiometry throughout the generalized optical spectrum. All NASA-borne, extreme-ultraviolet observation instruments have been calibrated at SURF since the 1970s, and SURF is used to measure and characterize systems for extreme-ultraviolet lithography. The **Center for Nanoscale Science and Technology (CNST)** performs research in nanotechnology through internal research efforts and running a user-accessible cleanroom nanomanufacturing facility. This so-called NanoFab is equipped with lithographic patterning and imaging tools, e.g., electron microscopes and atomic force microscopes.

Measurements and Standards: Handbook 44[1]

NIST supplies industry, academia, government, and other users with over 1,300 Standard Reference Materials (SRMs). These SRMs are certified as having specific characteristics or component content, used as calibration standards for measuring equipment and procedures, quality control benchmarks for industrial processes, and experimental control samples. **Handbook 44** was published by NIST after the National Conference on Weights and Measures (NCWM) annual meeting. Each edition is developed with the Committee on

Specifications and Tolerances of the NCWM and NIST's Weights and Measures Division (WMD). The purpose of Handbook 44 is a partial fulfillment of the statutory responsibility for cooperation among states in the USA for securing uniformity of weights and measures, laws, and inspection methods.

NIST has established government-wide identity document standards for federal employees and contractors to prevent unauthorized persons from gaining access to government buildings and computer systems. In 2002, the National Construction Safety Team Act mandated NIST to investigate the collapse of the World Trade Center buildings 1 and 2 and the 47-story 7 World Trade Center in New York following the September 11, 2001, terrorist attack. The investigation covered three aspects: technical architecture, fire safety investigation, and the factors contributing to the probable cause of the collapses. Simultaneously, NIST established a research and development program to provide the technical basis for improved building and fire codes, standards, practices, dissemination, and professional assistance programs. Its purpose was to engage the construction and community leaders in implementing proposed procedures, rules, and codes. NIST also supplies practical guidance and tools to prepare better facility owners, contractors, architects, engineers, emergency responders, and regulatory authorities to respond to future disasters. The final report on the WTC Towers – including 30 recommendations for improving building and occupant safety – was released in October 2005. NIST's notable safety and security work in conjunction with the Technical Guidelines Development Committee of the Election Assistance Commission to develop the Voluntary Voting System Guidelines for voting machines and other election technology.

Four scientific researchers at NIST have been awarded Nobel Prizes for work in physics: **William D. Phillips** in 1997, **Eric A. Cornell** in 2001, **John L. Hall** in 2005, and **David J. Wineland** in 2012. All four were recognized for their atoms' laser cooling and the atomic clock's development and advancement. In 2011, **Dan Shechtman** received the Nobel in chemistry for his work on quasicrystals in the Metallurgy Division from 1982 to 1984. Also, **John W. Cahn** was awarded the 2011 Kyoto Prize for Materials Science, and the National Medal of Science has been awarded to NIST researchers Cahn (1998) and Wineland (2007).

The NIST has been a reference and benchmark for other countries, spreading its standards globally. Although NIST was established in the USA, the work of the NIST has spilled over to the rest of the world by helping to develop common international standards. The cooperation with each nation's position in standardization, especially large countries, has many benefits that reduce the cost of producing goods and services, improve efficiency to contribute to economic growth, and help in promoting international trade.

Standards, Measurements, and Technology

Standards allow technology to work seamlessly and establish trust so that markets can function without problems. They provide a common language to measure and evaluate performance, make interoperability of components made by different companies possible, and protect consumers by ensuring safety, durability, and market equity. Standards also protect against monopolistic control over equipment and machinery, servicing, and repair. NIST's portfolio of services for measurements, standards, and legal metrology provides the solutions that ensure measurement traceability. This ability includes quality assurance and harmonizes documentary standards and regulatory practices. The tools, information, and training provided by NIST, and the contributions and results produced by its staff, support advancements in research and technological innovation globally. In addition, they promote the economy's drivers in invention, improvement, entrepreneurship, and commercialization. Thus, NIST functions are crucial to successful and repeatable innovation utilizing calibration services and conformity assessment.

NIST provides calibration services to disseminate the primary physical measurement standards for commerce, industry, and research. Calibration services allow customers to achieve the highest quality in their measurement systems and provide assurance by communicating the NIST measurement results for carefully selected instruments and artifacts. Conformity assessment demonstrates that specified requirements relating to a product, process, system, or body are fulfilled. The conformity assessment includes the supplier's declaration of conformity, sampling, testing, inspection, certification, management system assessment, and registration. It also provides the accreditation of those activities' competence and recognition of an accreditation program's capability. Under the National Technology Transfer and Advancement Act (NTTAA), NIST coordinates federal, state, and local documentary standards and conformity assessment activities. Documentary Standards can specify terms, classifications of components, delineation of procedures, specification of dimensions, materials, processes, products, systems, services, practices, test methods, and sampling procedures, or descriptions of fit and measurements of size or strength.

The **National Voluntary Laboratory Accreditation Program (NVLAP)** provides third-party accreditation to testing and calibration laboratories in response to legislative actions or requests from government agencies or private-sector organizations. NVLAP accredited laboratories are assessed against the management and technical requirements published in the International Standard, ISO/IEC 17025:2017. The NIST quality system for measurement services is internationally recognized and meets the needs of the **International Committee for Weights and Measures (CIPM) Mutual Recognition Arrangement (MRA)** for recognition of national measurement standards. In addition, the NIST quality system is recognized as conformant to the ISO/IEC 17025 and ISO Guide 34 by the Inter-American Metrology System (SIM) Quality System Task Force and the Joint Committee of the Regional Metrology Organizations BIPM (JCRB). The BIPM is the International Bureau of Weights and Measures.

NIST supports accurate and compatible measurements by producing and providing Standard Reference Instruments that transfer the ability to refer to measures or generate reference responses based on specific NIST reference instrument designs. NIST supports accurate and compatible measurements by certifying and providing more than 1,200 Standard Reference Materials® with well-characterized composition or properties. These materials are used to perform instrument calibrations in units as part of overall quality assurance programs, verify the accuracy of specific measurements, and support new measurement methods.

Standards.gov is the pathway to standards solutions. Maintained by the NIST Standards Coordination Office, this website provides tools, programs, services, and educational resources about documentary standards and conformity assessment. Whether needing to synchronize your computer's clock using our online tools or find data about recent leap seconds, NIST Internet Time Services (ITS) has the required information. NIST operates several stratum-1 network time servers, which means their time is linked to UTC(NIST), the official NIST time. ITS also provides information on protocols and authentication, such as the DAYTIME, TIME, and NTP protocols.[iii]

American National Standards Institute (ANSI)

ANSI was initially formed in 1918 when five engineering societies and three government agencies founded the American Engineering Standards Committee (AESC). In 1931, the organization became affiliated with the US National Committee of the International Electrotechnical Commission (IEC), formed in 1904 to develop electrical and electronics standards. In 1928, the AESC became the American Standards Association (ASA). The present name ANSI was adopted in 1969.

Before 1918, these five US founding engineering societies: American Institute of Electrical Engineers (AIEE, now IEEE), American Society of Mechanical Engineers (ASME), American Society of Civil Engineers (ASCE), American Institute of Mining Engineers (AIME), now American Institute of Mining, Metallurgical, and Petroleum Engineers), and the American Society for Testing and Materials (now ASTM International) had been members of the United Engineering Society (UES). At the request of the AIEE, they invited the US government Departments of War, Navy (combined in 1947 to become the Department of Defense or DOD), and Commerce to founding a national standards organization.

ANSI itself does not develop standards, but it accredits standards generated by other standards organizations, government agencies, consumer groups, etc. It oversees the development and use of standards by accrediting the procedures of standards-developing organizations. The standards are set in an environment that meets the Institute's openness, balance, consensus, and due process criteria. ANSI is the sole US representative and dues-paying member of the **International Organization for Standardization (ISO)**. As a founding member of ISO, ANSI also plays an active role in its governance. ANSI is also a member of the International Electrotechnical Commission (IEC). In

2009 ANSI and NIST formed the Nuclear Energy Standards Coordination Collaborative (NESCC) to address the need for nuclear industry standards. A national organization representing each country that belongs to ISO is called a "member body." Each member body has a mechanism for identifying issues and developing a national consensus on the work being done by ISO Technical Committees (TC). Different countries are members of various committees. This mechanism is called the ANSI-Accredited US Technical Advisory Group (TAG) to the specific ISO TC in the USA. It may be referred to as the US National Committee (USNC). ANSI accredits TAGs in the USA. They must follow specific ANSI procedures, known as the Model Operating Procedures for US Technical Advisory Groups, to ANSI for ISO Activities. The primary purpose of the TAG (or national committee) for each country is to develop and transmit that country's position on activities and ballots related to the work of each ISO TC. These groups are delegates actively involved in the international negotiation and preparation of international standards. ASQ is a member of ANSI and is accredited by ANSI to be a standards-developing organization. ASQ annually declares to ANSI that it follows and supports the consensus process of developing American National Standards.

The International Standards Organization (ISO)[2]

International standardization and measurement are critical to global trade, commerce, international investment in goods and services, and the advance of knowledge globally. These worldwide standards allow the world economies to function as a unit for the good of humanity. **ISO** is an independent, non-governmental international organization located in Geneva, Switzerland, with a membership of 165 national standards bodies. In London, in 1946, 65 delegates from 25 countries met to discuss the future of International Standardization. In 1947, ISO officially came into existence with 67 technical committees (experts focusing on a specific subject). Its members bring together experts to share knowledge and develop voluntary, consensus-based, market-relevant International Standards that support innovation and solve global challenges. It could be about making a product, managing a process, delivering a service, or supplying materials – standards cover many activities. Standards are the distilled wisdom of people with expertise in their subject matter and who know the needs of the organizations they represent, including people such as manufacturers, sellers, buyers, customers, trade associations, users, and regulators.

ISO standards are voluntary, and it does not regulate or legislate, although countries may decide to adopt ISO standards as regulations or refer to them in legislation. ISO is derived from the Greek "isos," meaning equal, and "Whatever the country, whatever the language, we are always ISO," and ISO has developed more than 23,669 standards. Their program ranges from standards for traditional activities, such as agriculture and construction, through mechanical engineering, manufacturing, distribution, transport, medical devices, environment, safety, information and communication technologies, and good practice and services standards. For example, quality management standards help workers be more efficient and reduce product failures. Environmental management standards help mitigate environmental impacts, reduce waste and be more sustainable. Health and safety standards help reduce accidents in the workplace. Energy management standards help cut energy consumption. Food safety standards help prevent food from being contaminated. IT security standards help keep sensitive information secure.

ISO has developed 23,669 International Standards for 97 total production, operation, and service fields. The following is one example of the selective ISO guidelines regarding medical devices for illustration purposes. ISO 13485 MEDICAL DEVICES provides a guide to managing quality throughout the life cycle of a medical device. ISO 45001 OCCUPATIONAL HEALTH AND SAFETY reduces workplace risks and ensures everyone gets home safely. And 22000 FOOD SAFETY MANAGEMENT inspires confidence in your food products with this family of standards.

ISO 13485 Updated ISO 14971, MEDICAL DEVICES (Standards Example)

No medical procedure is without risk, but there are many ways to minimize it. One such method is through applying sound risk management processes to medical devices. The International Standard to do just that has been updated and is **ISO 14971.** The application of risk management to medical devices specifies the terminology, principles, and process for managing the risks associated with medical devices. It includes software as a medical device (SaMD) and in vitro diagnostic (IVD) medical products. Primarily intended for medical device manufacturers, the ISO standard promotes the safety of machines and equipment used for medical purposes. It covers the risks of injury related to the patient's health, the operator, and other persons and potential damage to property, equipment, and the environment. The standard was updated to better align with changes in medical device regulations around the world. The ISO 14971 revision clarifies the standard's technical requirements by including more detailed information on manufacturers' steps to meet those requirements. It also includes new and updated terminology to reflect current market needs. The guidance has been moved to the standard's accompanying technical report ISO/TR 24971, Medical devices – Guidance on the application of ISO 14971, revised in parallel. ISO 14971 was developed jointly by technical committees ISO/TC 2101, Quality management and corresponding general aspects for medical devices, and IEC/TC 62, Electrical equipment in medical practice, of the International Electrotechnical Commission (IEC), and with the active involvement of many regulators from around the world.

The Medical Device Industry Standards

The following is how ISO functions in the critical Medical Device Industry. There is no other industry in which product conformity is as crucial as designing and manufacturing medical devices. With significant expertise in the medical device manufacturing sector, NQA is ideal for assisting clients in implementing ISO 13485 and other medical device manufacturing standards. The medical device industry is responsible for designing and manufacturing a wide range of products to diagnose and treat illnesses and improve patients' health. Products range from imaging equipment to artificial joints and other implants and are used globally in medical research centers, hospitals, and universities. Because medical devices are essential tools for healthcare and directly impact public health and quality of life, their safety is imperative. Companies must follow relevant medical device manufacturing standards to create desirable outcomes for all parties and prevent device recalls. These standards help ensure that a manufacturing or design process can consistently produce the quality required to serve patients and healthcare professionals.

Technological Advances in Manufacturing

Manufacturing is defined as any process that uses manual and machinery to make raw materials, usually conducted systematically with labor division for each step. In a more limited sense, manufacturing denotes the fabrication process or assembly of components into finished products on a large scale. The most important manufacturing industries are aircraft, automobiles, chemicals, textiles, clothing, computers, consumer electronics, electrical equipment, furniture, heavy machinery, refined petroleum products, ships, steel, and tools and die. Mass production represented another critical advance in manufacturing, enabled by the development of interchangeable parts. Mass production transformed the work organization and developed the machine-tool industry by 19th-century innovators. The result of fabricating precision equipment capable of producing many identical parts made at low cost and a small, trained workforce significantly increased total (labor and capital) productivity.

Two innovators of the First and Second Industrial Revolutions and mass production forbears include **Eli Whitney**, the Cotton Gin inventor, who introduced the concept of interchangeable parts for guns. And **Henry Ford (1863–1947 an American industrialist and business magnate)** was the automobile pioneer who created the continuous moving assembly line. Whitney used a master design to develop many exact duplicative parts, and interchangeable parts could be manufactured with mechanical devices on a massive scale. Interchangeable parts allow for easy and faster assembly of new products and repair of existing worn or broken products. One custom-designed piece can replace another without re-fitting its grooves. Interchangeability aided in the explosion of the assembly line that would become the foundation of modern mass manufacturing. Interchangeable parts made manufacturing a faster process, and the assembly line allowed for the continuous sequential manufacturing of certain products.

By creating the first automobile that middle-class Americans could afford, Henry Ford converted the car from an expensive curiosity into an accessible vehicle machine that significantly impacted human mobility and lifestyles.

Ford's continuous assembly line production concept was composed of moving assembly-line mass production and high wages for factory workers on the assembly line completing a repeated function. His determination to produce quality goods at low prices and increased wages for workers makes him one of the most influential and benevolent businesspeople.

Henry M. Leland (1843–1932, an American precision machinist, inventor, engineer, and automotive entrepreneur) refined Ford's production process to make it more precise and thus founded two premier American luxury automobiles Cadillac and Lincoln. At Cadillac, Leland applied new manufacturing principles to the beginning automotive industry, including interchangeable parts. Leland sold Cadillac to General Motors in July 1909 for $4.5 million but continued as an executive until 1917. He formed the **Lincoln Motor Company** and received a $10,000,000 contract to build the V12 Liberty aircraft engine.[iv] After the war, the company was reorganized, and The Lincoln Motor Company Plant was retooled to manufacture luxury automobiles. The Liberty engine's design influenced the V8 engine used in the first Lincoln automobiles. In 1922, Lincoln became insolvent and was bought out by the **Ford Motor Company**. Henry Ford's Model T automobile changed the nature of the transportation industry. Leland helped bring the precision mass production of interchangeable parts into automobile manufacturing.

The First and Second Industrial Revolution imparted rapid economic growth between nations that evolved into today's massive global trade market. Manufacturing has grown exponentially since the inception of the assembly line, mass production, and interchangeable parts. Although negative social and class situations developed at times from this industrial explosion, it shows how humans can significantly change their lives through innovation. Interchangeable parts are components that are, for practical purposes, identical. They are made to specifications to fit into any assembly of the same type without custom fitting. Interchangeable parts were achieved by combining several innovations and improvements in machining operations and machine tools, such as the slide rest lathe, screw-cutting lathe, turret lathe, milling machine, and metal plainer. Additional innovations included jigs for guiding the machine tools, fixtures for holding the workpiece in the proper position, and blocks and gauges to check the accuracy of the finished parts. Electric power allowed individual machine tools to be run by electric motors, eliminating line shaft drives from steam engines or waterpower. Thus, electricity promoted higher speeds, making modern large-scale manufacturing possible. In addition, modern machine tools often have Numerical Control (NC), which evolved into **Computerized Numeric Control (CNC)** as microprocessors became available.

Sustainability Costs of Manufacturing

Manufacturing produces goods involving labor and machines, tools, chemical or biological processing or formulation, and the secondary industry's presence.

Thus, the term refers to various human activities from handicrafts to high tech. It is applied to industrial design, in which raw materials from primary industry are transformed into finished goods on a large scale. Such finished goods may be sold to other manufacturers to include more complex products (aircraft, household appliances, furniture, sports equipment, or automobiles). Alternatively, they can be distributed via the tertiary industry to end-users and consumers, usually through wholesalers, who sell to retailers and sell them to individual customers.

Manufacturing engineering for the production process transforms raw materials into a final product. Some industries, such as semiconductor and steel manufacturers, use the term fabrication to describe the production process. The manufacturing process begins with the product design and raw materials specification from which the product is made. These materials are then modified through manufacturing processes to become the required part or product. Modern manufacturing includes all intermediate processes required to produce and integrate components. Manufacturing provides necessary material support for national infrastructure and national defense. Most importantly, it employs the labor force and provides psychological satisfaction from what is produced and how it is used. It provides income and benefits for workers and families that support a decent living standard.

Since the Second and Third Industrial Revolutions, society has learned about the social costs and environmental damage that were initially unknown as new jobs were created for workers. Most manufacturing involves energy, which has changed from waterwheel power to wood burning, then fossil fuels. Society learned about the social and environmental costs which have grown as the economy has expanded. The clean-up costs of waste, for example, may outweigh the benefits of a product that creates it, and hazardous materials may expose workers to serious health risks. These costs have become known, and today there are efforts to correct them by improving efficiency, reducing waste, using industrial symbiosis, and eliminating harmful chemicals. In addition, the growing concern about the damage to the earth's environment and increasing risks to human life from climate change have caused governments to initiate new and increasingly restrictive pollution standards for manufacturing. In August 2021, President Biden issued an executive order for auto manufacturers to shift to 50% electric car production by 2030 to combat climate change and tackle the nation's largest source of greenhouse gas emissions from the internal combustion engine.

The negative environmental costs of manufacturing are being addressed legally. Developed countries regulate manufacturing activity with labor laws and environmental standards. Manufacturers may be subject to regulations and pollution taxes to offset the environmental costs of production activities. Labor unions have played a historic role in negotiating worker rights and wages. Environment laws and labor protections available in developed nations may not yet be known in the third world. Tort law and product liability impose additional costs on manufacturing. These are significant dynamics in the ongoing process, occurring over the last few decades, of manufacturing-based industries relocating operations to developing-world economies where production costs are significantly lower than developed-world economies and environmental regulations are less restrictive. Manufacturing has unique health and safety challenges and is recognized by the National Institute for Occupational Safety and Health (NIOSH) as a priority industry sector and in the National Occupational Research Agenda (NORA) to identify and provide intervention strategies for occupational health and safety issues.

Evolution of Manufacturing Engineering

Manufacturing Engineering is a branch of professional engineering that shares many common concepts and ideas with other engineering fields such as mechanical, chemical, electrical, and industrial engineering. However, from a macro perspective, manufacturing engineering requires planning manufacturing practices, research and developing tools, processes, machines, and equipment, and integrating the facilities and systems to produce quality products with efficient capital allocation. The manufacturing or production engineer's primary focus is to turn raw material into updated or new products in the most effective, efficient, and economical way possible and in line with environmental regulations and industry standards. Manufacturing engineering is based on core industrial and mechanical engineering skills, adding essential elements from mechatronics, commerce, economics, and business management. This field also integrates various facilities and systems for producing quality products with appropriate expenditure by applying physics principles and manufacturing systems studies.

Manufacturing engineers develop and create physical products, production processes, and technology, including design and development. Manufacturing engineering is considered a subdiscipline of industrial and systems engineering and strongly overlaps with mechanical engineering. Manufacturing engineers' success directly impacts the advancement of technology and the spread of innovation. This field of manufacturing engineering emerged from the tool and die discipline in the early 20th century. It expanded further since the 1960s when industrialized countries introduced factories with numerical control machine tools, automated production methods, and advanced statistical quality control methods. These factories were pioneered by the electrical engineer **William E. Deming (1900–1993, an American engineer, statistician, professor, author, lecturer, and management consultant)** who was initially ignored. The same quality control techniques later turned Japanese factories into world leaders in cost-effectiveness and production quality. Industrial robots on the factory floor, introduced in the late 1970s, cut costs and improved production speed. These computer-controlled welding arms and grippers can quickly and flawlessly perform simple tasks such as attaching a car door 24 hours a day.

History of Factory Manufacturing

Many historians regard **Matthew Boulton's Soho Factory** established in 1761 in the UK, as the first modern factory. Similar claims can be made for **John Lombe's Silk Mill** in the UK in 1721 or **Richard Arkwright's Cromford Mill** in the UK in 1771. The Cromford Mill was purpose-built to accommodate the equipment and take the material through the various manufacturing processes. In the 19th century, British colonies built factories only as buildings where many workers performed hand labor, usually in textiles or sugar production. However, factories proved to be more efficient for administering and distributing materials to individual workers than earlier manufacturing methods, such as cottage industries or the putting-out system. Cotton mills used inventions like the steam engine and power looms to pioneer the industrial factories of the 1800s, where precision machine tools and interchangeable parts allowed greater efficiency and less waste.

Henry Ford further revolutionized the factory concept and manufacturing engineering in the early 1900s with mass production innovation. In Ford's case, highly specialized workers would build an automobile alongside a series of conveyor belts. This concept dramatically decreased production costs and reduced production time for all manufactured goods. It brought about the age of "consumerism." Modern manufacturing engineering includes all intermediate processes required to produce and integrate components. Automation is used in various manufacturing methods, such as machining and welding, and automated manufacturing refers to the application of automation to produce goods in a factory. The main advantages are higher consistency and quality, reduced lead times, simplified production, reduced handling, improved workflow, and provided better worker morale.

Computer Integrated Manufacturing, Robotics, and 3D Printing

The manufacturing sector has been undergoing significant changes by introducing more advanced technologies. Since the 1980s, machinery has become controlled by computers. **Computer Integrated Manufacturing (CIM)** can be considered an advanced production process that unifies a company's administration, engineering, and manufacturing. **Massachusetts Institute of Technology (MIT)** is credited with pioneering the development in CAD and CAM to meet aerospace industries' design and manufacturing requirements after WWII. Manufacturing technology available during the late 1940s and early 1950s could not meet the design and manufacturing challenges arising from the need to create sophisticated aircraft and satellite launch vehicles. The US Air Force approached MIT to develop suitable control systems, drives, and programming techniques for machine tools using computer electronic control. **Joseph Harrington** conceptualized CIM in his book in 1974 titled *Computer Integrated Manufacturing* (CIM) that served as an introduction to the field of CIM. In 1984 engineers began seeing the potential advantages of Harrington's approach. According to the US National Research Council, CIM improves manufacturing productivity by 40–70% by enhancing engineering productivity and quality. CIM can also decrease design costs by

15–30%, reduce overall lead time by 20–60%, and cut work-in-process inventory by 30–60%.

Information technology plays a significant role in planning and controlling the manufacturing process. It uses computers and communication networks to transform automated manufacturing systems into interconnected systems that cooperate across all organizational functions. The goal of CIM is to integrate all functions within an operation. This goal includes marketing, order entry, accounting, design, manufacturing, quality control, shipping, and other supporting departments to work closely together throughout the process. CIM requires a new management perspective and careful planning of each technical element. The value is the increased efficiencies, minimizing raw material input and waste, responding rapidly to current market trends and sales, adjusting requirements, and minimizing inventory. The result is a growing link between consumer demand customized CIM.

CIM provides information by linking each operation task by computer, giving decision-makers access to needed information. Tasks can be performed in parallel, not in sequence. CIM's potential lies in creating a network of people and activities to accelerate decision-making, minimize waste and speed up customer response while producing a high-quality product. CIM is a strategic policy within a company, and a total commitment is required at all company levels to provide the optimal benefit. There are several advantages of computer-integrated manufacturing systems. First is cost reduction because of the interlinkages of all the business segments. Second, improved and current information handling reduces manufacturing time, and enhanced accuracy and time savings translate into reduced costs and process time for an operation. Third, the preceding provides better use of capital resources through work automation, higher productivity, and lower overall business costs. Finally, the automation of the entire production process shifts management's emphasis from supervising people to supervising machines to being on top of changing market demands and tastes.

Notes

All dates, innovators' information, and events have been checked against the information in the following sources: *Encyclopedia Britannica, Encyclopedia Americana, Collier's Encyclopedia, Compton's Encyclopedia, Investopedia, and Wikipedia.*

i Evidence of the use of interchangeable parts can be traced back over two thousand years to Carthaginian ships that had standardized, interchangeable parts that came with assembly instructions insert "tab a into slot b" marked on them. In East Asia, during the Warring States period bronze crossbow triggers and locking mechanisms that were mass-produced and made to be interchangeable.

ii A jig is a device that holds a piece of work and guides the tools operating on it.

iii The foregoing information has been adopted from www.nist.gov (Accessed May 18, 2021.

iv The Liberty L-12 was an American 27-liter (1,649 cubic inch) water-cooled 45° V-12 aircraft.

9 Innovation and the Future of Earth

Earth is a body of fixed natural resources. To avoid the limits of these resources, humanity must develop new ways of using them by expanding total factor productivity to elevate the standard of living and continue to progress. This process is accomplished through innovations initiated by inventors and implemented by entrepreneurs applying new technologies created using scientific knowledge for beneficial purposes.[i] An entrepreneur sees a business opportunity using the latest technology and convinces investors of the value of taking on greater than normal financial risks to implement the creative, disruptive innovation. All the required components for innovations to occur are sensitive to different risks. Innovations help avoid the limits of nonrenewable natural resources and support increased adoption of sustainable technologies prolonging life on Earth. International trade in goods and services, global capital flows, and immigration transmit growth and development most efficiently worldwide.[ii] We have identified and traced significant disruptive innovations that changed how humans improve their living standards on Earth. While a few entrepreneurs and their creations stand out as significant disruptive innovations identified in the Case Study Boxes, many inventors and innovators contributed along the way.

Robots are replacing workers in the manufacturing sector, and the Covid pandemic may accelerate this process. Rising unemployment and underemployment will curtail consumer income and demand for goods. Past patterns suggest that these workers move into the services sector without other opportunities, often with lower compensation. Thus, the decline in the population growth rate may continue as income disparity expands.

Key Innovation Tends[1–4]

Innovations are expected to continue increasing, but they will become more expensive and complex. Several trends emerge from the First through the Third Industrial Revolutions, which will impact future entrepreneurial activities and innovations in the Fourth Industrial Revolution. The following sections provide context for each of the eight emerging trends.

DOI: 10.4324/9781003024675-12

First: Innovations in Global Finance Expand[5–7]

Global finance, including banking and insurance, is currently dominated by a few large multinational institutions of universal commercial and investment banks and insurance companies. Developed countries have followed an open-door policy concerning freedom of capital flows between countries, except for anti-money laundering and financing of terrorism, to seek its best risk-adjusted return. The US dollar remains the key global currency for international transactions and countries' reserves, and the Federal Reserve continues its responsibility for global financial stability. Global banking and insurance have faced rising costs as they have added new technologies, products, and branches, and loan losses from the financial crises in 2007–2008. The COVID pandemic has hindered lowering the cost of financial services for clients. Historically, significant banking institutions have evolved with separate internal business silos, with stand-alone custom technology making communication difficult. Banks want clients to use more of the services they provide. However, financial services clients, both companies and individuals, like a more integrated approach to their total financial picture, at a lower cost. This situation is changing with the emergence of non-bank financial technology innovations enabling consolidated and simplified transactions information at a lower cost to bank clients. The digitalization of currency, expansion of online internet financial transaction processes, near-global access to cloud computing, and the expanded use of blockchain security make worldwide financial transactions simpler, more secure, and less expensive. **Applied Positioning Interface (API)** or "open banking systems" technology, provides access to all financial accounts even if at different banks. Non-bank Fintech companies can now offer a current, total financial picture of any client's accounts electronically at a low cost.

Significant innovations in the financial service sector are just beginning and are a substantial component of the Fourth Industrial Revolution. Banks' competitive response includes adopting Artificial Intelligence (AI) smartphone robots for customer service questions. Increased M&As are consolidating the number of banks and closing neighborhood bank branches. Banks are increasingly outsourcing operating and regulatory reporting functions to non-bank Regtech companies to supply regulatory compliance reports, account verification, and data capture and integration, enabling enhanced analytics to avoid errors and violations. Non-bank mortgage companies use technology to appraise real estate, run credit reports, and compile income and credit histories and scores immediately online. Mobility software solutions help insurance agents instantly catalog damage claims, file reports, and access customer insurance and payout information. The global digitalization of banking and lower funds transfer costs via smartphones stimulates the flow of funds worldwide. It opens new opportunities for payments and investment even in developing countries, including Africa.

Second: Inventions and innovations increasingly require additional and higher levels of education and skills in STEM and Medical and Biological Sciences. The Medical and Biological Sciences are just entering a period of increased use and development of innovative technologies. Artificial Intelligence to diagnose patients' illnesses and recommend treatment advances with increasing accuracy, supported by big data analytics. Cloud access to these improved diagnoses and new surgical procedures with medical robots is becoming more widely available. COVID-19 and the development of new vaccines such as messenger RNA (mRNA) vaccines teach our cells how to make a protein that will trigger an immune response inside our bodies. Another new vaccine type is Viral Vector Vaccines (VVV) which use a modified version of a harmless virus that is different from the virus being targeted to deliver important instructions to our cells on how to counteract the unwanted virus. According to the Center for Disease Control (CDC), VVV enters the muscle cells and uses the cells' machinery to produce a harmless piece of a spike protein on the surface of COVID-19. Our immune system recognizes that the protein does not belong there, which triggers our immune system to produce antibodies and activate other immune cells to fight off an infection.

Research is advancing using animal organs to replace inoperative human organs, and 3D custom printing of human body parts is proceeding as a new way to repair human medical issues. The World Health Organization (WHO) recently approved using the RTS,S/AS01 (RTS,S) malaria vaccine for children in sub-Saharan Africa and other regions with moderate to high *P. falciparum* malaria transmission. The recommendation is based on results from an ongoing pilot program in Ghana, Kenya, and Malawi, reaching more than 800,000 children since 2019. Malaria causes illness and death of 260,000 children annually in sub-Saharan Africa.

Following college graduation, industry-relevant, life-long learning is necessary to continuously update specialized skill-based training for managers and employees in every industry to understand and apply new technology effectively. More employees with advanced graduate degrees in STEM and Medical Sciences are required. There are three ways for governments and companies to address this shortage. Encourage and provide more opportunities for greater diversity and inclusiveness of cultures, races, and nationalities seeking higher education. Second, continue supporting women entering STEM and Medical and Biological Science fields. Third, recruit more qualified foreign graduate students and degreed professionals. These options could be accelerated with scholarships or subsidizing student debt for each postgraduate semester in STEM or Medical and Biological Sciences areas. It is also essential to ensure equal compensation for all sexes after completing their degrees for similar performance. Attracting more foreign graduate students may require continuing and extending the visa status to 10 years for practical experience after graduation for exceptional masters and doctorate experienced professionals. With only 20% of domestic high school graduates ready for the rigors of STEM majors, the USA must support the recruitment of more top international scientists.

A less expensive option to recruit more students in STEM and Medical Sciences is to encourage students to begin their education at local Community Colleges. In the USA, Community Colleges and Technical Schools are crucial in preparing students to enter the workforce with associate degrees, certificates, and skill-based programs for transition to four-year educational institutions. In some cases, the low tuition is even subsidized, and all 4-year colleges and universities accept transfer credits for all courses taken at Community Colleges. In 2017, US Community Colleges awarded 93,000 associate degrees in Science & Engineering (S&E) fields and another 133,000 in S&E technologies. More multinational companies are following the example of **Intel** which in 2020 launched an "Artificial Intelligence (AI) for Workforce Program" to improve students' employability in the digital economy. Intel collaborates with Community Colleges to provide 200 hours of AI instruction to train the trainer. This year, after a successful pilot at Arizona's Maricopa County Community College District, it is expanding the Intel AI program to 18 different schools across 11 states providing this learning opportunity to more than 800,000 students.[iii]

Looking into the future from an international competitive standpoint, US eighth-graders rank in the middle of advanced economies in mathematics and science assessments with minor changes over the past decade. Countries that rank above the USA in Science and Technology scores include Singapore, South Korea, Taiwan, Hong Kong, Japan, and Russia. The USA awarded 800,000 Science & Engineering (S&E) university bachelor's degrees in 2016, compared with 1.0 million for the EU and 1.7 million for China, which has doubled over the past ten years. In terms of doctorate degrees, in 2016, the USA awarded 40,000 S&E doctorates, the EU had 77,000, and China 34,000.

Third: All employees' jobs are becoming more specialized and focused and require a more detailed understanding of their significance and industry importance. This trend reinforces the need for additional high-level education. Since the First Industrial Revolution, every industry's production process has become increasingly complex and specialized. Thus, more detailed and sophisticated knowledge and skills are required to perform effectively and add value. Applying higher levels of technology to every aspect of a job requires more detailed specialized skills every year. If a person does not have the knowledge and education to function at this higher level of technology today, they cannot communicate with their direct report or fellow employees. How will the worker operate with tomorrow's technology if they cannot understand how today's works and do not understand the terminology to explain it to them?

Fourth: The future economic growth and innovation sector for advanced developed countries is expected to continue primarily in the services industries, which favors local labor. The service sector began expanding during the First Industrial Revolution partly because of the reduction in the agricultural sector employment with the increased mechanization and size of farms. The differing employment percentages for the three major sectors of an economy, agriculture and extractive, manufacturing, and services, indicate the stage of a country's economic development. In more developed countries with rising economies of scale, an increasing share of income comes from capital-intensive instead of labor-intensive industries.

Comparing stages of development today, both the USA and Canada have about 2–3% of their labor force working in agriculture compared to 4% in Japan, 5% in the EU, and 10% in Russia. In developing countries like India, the percentage is 47%, Indonesia 38%, China 27%, Mexico 14%, and Brazil 10%. The service sector (public and private) in the USA and Britain today employs 80% of the workforce, and in Japan and EU, it is 68%, Russia 63%, Brazil 58%, Indonesia 49%, China 46%, and India 31%. As incomes rise, people and companies in developed countries can specialize more in using their scarce time, and it is less expensive to pay others to take care of an increasing share of their service duties and needs.

Following two world wars, during the Third Industrial Revolution or Digital Revolution, countries experienced more capital-intensive investments. In the manufacturing sector, increased outsourcing of services has allowed a business to concentrate on critical capital-intensive activities to boost its success. Today the primary service sector growth areas comprise warehousing and transportation services; information services including education; financial, securities, and other investment services; professional services including consultancy, training, or marketing; waste management; health care and social assistance; and arts, entertainment, and recreation. The largest employment service sectors are the professional and business services, healthcare and social services, retail, leisure and hospitality, and financial services.

The rise in people's income in the middle and upper-income categories has enabled them to pay for more support services that earlier were not available or could not be afforded. Increasingly, services are being traded, both within and across borders digitally. This trend will continue to increase as more people connect to the internet and trade digitally with the rest of the world. The emergence of public and private cloud computing and data storage further facilitates the expansion in the use of outside service providers in all areas of corporate activities. With services increasing tradability and rising importance as inputs to traded goods, the service sector is poised to play an increasingly vital role in many countries' economic growth.[iv]

There is a strong empirical correlation between economic progress as measured by the growth in per capita GDP and services' share of total employment. A significant source of this shift has been the new employment of women in the labor force. Many women left unpaid household duties for paying jobs and recruited service people to take over their household chores. Similarly, more health care and other services become required with the aging population. The future economic growth sector for advanced developed countries is the services sector. It is already the most prominent and growing employment sector and the primary contributor to advanced countries' GDP growth. The manufacturing and service components of the economy are increasingly intertwined and support each other. Like the manufacturing sector, the service sector also requires specialization in a person's chosen field of competence. One needs to know how a piece of machinery operates and how to repair or improve its operation. More companies are outsourcing various parts of the organization's functions to reduce costs and free time to focus on their primary business. The services sector will continue to experience the most significant innovations and provide employment opportunities for workers displaced in the manufacturing industry as the role of robots expands. There are also increasing indications that robots may become used in specific service sectors. Historically, employment opportunities continue to grow with economic advancement in every service industry sector in developed economies.

Economies are divided into three economic development sector categories contributing to GDP: the primary sector activity consists of agriculture, mining, forestry, hunting, and fishing. The secondary sector activity category is product-producing and includes construction and manufacturing, metalworking, chemical and engineering, bottling, and textiles. The tertiary sector activity is services consisting of government and private services. Today's service to manufacturing employment ratio is 10-to-1 compared to 2-to-1 in 1940. Most of the service expansion in employment has been in professional business services, wholesale and retail trade, education and health services, and leisure and hospitality. Many of these new jobs are higher-paying at above $51,000 a year.

Different components of the US service sector have contributed to real GDP growth in each expansion cycle. For example, the increased growth of the service sector beginning in the Third Industrial Revolution was driven by the rapid rise in technology and advance in global communications with the launch of the internet and the use of computers and cell phones. Consequently, the USA has transferred from a major manufacturing economy into the largest, most extensive service-based economy. The most significant contributor to GDP within the service sector industry is the Finance, Insurance, and Real Estate industry, representing over one-fifth of total GDP. However, its contribution to GDP growth has not been significant over the past decade since the 2007–2008 financial crisis. This lack of development is expected to improve over the next ten years with the advance of Fintech. New non-bank technology financial service startup companies are beginning to replace traditional banking activities, including branch activity, with online digital banking and investing services. These innovations will reduce the cost of certain financial transactions for consumers as modern technologies replace large banks' oligopolistic control over banking and financial services.

The information industry was the most important contributor to GDP growth during this past decade and was one of the fastest-growing sectors reflecting a period of digitalizing of data. The growth of the service sector enhances the productivity in other sectors as it is an essential part of any economic sector. This sector includes publishing, broadcasting, data processing, telecommunications, motion pictures, and recordings. A second fast-growing sector was health care, social assistance, and education, driven by an aging population. The world is amid a significant demographic transition as population growth is slowing, reducing the share of young people. At the same time, the percentage of older people is rising sharply, especially in the USA and other advanced countries. Despite the rise in the standard of living, fertility rates have declined while life expectancy has been extended. World population growth is slower, and more people are aging. Globally, the share of the working-age population in developed nations is expected to fall by 25% from 19% in 2020 to 14% in 2050. Together with the aging of the population, these factors are expected to slow per-capita GDP growth. However, in all developing countries, the working-age share of the population is estimated to rise from 80% in 2020 to 86% in 2050, increasing per-capita GDP growth and boosting higher saving and investment.

The third fastest-growing component of the service sector was professional and business services, followed by manufacturing, trade, transport, and warehousing. COVID has recently increased the health services sector. During the contraction periods 1973–1975, 1979–1982, and 2007–2008 there were significant declines in the private goods-producing sector but moderate increases in the private services-producing industries. In contrast, construction and durable goods manufacturing led to reductions in real GDP during all the recession periods. The size of the service sector is increasing in all countries. The service sector represents half of the real GDP growth in many emerging market economies. Usually, the service sector's most robust growth components are financial services, health, education, and tourism.

Economists have separated a part of the service sector to create the quaternary sector. They assign areas of research, information technology, education, consulting, and various other elements of what has become known as the "knowledge-based economy," Subsequently, the quaternary or fourth part of the service sector was further divided into the quinary or fifth sector. The quaternary category or knowledge economy includes intellectual activities associated with technological innovation such as libraries, scientific research, education, information technology, and government. The quaternary sector accounts for 25% of total employment in the USA and is expected to become increasingly significant in the Fourth Industrial Revolution, which began in 2010. The quinary fifth category is a subset of the fourth category or people in the highest decision-making levels or top executives of the quaternary sector. This category consists of the top executives in the C-suite and the Board of Directors in scientific firms, universities, nonprofits, health care, media, and the government. It is estimated that 14–15% of the US labor force are employed in the quinary subsector. Table 9.1 : Sectoral Shares in US GDP shows that the fastest-growing sector between 1947 and 1985 is the Quaternary rising 13.3%. This increase was not due to the government sector, which declined from 14.6% to 11.2%, significantly elevating the private quaternary sector's importance as a percent of GDP. Furthermore, between 1967 and 1977, the Quaternary value-added

Table 9.1 Sectoral Shares of Value Added to US GDP

Sector	*1947*	*1969*	*1979*	*1985*	*1947–1985 %Δ*
Primary	11.5	8.0	6.6	6.2	−46.0
Secondary	28.4	29.8	27.7	26.6	−6.3
Tertiary	24.2	23.2	25.6	26.5	+9.5
Quaternary	36.0	39.0	40.2	40.8	+13.3

Percentage change in 1982 dollars.

Source: Survey of Current Business, April 1986 p. 6. Adapted from Michael Urquhart, "The Employment Shift to Services: Where Did it Come From?"

share rose from 70.6% in 1967 to 74.4% in 1977, whereas in the other three sectors, value-added declined.

The significance of the shifting of employment and contribution to real GDP to the service sector category also reflects the most significant unicorn technology companies' innovations and additions to the service sector. For example, Jeff Bezos launched Amazon in 1995, Bill Gates & Paul Allen created Microsoft in 1975, Mark Zuckerberg launched Facebook in 2004, Larry Ellison started Oracle in 1977, Larry Page & Sergey Brin developed Google in 1998, Warren Buffett purchased Berkshire Hathaway in 1964. Except for Warren Buffett, all the other innovations are more recent. In contrast, the only significant recent non-service manufacturing innovation is Elon Musk's Tesla electric car production purchased in 2004. Tesla was founded (as Tesla Motors) in July 2003 by **Martin Eberhard (1960–, an American engineer, a Silicon Valley entrepreneur, and inventor)** and **Marc Tarpenning (1964–, an American engineer and technology entrepreneur**) in San Carlos, California. These greatest fortunes ranked above started as creative ideas from people with the creativity, drive, and connections to make them take off. Their success relied on competitive markets, but sometimes the innovation is so unique and original that it becomes a monopoly.

In contrast, the only significant recent disruptive non-service manufacturing innovations are those by **Elon R. Musk (1971–, South Africa Born, Canadian and American Citizen design engineer, entrepreneur, and business magnate).** Musk purchased a startup, **Tesla Motors** electric car production, in 2004. Under Musk's guidance, Tesla has made significant advances in the automobile industry with its clean energy advances. And, with a rising market capitalization above $580 billion, it has risen to the most prominent auto producer. In addition to Tesla, Musk is an active entrepreneur in several other areas, including space travel (see Case Study 9.1).

Case Study #9.1 Significant Disruptive Inventors and Innovations – Transportation: Electric Car and Space Travel

Key Disruptive Inventors	**Elon R. Musk (1971–, South Africa Born, Canadian, and American Citizen design engineer, entrepreneur, and business magnate)**
Location	**South Africa, Canada, USA**
Disruptive Invention	Entrepreneurial activities include starting and acquiring the following companies. Zip2 software company, X.com acquired by PayPal, Tesla electric car production, SpaceX rocket manufacturer for space travel, Neuralink interfacing the computer and human mind, The Boring Company reducing intra-city transit congestion, SolarCity energy generation system acquired by Tesla.
Problem Resolved	Musk helped reduce the cost of payments systems, and is creating a more environmentally friendly car driven by electricity.
Solution Impact	Most of the companies started by Musk have reduced the cost of various services in their industries and been less damaging to or helped improve the environment.
Economic Impact	Musk entrepreneurship stimulates the growth of new jobs and provides a less expensive way of undertaking activities with electric cars. His commercial space exploration at lower costs than others give him an excellent first-mover advantage business opportunity. This early mover advantage and business investment and GDP growth and reduced environmental damage.
Cultural Impact	Made consumer payments easier and made electric cars a way of preserving the environment vs. gas engine cars.
Inventors Education & Training	Born and raised in Pretoria, and at age 12, he learned computer programming using a manual and sold the code of a BASIC-based video game he created. In South Africa, he went to the University of Pretoria. His father was a South African electromechanical engineer, pilot, sailor, and property developer, and the family was very wealthy in Elon's youth. Musk then moved to Canada and enrolled at Queen's University in Kingston, Ontario. He transferred to the University of Pennsylvania and received a BA in economics and a BS in physics in 1995. Musk was accepted for a Ph.D. program in materials science at Stanford University in California but instead decided he would start a business. He, his brother, and a friend began Zip2 in 1995, which developed and marketed an Internet city guide for the newspaper publishing industry, with maps, directions, and yellow pages.
Innovation Environment	Musk and his brother lived in Palo Alto near Stanford University and were part of the Silicon Valley computer technology boom years in innovation.

Financing	Elon and brother Kimbal had little money and worked 24/7 when they started the web software company **Zip2.** In 1999 Zip2 was acquired by **Compaq,** a software company based in Silicon Valley, for $305 million, Elon received $22 million, and Kimbal got $15 million. Musk immediately co-founded an online bank **X.com**, which merged with **Confinity** in 2000 to form **PayPal,** a multinational financial technology company operating an online payments system. In 2002 **PayPal** was bought by **eBay** for $1.5 billion, with Musk receiving an estimated $165 million. In the same year, to reduce the cost of space exploration, Musk founded **SpaceX**, an aerospace manufacturer and space transport services company, of which he is CEO and Chief Engineer. SpaceX has launched 144 rockets as of 2022; 84 have been reflown. The privately held company is currently valued at over $100 billion and is now providing space travel for the US government. In 2004, Musk joined electric vehicle manufacturer **Tesla Motors, Inc.** (now **Tesla, Inc.**) as chairperson and product architect, becoming its CEO in 2008. Tesla's current market cap exceeds $550 billion. In 2006, he helped create **SolarCity,** a solar energy services company later acquired by Tesla for $2.6 billion and became **Tesla Energy**. In 2015, Musk co-founded **OpenAI,** a nonprofit artificial intelligence (AI) research company aiming to develop Artificial General Intelligence that promotes social and safe artificial intelligence. Its objective is to be the first company to design a machine with the learning and reasoning powers of the human mind. In 2016, Musk co-founded **Neuralink**, a neurotechnology company focused on developing human brain–computer interfaces, and as of 2022, more than $360 million has been invested in the effort. Musk also founded **The Boring Company** in 2016 as an intra-city tunnel construction company. Its first project was in Las Vegas, creating two parallel tunnels almost 2 miles long. In 2013, Musk announced plans for a version of a vactrain (or vacuum tube train) and delegated several engineers to establish the conceptual foundations and create initial designs and is still under development. Musk was first listed on the *Forbes Billionaires List* in 2012, with a net worth of $2 billion, and by 2022, he was ranked number one at $220 billion.
International Commerce	PayPal has helped make international payments simpler and less expensive. Tesla electric cars are being sold in more countries outside the US. Tesla produced over 930,000 electric vehicles worldwide. Tesla not only

(*Continued*)

(Continued)

	benefited from a solid shift to electric cars in major global markets, especially in the prosperous European Union region, but also from Model Y production in Shanghai, adding almost half a million vehicles per year capacity. Tesla has an overseas production capacity of half a million each for the Model 3/Y in factories in Shanghai and a similar degree in the new factory in Berlin.
Major Success Factors	Musk is excellent at identifying business bottlenecks and figuring out ways to get around them less expensively than others, using his understanding of technology, research abilities, creative imagination, and determination to execute and deliver on his ideas and dreams.

Most service sector workers and jobs tend to have lower income employment, requiring less training and education to perform well. For example, 62% of service workers make $50 thousand or less per year, while 38% make more than $51 thousand annually. Both parts of the service sector are likely to continue to experience expansion for several reasons, but the quintenary will be the guiding innovation star. First, over 60% of the workers are in lower-skill jobs because of less education. Many are also older and find it challenging to qualify for academic education or specialized skill programs, which are becoming increasingly expensive and time-consuming. Some immigrants find work at this lower level because they cannot quickly transfer degrees or certificates from other countries and are willing to accept a less stressful position at lower pay. Second, time is increasingly scarce and an essential commodity for wealthy people. Consequently, the demand for services provided by lower-income workers is expanding. Even middle-income families can afford to employ people in the services sector to save time for other, more enjoyable activities. Third, service sector demand is rising as populations are aging, the need for health care support is expanding, and increasing medical and health service workers are required for both part-time and full-time work. As service sector employment grows at all levels, increasing consumption expenditures and supports continued strong economic growth.

A second meaningful change in innovations is the shift from manufacturing product innovations to service sector innovations. The USA has experienced intense competition from selected countries for increasingly vital manufacturing innovations and competitiveness in manufactured products. This manufacturing competition has come from Japan, South Korea, Taiwan, Hong Kong, and China as part of the natural progression of economic development. When a company becomes a monopoly in an industry or sector of an enterprise, this tends to suppress competitive forces required to provide new innovations, productivity increases, and promote economic growth. This description, in many cases, fits the present situation in the service sector as represented by the dominance of the new unicorn technology companies mentioned earlier, particularly in the USA. Given the service sector's already large and growing significance, the potentially damaging impact on the economy's largest sector is an increasing concern. This service sector damage concerns the widening income diversity between the top 1% and the rest of the population in developed countries, particularly in the USA. This widening income gap also threatens the US international competitiveness, continually worsening its global trade deficit as the USA increases its reliance on imports from foreign countries. A significant percentage of service sector workers rely on less expensive products imported from other countries. Undoubtedly, labor unions in the manufacturing sector will use this widening gap to pressure import restrictions. Anti-globalization politicians could use this to justify establishing additional protectionist trade barriers against foreign countries' imports to preserve jobs in inefficient industries. If they are successful, the result would further strengthen monopolist companies' control, causing rising prices on goods and services. The challenge is breaking up the present monopoly position of the technology giants without sending a discouraging message to future service sector innovations required for continued economic growth, employment, and competitiveness.

Fifth: Innovation flourishes in a competitive environment. Innovation is dependent on the creative capacity, level of knowledge, and empowerment of people and industry to be entrepreneurial. A country's competitiveness is based on its creation of knowledge and dependent on the ability of its initiative to innovate and implement change without government assistance. A company's or industry's competitiveness is measured by its relative competitive advantage in exports of goods or services. It is challenged to succeed in the global marketplace against all competitors. This competitiveness implies that the company or industry has gained a competitive advantage in its home country's market, where the environment is also competitive, expanding, and innovative in its field.

Competitiveness is required for leading-edge employment creation, increased productivity, market-determined international comparative advantage, and continuous invention and innovation. Consequently, domestic monopolies and oligopolies are detrimental to achieving a company's or an industry's sustainable global competitiveness. Interrupting the flow of innovation may result in a misallocation of resources and contribute to inflationary pressures and loss of competitiveness as market forces become distorted. They should be appropriately re-organized to re-establish a domestic competitive environment.

The evolution of innovations changed significantly since the First Industrial Revolution when most inventions and innovations resulted from a single person or a few people funded by family and friends. There have still been a few families and friends who funded successful startups. However, since the late 1800s, corporations have taken over, refined, and developed a research procedure for becoming the predominant source of entrepreneurial activity for inventions and innovations. Through their research laboratories modeled after the Research Laboratory first established by Thomas Edison in 1876, and in-house R&D departments, corporations have increased their control over new inventions and innovations. Developing innovations have become part of a corporation's competitive strategy. In addition to their innovation Lab and R&D efforts, they also help fund University faculty research in areas of importance and capitalize on the promising research outcomes and ideas by hiring the researcher, licensing, or acquiring the invention. The USA is serious about stimulating innovations and maintaining its competitiveness as an estimated 16,000 US firms operate industrial research Labs. In 2020, the countries spending the most significant amount on R&D ($ billions) included the following: the US $597, China $533, Japan $191, Germany $128, India $96, S. Korea $90, France $69, Russia $61, UK $53, and Brazil $39. The companies with the most significant spending in 2020 on R&D ($ billions) include Amazon $43, Alphabet (Google) $28, Microsoft $19, Apple $19, and Facebook $19. Huawei $22 was the only foreign (China) company in this group. In 2018, the top 10 US companies' R&D spending was $98.1 billion, and the top 10 global companies' expenditures on R&D totaled $149 billion in 2020, with half this expenditure coming from US companies. In 2019 with the arrival of COVID-19 total global pharmaceutical spending hit $210 billion as companies searched for a COVID vaccine with the top R&D spending ($ billions) by Roche $10.3, Johnson&Johnson $8.8, Merck $8.7, Novartis $8.4, Pfizer $8.0, Sanofi $6.1, Bristol-Myers Squibb $5.9, Eli Lilly of $5.6, AstraZeneca $5.3, and AbbVie $5.0.

Corporations also purchase new promising startups if they think it has a good business innovation to add to their portfolio of products or services. Or, if the startup has an invention that might threaten their current products' leadership position, companies will purchase the startup and put the idea into their vault until they think the market for their existing products has been exhausted. What is wrong with this behavior is that it is a monopolistic practice to strengthen their position by controlling potential competition to retain their monopoly at the expense of the consuming public and nation. This action is a form of price control by eliminating any competition, and as a result, the consumer and the country lose. At the same time, innovations are becoming more complex and expensive to launch successfully, which works to the advantage of corporations rather than individuals. These corporate practices limit productivity growth and curtail the economies' development, adversely impacting the workers' living standards. This monopolistic action is condoned by the current Patent protection time of 20 years, which could be reduced, and the renewal fee increased.

Corporate control of new innovations through their research laboratories and R&D departments and the recent formation of technology oligopolies and monopolies conflict with the environment that supports increased innovations. Great care should be taken by the justice system, not the political system, to avoid something like the recent Chinese approach to punishing this vital sector, which offers many jobs to labor in the economy's service sector. One option might be to assign higher corporate taxes levels to companies considered oligopolies and monopolies. A second option would be the traditional legal breakup, restructuring, and sale of parts of the monopoly. A third additional option might be to shorten the patent protection time to less than 20 years to support further innovations. This patent protection period has condoned the recent tech monopolies by disadvantaging new startups that might be helped if the patent period were reduced and the renewal fee increased. The objective is to support a competitive environment that encourages new innovative company startups and helps reduce the gap between income levels by promoting new higher-paying service sector employment opportunities.

Identifying Productivity Competitiveness[8–13]

Why does one manufacturer generate more revenue per total hours worked than another? The US Census Bureau and Bureau of Labor Statistics have begun a new effort to measure the productivity differences between more and less productive plants in an industry shown as differences in revenues per total hours worked. Based on 1997–2015 data, they have found that plants show significant differences in real revenue per total hours worked. For example, more productive plants in the top 75% of productivity distribution generate about 150% more revenue per hour than less productive plants in the lower 25%. There may be several reasons underlying the difference, including varying quality of products, market demand and price, different customers and markets by location, more contemporary technology and business management, better ability to adjust scale and operations mix, and adaptability to new products and processes. The first-mover advantage in adapting to modern technologies tends to be more productive in revenue per hour. The cause of the higher dispersion may vary between difficulty in adjusting the labor force to a change in the business climate, or the rise may reflect a significant amount of experimentation and innovation. More productive factories are likely to grow and survive and may become larger by absorbing resources of less productive plants. In addition to measuring productivity using output per hour or real revenue per hour, value-added per worker and multifactor productivity are also measured.

Sixth: Inventions must pass sustainable growth requirements as a condition of being patented and allowed to become innovations. As indicated throughout this book, some significant innovations by entrepreneurs conflict with sustainable development, discovered years after their invention and innovation. If all patents required an environmental impact study before award, this would help prevent future innovations from conflicting with sustainable growth. Any innovation application that does not entirely support sustainable economic development should <u>not</u> be approved or granted a patent. This policy reinforces the current practice of major financial institutions not financing major projects unless they are convinced that the project will not be a future ecological liability.

Innovations during the First and Second Industrial Revolutions were launched at a time and during a period when pollution was low, and concern about pollution or sustainability was not an issue. It was not until the 20th century that some people began to be concerned about the damage to the environment and people's health, such as using coal to power the steam engine. Coal was also used as the energy source in the production of iron and eventually steel in large manufacturing and processing factories. Even though the steam engine is gone and the process of producing steel has changed, coal is still in use today in many countries and continues damaging the environment.

The Second Industrial Revolution in 1850–1914 introduced a new, cleaner source of power in electricity, electric motors, and the light bulb. However, we continue to suffer from the negative consequences of generating electricity, which should be changed to comply with sustainable development. We also saw the invention of the automobile powered by an internal combustion engine burning gasoline, a petroleum product generating CO_2, which does not support sustainable development. Efforts to reduce the environmental damage by requiring catalytic converters on all cars have helped but are not 100% effective. The invention of the electric car motor has helped. Still, it is essential to ensure that all parts of this car support sustainable growth, including its newly developed batteries, when replaced or rebuilt.

The world has gone through three major industrial revolutions. The Fourth Industrial Revolution's launch began when the COVID pandemic accelerated the need to adopt new technology to work and communicate. It is believed that the COVID pandemic results from climate change-related rise in the Earth's temperature caused by several types of pollution. The COVID-19 virus exposed weaknesses in the national and global production and distribution systems. First, the pandemic prevented many workers from going to work to stop the spread of the virus. Many large and small companies closed, and workers lost their jobs. A second problem caused by COVID was that global supply chains were severely disrupted. Many open or re-opened companies could not get the necessary parts to complete their products for various essential products. And most, 80+% of US multinational companies surveyed reported they planned re-shoring their global supply chains to prevent or gain better control of future disruptions. US companies' corporate response to COVID closures is to accelerate substituting robots for labor. The re-shoring process will help reduce imports from US foreign production facilities relocated to the USA, reducing the trade deficit. It will also increase corporate tax revenue from re-shored companies reducing the budget deficit. Finally, depending on the extent to which robots are substituted for workers, re-shoring may not significantly increase manufacturing jobs. The latter point will only help reduce unemployment if qualified workers can be trained and are located where jobs are found. The COVID pandemic is believed to be due to climate change caused by pollution of Earth's environment resulting from the first three Industrial Revolutions. Several COVID vaccine innovations may help control future pandemics, but they do not address the cause – climate change.

Seventh: The current patent protection time may no longer be appropriate for the much more rapid pace of inventions today and may be conflicting with a competitive environment delaying innovations. A US utility patent is granted for 20 years from the date the patent application is filed, with periodic fees required to maintain the enforceability of the patent. However, today new inventions are occurring at a much more rapid pace than they were more than 230 years ago when three patents were awarded in 1790. For example, in 1850, there were 2,193 utility patent applications and 884 patents granted, whereas, in 2020, there were 597,175 utility applications and 352,066 patents awarded in the USA alone.[v] A 20-year monopoly provided by current patent law has enabled several leading technology companies to control their industry and are currently facing Congressional investigations for their dominant near-monopoly control of their markets.

Eighth: Innovation in other countries outside the USA is expected to increase faster as further developed and developing countries experience economic development, global trade benefits, and knowledge transfers. The outsourcing to low-labor cost developing countries has historically helped to expose international managers and workers to some aspects of more advanced technology. SONY and Canon's stories in Japan are excellent examples of developing innovations and building a strong comparative advantage in electronics. Similarly, Israel has also become an innovation powerhouse in several areas. Some of Israel's high-profile recent startup exits included community-based navigation app **Waze** acquired by Google for $1.1 billion, self-driving car technology firm **Mobileye** acquired by Intel for $15.3 billion, and fraud-prevention firm **Trusteer** acquired by IBM for $1 billion. While Taiwan started the low-cost production of computer chips, it is now the leader in innovating and developing the world's most advanced chips. Taiwan has developed a formidable reputation for hardware and software innovations. **Taiwan Semiconductor Manufacturing Co. (TSMC)** is ranked one of the top 10 world-leading technology companies and a leader in advanced nanochip development. Another Taiwan company **Foxconn** is also the world's largest multinational electronics manufacturing company by producing chips for Apple, Google, and others. It has an excellent chance to develop a globally competitive startup ecosystem in AI, software, and semiconductors. The South Korean companies **Samsung** and **LG** have also become well known for their smartphone technology, advanced television, and appliance technologies. Samsung is a global leader in screen technology, TVs, batteries, and chip design. LG has become a lead innovator in solar technology. The four areas of **Hong Kong's** innovation and technology industry are biotechnology, artificial intelligence, smart city, and financial technologies. In 2019 and 2020, the top companies from developing countries awarded patents included Samsung, LG, Canon, Huawei, and TSMC. Other top 20 developing countries receiving patents include Australia, India, Brazil, Indonesia, Mexico, South Africa, Israel, and Singapore.

The COVID pandemic event reflects the subject of a paper by Prof. Nathan Rosenberg of Stanford University on "Innovation and Economic Growth," OECD, 2004. His article builds on an earlier document written in the 1950s by his colleague at Stanford, Prof. Abramovitx. Abramovitx's paper measured the growth of capital and labor inputs against the increase in output between 1870 and 1950 and found that they only accounted for 15% of the actual change, leaving an unexplained residual of 85%, the result of technology, organizational, or management improvements. Business investment in new plants and equipment also is known to have a multiplier impact on economic output growth, and that process is also subject to many uncertainties. Other economists, including **Robert Solow**, have found comparable results indicating the importance of technological change or "creative destruction" for economic growth. Rosenberg identifies a single feature that he argues dominates the search for new or improved technologies. That is high "uncertainty," which he then relates to several causal factors explaining the missing 85%. Including that R&D in high tech is costly and that R&D spending faces many financial risks.

A Positive Change in People's Environment Triggers Innovations[14–16]

Several noteworthy events set the stage for the First Industrial Revolution, which started to change the way people think and behave. These events, which made people feel free, positively impacted people's creativity and exhilarated the First, Second, and Third Industrial Revolutions. Following the multiple wars and famines of the Middle Ages, the Crusades significantly impacted European society between the 11th and 13th centuries. They set an awful precedent for holy wars as they were too costly and deadly. On the positive side, the Crusades exposed Europeans to how other cultures lived, their customs, foods, music, art, beliefs, and other thinking methods. The Crusades were followed by the Black Plague, or bubonic plague occurring in Afro-Eurasia from 1346 to 1353. It is the most fatal pandemic recorded in human history, killing between 75 and 200 million people in Eurasia and North Africa and striking Europe from 1347 to 1351. It caused great pain, fear, and uncertainty, and in the end, people yearned for health, freedom, and happiness.

The ending of these destructive events triggered the Renaissance, a vibrant and dynamic period of European cultural, artistic, political, and economic "rebirth." The feeling and expression of freedom and creativity became the Renaissance, which lasted from the 14th to the 17th century and promoted classical philosophy, literature, music, art, and creativity. It was a period of significant disruptive innovations in reasoning, philosophy, the scientific method, literature, music, the arts, the discovery of new lands, and the construction of unique and inspiringly creative architecture. It changed the way people think to be more positive, adaptive, driven, and fearless. The replacement of uncertainty with freedom was the source of innovative ideas launching the First and Second Industrial Revolutions.

A second major positive event was the ending of the great depression and WWII which was followed immediately by The Korean War (1950–1953, US 36,574 dead, 103,284 wounded, 4,714 prisoners) and the Vietnam War (1955–1975, US 58,193 dead, 304,000 wounded, 78,750 missing). In March of 1985, Mikhail Gorbachev became the leader of the Soviet Union. Gorbachev became a transformative figure in the USSR as he ushered in new domestic and foreign policy reforms to salvage the crumbling Communist system. One of the critical decisions was agreeing to nuclear disarmament deals with the USA, some of the first steps toward ending the Cold War. By the early 1990s,

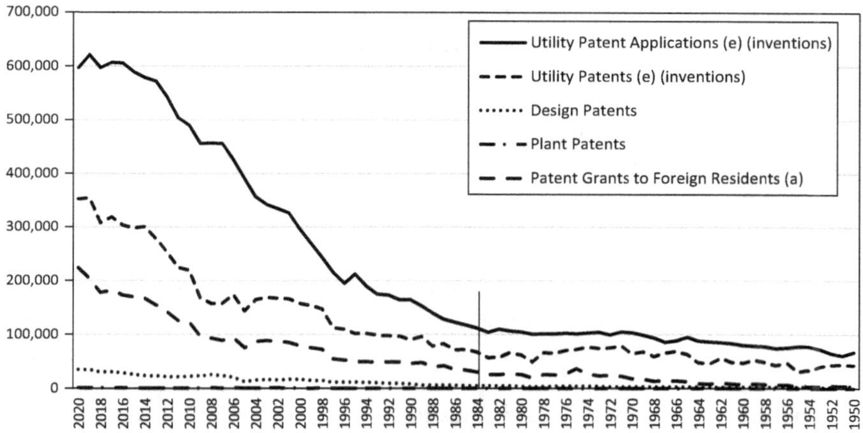

Figure 9.1 US Patents: Applications and Awards

Source: US Patent Office.

his reforms had worked, and the Soviet Union was dissolved. He resigned in 1991 as the transition to democracy began.

In 1984 a new period of inventions and innovations began, impacting the service and manufacturing sectors. These events improved the environment and resulted in another "renaissance" and the Third Industrial Revolution, led by creative innovations in communications (television and the internet, and jet air travel). It also caused the shift from mechanical office equipment to electronic computers and the internet, advances in medicine to contain flu viruses, and eventually data digitalization. As seen in Figure 13.3 in 1984, US patents awards rose more sharply and never stopped growing, including US patents awarded to foreign residents in the USA. Similarly, the recovery from the unexpected global COVID-19 pandemic triggered the re-launching in 2022 of the Fourth Industrial Revolution.

The Fourth Industrial Revolution (2010–) of Cyber-Physical Systems[vi][4,17,18]

In 2010 Germany introduced a high-tech strategy of the computerization of manufacturing. The idea of digital manufacturing was introduced in the early 1970s by **Joseph Harrington**, *Computer Integrated Manufacturing*, 1973. Still, it was not until 1984 that it began to be developed by manufacturers. **Computer Integrated Manufacturing (CIM)** is the complete automation of a manufacturing facility where all processes are controlled by a computer supplied with continuous digital information. **Computer Integrated Manufacturing Open System Architecture (CIMOSA)** was vendor-independent and constructed with standardized CIM modules. CIM has emerged into the "lights-out factory," completely independent of human intervention. Combining manufacturing and computer hardware with AI-driven productivity optimizing software and biology is the future of innovation at the corporate level. It involves the application of the Fourth Industrial Revolution. This innovation consists of integration, connectivity with wireless 5G smart technologies, and physical and digital convergence with information and operations technology autonomously controlled by AI.

Corporate manufacturing and operations processes are linked to smart chip-sourced big data and a digital supply and demand network. More timely data creates a three-dimensional vertical and horizontal integration – an intelligent, innovating corporation. This process involves machine-to-machine automation and improved communication using smart technology, the Internet of Things (IoT), 3D printing for mass customized production, self-monitoring, diagnosing, and adjusting issues without human intervention. Once the corporate leadership and Board of Directors agree upon the values and goals, the software programmers can set the AI software objectives. Then the innovative attributes of the Fourth Industrial Revolution will continuously, 24/7, self-optimize performance. The cloud-based continually evolving process network will self-optimize efficiency and productivity to lower costs and mass produce customized products and services. It will be guided automatically through AI-driven 3D printing production robots to respond to changing consumer demands or mass-customized production.

This responsive, proactive, agile, and resilient process is the new operational format of the human-technology interface to achieve sustainability and higher productivity. The design principles are based on the interconnection of machines, computers, data sensors, AI managers, and technologists using the IoT to communicate. Information transparency of comprehensive data from all parts of the process enables better decisions in which the technical facility of the systems assists humans in decision-making and problem-solving. Decentralized decision capability by cyber-physical systems using elastic cloud computing, cognitive computing, and AI would allow autonomous decisions in real time to adapt to changing needs of consumers. The smart or intelligent factory could autonomously manage smart production and logistics, monitoring physical processes and suppliers with a virtual copy of the physical world and harmonized decentralized decisions. 3D printing allows immediate customized mass production and reduces supplier dependence, and smart wireless sensors drive the central forces of innovation.

The result of the Fourth Industrial Revolution is the "Knowledge Economy" in which products and services are based on knowledge-intensive activities, accelerating the technical and scientific advance as well as rapid creative adaptability. The Knowledge Economy removes the reliance on physical inputs and natural resources and emphasizes intellectual capabilities. Big data and digital transformation of everything, together with the expansion of the Internet into billions of computing chip devices, is at the heart of the Fourth Industrial

Revolution. This ability will enable constructing the intelligent factory with manufacturing technologies, input logistics, product distribution, financing, and real-time market demand data to self-optimize. It will be supported with IoT, cloud computing, cognitive computing with AI, self-modifying, and reprogramming itself for continuously improved efficiencies.

Creating the Knowledge Economy has high economic and investment costs and must be customized to each business model and its objectives. It will also require a more sophisticated labor force with advanced technological skills for programming lead robots and autonomous maintenance, repair, servicing, and updating robotic teams. A positive development is that digitalization provides online open access to all new scientific information for all subjects globally. Virtual and physical manufacturing systems increasingly use mobile robots embedded with AI in production to self-correct and respond to dynamic global marketing trends reflecting changing consumer demands. New technological innovations in digitalization cloud computing are expanding rapidly. They will make a meaningful change in how humans live with growing big data driving increased reliance on AI automation.

Innovations, including intelligent robot teams run by AI, controlling the Internet of Things, 3D printing, computer-driven manufacturing, etc., enable increased output per unit of labor, raising a country's productivity. Labor productivity expands as technological innovations replace labor time and effort with physical capital intelligent machines. Many innovations will result in circumventing nonrenewable resources for economic growth. High or rising prices of scarce natural resources stimulate modifications to promote growth depending on the innovator's knowledge, experience, and creativity. AI is increasingly improving in making better decisions than humans in specific learning and decision-making areas. It may someday become a significant contributor to extending the human mind's powers to become "creative" and develop future innovations. Applying AI and Applied Positioning Interfaces (API) to manufacturing plants and "smart" infrastructure projects will improve efficiency, productivity, and sustainability. Increasingly, computers and manufacturing are interlinked for faster and more precise production of complex parts reducing waste. Companies are developing electronic "dual" company models that can apply simulations of various production-related decisions or risk scenario analysis to see the company's operational and financial results before the actual decision is executed. This risk-vulnerability procedure will stress-test a company's operations against potential shocks or unexpected events to assess its operating and financial damage and vulnerabilities and determine how to respond cost-effectively and least damaging manner.

The Fourth Industrial Revolution is expected to impact every aspect of our lives, including transportation, communications, financial services, new medicines, medical robotics, AI, and big-data-driven autonomous manufacturing. Innovations are expected with new vaccines and other advances in specific illness-targeted drugs. Also expected are further advances in 3D printing in medical and pharmaceutical production areas. Further expansion of electric auto, airplane, ship transportation, self-driving cars will change our lives. The Fourth Industrial Revolution will increase productivity and real GDP growth while supporting sustainability.

The current Fourth Industrial Revolution, referred to as the Second Machine Age, was temporarily interrupted by COVID-19. As developed countries escape COVID, the Second Machine Age is expected to be the most transformative in human life, changing the functioning of societies and the global economy. It will provide better immunity to future pandemics. It is expected to be most important in impacting our lives by replacing humans with robots managed by Artificial Intelligence (AI). We will witness advances in introducing intelligent medicines and drugs and expanded 3D-Printing of replacement body parts. It is anticipated to begin reversing the environmental costs and damage of previous Industrial Revolutions. It will support a transition to sustainable growth, emphasizing renewable energy sources and healthier and longer life on Earth.

The New Future of Earth[1,17]

We end this book positively by reemphasizing the beginning of the Fourth Industrial Revolution's innovations and the Knowledge Economy based on the emergence of the quaternary sub-component of the services sector. The Knowledge Economy is a new form of globalization in which sustainability, technology, science, and global commerce become the major forces driving economic globalization guided by intellectual service activities. The Fourth Industrial Revolution is research, innovation, and capital intensive and will disrupt existing manufacturing and labor markets as the nation's service sector continues expanding. Major multinational manufacturing companies are leading this transition in developed countries as they re-shore. Intelligent robots will replace assembly workers. Many traditional jobs will become automated as the new innovative modern economy will be driven by the rapid generation, analysis, and dissemination of information and autonomous decision-making. Future innovations will continue improving manufacturing automation and its services, communications, transportation, and logistics.

Manufacturing automation includes self-servicing and repair abilities, all without human intervention. Innovative companies, cities, and nations will gradually emerge with commercial products or services with a competitive advantage in international trade. The scientific expansion of knowledge led by universities and corporate R&D Departments and their Laboratories will become increasingly disseminated through online learning education sessions supporting entrepreneurial innovations. To become and remain domestically and internationally competitive, individuals, companies, and nations must constantly be creative and innovative. This goal involves continuous training and educating the nation's labor force to understand the forces driving the latest developments in its products, services, and industry. As we enter the Fourth Industrial Revolution, there are three significant uncertainties: the human–computer interphase and AI's role, better security systems to strengthen cybersecurity defenses. The role of labor will change, and humanity will face new challenges and lifestyles yet to be determined. This change will adversely impact the lower labor cost countries, which had attracted multinational companies to developing countries.

Notes

All dates, innovators' information, and events have been checked against the information in the following sources: *Encyclopedia Britannica, Encyclopedia Americana, Collier's Encyclopedia, Compton's Encyclopedia, Investopedia, and Wikipedia.*

i Schumpeter, Joseph A., "Theoretical Problems of Economic Growth," Journal of Economic History Supplement, 1947, pp. 1–9.
ii Akcigit, Ufuk, John Grigsby, Tom Nicholas, "When America Was Most Innovative," Harvard Business Review, March 6, 2017.
iii David Mantey, "Intel's AI Degree Program Expands, Opportunity for More Than 800,000 Students," Thomas Industry Insights, August 26, 2021.
iv Buckley, Patricia, and Rumki Majumdar, "The services powerhouse: Increasingly vital to world economic growth," Deloitte Insights, July 2018.
v Patent awards normally take about two years after receiving a patent application.
vi NIST – Cyber-Physical Systems (CPS) comprise interacting digital, analog, physical, and human components engineered for function through integrated physics and logic. These systems will provide the foundation of our critical infrastructure, form the basis of emerging and future smart services, and improve our quality of life in many areas. CPS comprise interacting digital, analog, physical, and human components engineered for function through integrated physics and logic. Other phrases that you might hear when discussing these and related CPS technologies include Internet of Things (IoT), Industrial Internet, Smart Cities, Smart Grid, "Smart" Anything (e.g., Cars, Buildings, Homes, Manufacturing, Hospitals, Appliances).

Bibliography

Chapter 1

1 The Merriam-Webster.com Dictionary, *Merriam-Webster Inc.*, www.merriam-webster.com/dictionary/initial%20coin%20offering (Accessed January 3, 2020).
2 Christensen, Clayton M. (1997), *The Innovator's Dilemma: When New Technologies Cause Great Firms to Fail*, Harvard Business Review Press.
3 Halpern, Diane F. (2003), *Thought & Knowledge*, Lawarence Erlbaum Association, Ch. 1.

Chapter 2

1 Smiles, Samuel (2010), *Industrial Biography: Iron Workers and Tool Makers*, Europ Ischer Hochschulverlag Gmbh & Co. Kg.
2 Rosen, William (2010), *The Most Powerful Idea in the World: A Story of Steam, Industry, and Invention*, Random House.

Chapter 3

1 Cooke, A. J. (1979), "Richard Arkwright and the Scottish Cotton Industry," *Textile History*, vol. 10, no. 1.
2 Fitton, R. S. (1989), *The Arkwright's: Spinners of Fortune*, Manchester University Press.
3 Postrel, Virginia (2020), *The Fabric of Civilization: How Textiles Made the World*, Basic Books.
4 Barraclough, K. (1990), *Steelmaking 1850–1900*, Institute of Metals.
5 "Carl von Linde – Developer of Refrigerators & Gas Separation Technology" (December 2019), *World of Chemicals*, http://scihi.org/carl-von-linde/.
6 Gale, W. K. V. (1969), *Iron and Steel*, Longmans.
7 Oberg, Erik and Franklin Day Jones (2018), *Iron and Steel; a Treatise on the Smelting, Refining, and Mechanical Processes of the Iron and Steel Industry*, Franklin Classics.
8 Thallner, Otto (2019), *Tool-Steel: A Concise Handbook on Tool-Steel in General, Its Treatment*, Wentworth.
9 "Carl von Linde | German Engineer" (December 2020), *Encyclopedia Britannica*, https://www.britannica.com/biography/Carl-Paul-Gottfried-von-Linde.
10 Siemens, C. W. (June 1862), "On a Regenerative Gas Furnace, as Applied to Glasshouses, Puddling, Heating, etc," Proceedings of the Institution of Mechanical Engineers 1847–1982, Institution of Mechanical Engineers.
11 Stokes, Raymond (2015), *Building Upon Air: A History of the International Industrial Gases Industry from the 19th to the 21st Centuries*, Cambridge University Press.

12 Park, Benjamin (1898), *A History of Electricity: The Intellectual Rise in Electricity from Antiquity to the Days of Benjamin Franklin*, translation of Girolamo Cardano, John Wiley & Sons.

Chapter 4

1 Berger, Michael L. (2001), *The Automobile in American History and Culture: A Reference Guide*, Greenwood Publishing Group.
2 Black, Edwin (2006), *Internal Combustion: How Corporations and Governments Addicted the World to Oil and Derailed the Alternatives*, St. Martin's Press.
3 Clarke, Sally H. (2007), *Trust and Power: Consumers, the Modern Corporation, and the Making of the United States Automobile Market*, Cambridge University Press.
4 Harris, Philip R. and Robert T. Moran (2000), *Managing Cultural Differences, Leadership Strategies for a New World of Business*, Gulf Professional Publishing.
5 Kay, Jane Holtz (1997), *Asphalt Nation: How the Automobile Took Over America, and How We Can Take It Back*, Crown Publishers.
6 Krarup, M. C. (November 1906), "Automobiles for Every Use," *The World's Work: A History of Our Time*, vol. XIII.
7 "New England in Motor History; 1890 to 1916" (February 25, 1916), *The Automobile Journal*, vol. 41: 9, https://books.google.co.in/books?id=V_9YAAAAYAAJ&pg=RA1-PA7&redir_esc=y.
8 Norman, Henry (April 1902), "The Coming of the Automobile," *The World's Work: A History of Our Time*, vol. V: 3304–3308 (Accessed July 10, 2009).
9 DuFour, H. R. and Peter J. Unitt (1997), *Charles E. Taylor: 1868–1956, the Wright Brothers Mechanician*, Prime Printing.
10 House, Robert J., Paul J. Hanges, Mansour Javidan, Peter W. Dorfman and Vipin Gupta (2004), *Culture, Leadership, and Organizations, the GOBE Study of 62 Nations*, Sage Publications.
11 Tarbell, Ida M. (1904), *The History of the Standard Oil Co.*, The Famous Original Exposé in McClure's Magazine of Standard Oil.
12 Williamson, Harold F. and Arnold R. Daum (1959), *The American Petroleum Industry: The Age of Illumination, 1859–1899*, vol. 2; (1964), *American Petroleum Industry: The Age of Energy 1899–1959, The Definitive History of the Oil Industry*, the online edition of vol. 1, Northwestern University Press.
13 Yergin, Daniel (1991), *The Prize: The Epic Quest for Oil, Money, and Power*, Simon & Schuster.

Chapter 5

1 www.britannica.com/technology/computer/History-of-computing
2 Nguyen, Tuan C. (January 26, 2021), "The History of Computers," *ThoughtCo*, thoughtco.com/history-of-computers-4082769; www.computerhistory.org/timeline/computers; www.javatpoint.com/history-of-computer; https://plato.stanford.edu/entries/computing-history.
3 Strickland, Jonathan, "Do Wars Drive Technological Advancement?" www.livescience.com/20718-computer-history.html.
4 Nowell, Gregory P. (1994), *Mercantile States and the World Oil Cartel, 1900–1939*, Cornell University Press.
5 Tarbell, Ida M. (1904), *The History of the Standard Oil Co.*, The Famous Original Exposé in McClure's Magazine of Standard Oil.

6 Williamson, Harold F. and Arnold R. Daum (1959), *The American Petroleum Industry: The Age of Illumination, 1859–1899*, vol. 2; (1964), *American Petroleum Industry: The Age of Energy 1899–1959, The Definitive History of the Oil Industry*, the online edition of vol. 1, Northwestern University Press.
7 Yergin, Daniel (1991), *The Prize: The Epic Quest for Oil, Money, and Power*, Simon & Schuster.

Chapter 6

1 Schwab, Klaus (2016), *The Fourth Industrial Revolution*, Crown Business.
2 Siebel, Thomas M. (2019), *Digital Transformation: Survive and Thrive in an Era of Mass Extinction*, Rosetta Books, www.energystar.gov/ia/business/industry/41724.pdf.

Chapter 7

1 McAfee, Andrew and Erik Brynjolfsson (2017), *Machine Platform Crowd: Harnessing Our Digital Future*, Norton.
2 Schwab, Klaus (2016), *The Fourth Industrial Revolution*, World Economic Forum.
3 Bank for International Settlements, www.BIS.org.
4 Bhatia, Anurag (May 26, 2020), "Top 10 Fintech Trends for 2020," *Global Banking & Finance Review*.
5 Brynjolfsson, Erik and Andrew McAfee (2014), *The Second Machine Age*, Norton.
6 Greenspan, Alan (2007), *The Age of Turbulence*, Penguin.
7 Hall, Bronwyn H. (December 2005), *The Financing of Innovation, Management*, Ludwig-Maximilien University.
8 Shiller, Robert (2005), *Irrational Exuberance*, 2nd ed., Princeton University Press.
9 Smil, Vaclav (2004), *Enriching the Earth: Fritz Haber, Carl Bosch, and the Transformation of World Food Production*, MIT Press.
10 Mishkin, Frederic S. (2018), *Economics of Money, Banking and Financial Markets*, 12th ed., Pearson.
11 Reinhart, Carmen M. and Kenneth S. Rogoff (2009), *This Time It is Different: Eight Centuries of Financial Folly*, Princeton University Press.
12 Ritter, Lawrence S., William L. Silber and Gregory F. Udell (2018), *Principles of Money, Banking & Financial Markets*, 12th ed., Addison-Wesley.

Chapter 8

1 NIST Handbook 44. https://www.nist.gov/document/2022-handbook-44
2 ISO. https://www.iso.org

Chapter 9

1 Boden, Margaret A. (2016), *AI: Its Nature and Influence*, Oxford University Press.
2 Brooks, Frederick Jr. (1995), *The Mythical Man-Month: Essays on Software Engineering*, Addison-Wesley.
3 Brynjolfsson, Eric and Andrew McAfee (2014), *The Second Machine: Work, Progress, and Prosperity in a Time of Brilliant Technologies*, Norton.
4 Schwab, Klaus (2017), *The Fourth Industrial Revolution*, WEF.
5 Dalio, Ray (2017), *Principles*, Simon & Schuster.

6 Dalio, Ray (2021), *Principles for Dealing with the Changing World Order: Why Nations Succeed and Fail*, Avid Reader.
7 Mayer-Schonberger, Victor and Thomas Ramage (2018), *Reinventing Capitalism: In the Age of Big Data*, BasicBooks.
8 Daugherty, Paul R. and H. James Wilson (2018), *Human + Machine: Reimagining Work in the Age of AI*, Harvard Business Review Press.
9 Drucker, Peter F. (1999), *Management Challenges for the 21st Century*, HarperBusiness.
10 Ford, Martin (2015), *The Rise of the Robots: Technology and the Threat of a Jobless Future*, Basic Books.
11 Kenett, Ron S., Robert S. Swarz and Avigdor Zonnenshain (Editors) (2020), *Systems Engineering in the Fourth Industrial Revolution: Big Data, Novel Technologies, and Modern Systems Engineering*, Wiley.
12 OECD (2010), *The OECD Innovation Strategy: Getting a Head Start on Tomorrow*, OECD.
13 Porter, Michael E. (1985), *Competitive Advantage: Creating and Sustaining Superior Performance*, The Free Press.
14 OECD (2017), *Entrepreneurship at a Glance 2017*, OECD.
15 Pisano, Gary P. and Willy C. Shih (2012), *Producing Prosperity: Why America Needs a Manufacturing Renaissance*, Harvard Business Review Press.
16 Schwab, Klaus and Nicholas Davis (2018), *Shaping the Future of the Fourth Industrial Revolution*, WEF.
17 Siebel, Thomas M. (2019), *Digital Transformation: Survive and Thrive in an Era of Mass Extinction*, Rosetta Books.
18 Smil, Vaclav (2015), *Made in the USA: The Rise and Retreat of American Manufacturing*, MIT Press.

Index

For Product Safety Concerns and Information please contact our EU representative GPSR@taylorandfrancis.com
Taylor & Francis Verlag GmbH, Kaufingerstraße 24, 80331 München, Germany

www.ingramcontent.com/pod-product-compliance
Lightning Source LLC
LaVergne TN
LVHW021122300926
849160LV00010B/822
* 9 7 8 1 0 3 2 3 9 8 8 3 9 *